Wholebody

Neural Pathways to Prosperity, Health and Wisdom

By Alex Maunder

Copyright © 2017 Alex Maunder

ISBN: 978-1-326-97891-4

All rights reserved, including the right to reproduce this book, or portions thereof in any form. No part of this text may be reproduced, transmitted, downloaded, decompiled, reverse engineered, or stored, in any form or introduced into any information storage and retrieval system, in any form or by any means, whether electronic or mechanical without the express written permission of the author.

The views expressed in this work are solely those of the author and do not necessarily reflect the views of the publisher, and the publisher hereby disclaims any responsibility for them.

PublishNation
www.publishnation.co.uk

Dedication

This book is dedicated to the genius of two men, FM Alexander and Eugene Gendlin, whose work I have built upon. Also to my great friend and Focusing partner Kevin McEvenue, whose listening skills when in deep grounded presence, helped me to formulate my ideas.

Contents

Foreword – Writers Block.. 3
Chapter 1
The Shift into Embodied Thinking............................ 10
Chapter 2
Brain Basics 31
Chapter 3
The Neuroscience of Positive and Negative Emotions..52
Chapter 4
What is the A.T and what is Focusing? 69
Chapter 5
Tools for Staying in Contact with the Flow of Our
Experience at a Deeper Level 86
Chapter 6
A Manual of Wholebody Focusing 108
Chapter 7
Relationships and our Energetic Interconnectedness..135
Chapter 8
Quantum Physics and Living in an Interconnected
Universe..158
Chapter 9
WBF & Neural Pathways to Prosperity 172
Chapter 10
WBF and Neural Pathways to Health 183
Chapter 11
WBF and Neural Pathways to Wisdom....................201
Chapter 12
WBF and Therapy.. 220
Chapter 13
Wholebody focusing and Neuroscience Research on
Client X 250
Chapter 14

How EMDR can be integrated with WBF in the Treatment of Trauma 276
Chapter 15
Short Meditation for Inducing Alpha Wave Rhythms in your Brain 285
Useful Addresses and Website Links 291
Bibliography..292

Foreword – Writers Block

It is feels so hard for me to sit down and write this book. I imagine that some people have a naturally focused mind and are able to set clear time boundaries and just get on with it. Not me, I have been meaning to write this book for a long time, I have even set aside time in my summer holiday to do it, but I never seem to get around to. I manage to write the book plan and a few chapters but the book itself never gets completed. Until one day I wake up and realise - I'm suffering from writers block. I 'm supposed to be writing a book on Wholebody focusing and I cannot even get my act together! When I sit down to analyse the situation I realise that its not just lack of willpower. It is not a question of getting up earlier, "getting more focused", drinking more tea or coffee and working longer hours. Part of it is just a deep-seated belief pattern that I don't have anything worth saying. There is a voice inside my head saying "you're stupid, you don't have anything to say, other people have already written so much good stuff on this subject". It is the vicious internal critic at work, a part of my personality that keeps me feeling stuck and full of fear and for some reason it does not wish we to move forwards and to complete this project. I am curious about this part of me and I know that unless and until I work with reconciling and reintegrating this fearful and vulnerable part of myself all my efforts to write this book will be in vain. This inner critic is actually linked to a certain feeling in my body. Its a familiar feeling of being ungrounded and slightly panicked, like all my thoughts are racing, chasing each other around in big circles in my head. I cannot seem to think clearly or get focused, and life feels slightly out of control.

So I retire to a quiet room to work on myself in a Wholebody focusing way. I know that this routine will take about 20 minutes of my time but that I will come away feeling immeasurably refreshed and revitalised. The whole day will be different, with a clearer mental focus and energy flow. At the end of the day more will get done and the quality of the work will have been higher than if I had just forced myself to work towards my goal, ignoring all the signs of resistance and the blocked energy flow in my mind and body. Paying attention to my body sensations will help me to define the problem more clearly and Wholebody focusing will help me to transform the situation.

Standing in a comfortable position with the feet about shoulders distance apart, I start rocking gently from side to side in a kind of slow soothing rhythm that helps me to calm down and to get grounded. I say to myself "I'm putting all of that stuff on hold", everything that has been bugging me, I'm not going to think of it at all for the next 5 minutes until I am properly grounded and connected with my body.

I need to stop being so goal orientated and work with an inner understanding to transform the physical and emotional blockages first before I can get the energy and the mental focus needed to write the book. Rather than fighting it, there has to be a befriending of the wounded part and I need to take some time to understand its perspective. So firstly, I take time to focus on the physical sensations of that whole thing about "writing the book" and what seems to need attention there. I feel that there is a "contracting pressure" in my head, I feet closed in on myself, a bit depressed. This part in my head feels painful and pressurised; it feels "I'm the bad one", this part wants to cut off and it thinks, "what's the use of even trying?" It seems that I just want to give up whenever I encounter difficulties in life and then I feel depressed as a result of not achieving anything. Also I notice that my shoulders feel tensed and my chest feels slightly collapsed inwards.

Part of me just wants to wallow in self-pity with the justification "this is the way its always going to be, no matter how hard I try I won't get what I want". Making room for that place, I can begin to feel the first stirrings of compassion for myself. So the first step is to have the courage to name what is happening and not to be afraid to stay with that wounded part, however difficult that may be.

So I start a swaying motion with my whole body swaying from side to side as I am standing with my feet wide apart and knees slightly bent. I can feel my connection with gravity and that the whole of planet Earth is supporting me. I keep swaying for about 5 or 10 minutes, until I reach a place of stillness, a place of calmness and place of grounded presence. From a still point of knowing that I am grounded within myself, I use the next steps of this six-step technique of Wholebody focusing (that will be described in more detail later on in this book) to transform this issue. I open myself, through the power of awareness to the greater potentialities that exist as my inner world connects with a sense of something bigger out there that is supporting me. I stop "doing" and I simply start "being".

I realise that I will not be able to force myself to write this book, because there are parts of me that are resisting and blocking and they are just as strong as the part that wants to write the book, so there is a stalemate. I need to understand this part of me in a compassionate way, what is it so afraid of? What is it that this part wants or doesn't want to happen?

I begin to get a sense of an inner wisdom inside of me that knows more than I think that I know at this point in time, that can get a bit of distance to this wounded part and yet still stay in relationship with it. There is a sudden flash of intuition and I know that this part is reluctant to write the book because of a fear of what the critics might say. Some people are going to like it, and some people are going to dislike it, and when I get critical feedback something inside me feels so hurt and vulnerable, that I just want to curl up and die. Its because I can't stand up and defend myself and I hate confrontation. There is a sudden wave of self-compassion, "Oh, I understand why you feel this way sometimes!" I decide to allow myself to hold both parts equally, the part that wants to write the book and the part that is afraid of writing the book, and let them both be there in total self compassion and without any judgments about relative worth, as they both have something to say. Something inside says, "Just trust, stop trying so hard and see what happens from a place of trust rather than from that frustrated act of trying to force things against an inner resistance that seems equally powerful".

As I reach a state of calmness and detached awareness several subtle bodily shifts and releases begin to take place and my consciousness clarifies itself. As I make the effort to hold the attention steady things begin to shift, my heart begins to fill with a sense of the fullness of life, "life is beautiful, my heart is uplifted, I'm so glad to be alive when there is a sense of connecting to the larger life all around me, a sense of the vibrancy and aliveness in everything".

I also feel something shift in the position of my head, as my head lifts itself and I am suddenly looking forwards, seeing everything really clearly and in sharp focus. My vision widens into peripheral vision as well, I can literally see the larger perspective, like the landscape suddenly becomes more alive, and it becomes vibrant and seems bigger. I am aware that I am "looking forwards to life". I think to myself, "Life is exciting, its full of possibilities". Instead of feeling defeated I feel pro-active and that I have an abundance of energy to make things happen". There was a tingling sensation within my whole body, which now feels expanded, and a sense of deep joy in my heart. I feel that I have regained a wonderful sense of spaciousness in my body; a lightness of being, and in that space there is now room for a free flow of energy and intelligence. At the same time I shift into a more relaxed and confident mood, feeling alive and energised with a vibrant sense of self worth.

I notice how there are many subtle shifts within my posture, musculature and alignment that have occurred in a natural whole body process. There is an opening of my whole body, with my chest expanded, an upward flow of energy in the body which lifted my head up, making me feel "open to the world". It felt like my eyes are letting in more light, more clarity to see the goodness of the world that exists all the time, in the present moment, all around me and in my heart. Above all there is a shift in consciousness to a place of detached perspective I am aware of my whole energetic body......supporting and sustaining me...of my body working when I ask it to move into action......I am aware of my mind working smoothly and calmly when I want it to......of my intuition clicking in when I need to know something extra about the situation.....I suddenly realise "Its not about fighting against the blockages, its about living in the flow of the moment".

In fact, now that I have stopped trying so hard to achieve and just reached stillness and clarity, this inner wisdom knows how to write perfectly, eloquently in a smooth flow of words that come from a place of deep intuitive knowing.

Several other thoughts rise strongly to the surface of my consciousness:

Feeling stuck in life is only an energy that has become blocked. Through the power of awareness that blocked energy can be released into a positive, forward moving life direction. Something positive can be achieved, in a seemingly effortless way. Its the same energy; just that what was blocked has now become free flowing.

I realise that first I had to deepen my awareness, to recognise and to name my stuck, depressed situation. Paradoxically, it is only by staying with the reality of what is happening inside me now and owning it, that enables me to change and move on from it.

It is painful to admit responsibility for my mistakes, to see the part that I have played in creating this whole situation. It is easier to go into victim mode and to blame others for my suffering, thus making them the persecutors. However, if I do have the courage to take responsibility for my part of the mess that I am in, then it empowers me- because then I can change that part. My behavior pattern starts to exhibit less of the unconscious saboteur and more conscious self-direction. Taking responsibility enables me to grow.

Previously, my life story kept repeating the theme of cutting off from myself and disempowerment. Now, finally my bodymind has shifted beyond that, to a different more alive and energised place and I no longer believe the old messages stored in my subconscious mind.

I have a real sense of self-worth now, which I can feel it in my body as a positive, expansive feeling. It is the aliveness of my energetic body, which is vibrating in every cell of my being. There is a golden glow within, a real physical sensation of expansion and upliftment. There is a positive energy that has been liberated from the wounded part.

Feeling calm and clear I focus my attention on the bodily shifts that had taken place and ask myself what they mean for me. I feel completely different in several key areas. Several words come clearly to mind that describe the shift. I write them down:

"I feel grounded and I feel alive,
My head is up and my eyes are looking forwards.
My heart feels uplifted.
Life is beautiful, I'm so glad to be alive,
I am connecting to a sense of the larger life, within and all around me,
Where there is a vibrancy, an aliveness in everything.
My Life is full of possibilities".

Now I can start to write this book about Wholebody focusing, which is about using my power of awareness to process all the blockages and stuck energy in my life into a positive, forward moving life direction.

Chapter 1. The Shift into Embodied Thinking

There is an important difference between our normal cognitive thinking and "embodied thinking" and a distinct difference to the whole body feel of embodied thinking. This embodied thinking involves getting into a timeless, expanded, spacious zone, where you are smoothly focused on the object of concentration, but also able to softly relax and widen out into greater awareness of your body and the surrounding environment, riding the energy wave of pure awareness from time to time. Everybody knows about cognitive thinking, you do not have to learn it, the thinking, planning, and decision making capacity of the pre-frontal cortex is there all the time. But the limitations of relying on cognitive thinking in isolation only start to appear when confronting the huge life problems that are way outside of your comfort zone, when you have to start thinking outside of the box in order to find creative answers. The problem arises with trying to use the pre-frontal cortex on its own, un-integrated with input from other parts of the brain. That's when you feel overwhelmed by the complexity of the subject and unable to reach clarity or any original and creative ideas.

Added to that is the problem of emotional hijacking. You can get triggered; when a particular thought, sensation or image arises that has powerful associations in your memory with a stressful or traumatic incident from the past. Often however, this is implicit, subconscious memory, so something feels wrong, but it is murky and just below the level of consciousness. You are aware that something is not quite right, but you are not aware of what it is exactly.

The real question is how to integrate the pre-frontal cortex effectively and this it not just a question of blocking out unwanted, distracting thoughts – which is a negative method, but how to find a positive method so all of your thoughts are flowing in a one directed stream of clear intention and awareness. When you first start to learn meditation techniques you realise how much the mind wanders into unwanted areas when you are trying to keep it focused on one particular line of thought or awareness and you need to learn specific techniques to direct your thoughts so that they are focused but also broaden them out so that they are receptive. Most of all, if you just allow your thoughts to come and go at random, without any awareness at all – then you are living with a reactive mind rather than a truly creative mind and the quality of your life suffers.

The 17th-centaury French philosopher Rene Descartes sums up the purely cognitive, un-integrated pre-frontal cortex in the famous statement: "Cogito ergo sum", "I think therefore I am". This summed up his rationalist philosophy and influenced European thought for centuries. He divided nature into the realm of the mind, *res cognitans*, and the realm of matter, *res extensa*. Human beings were defined as isolated minds, separated from God, from their physical bodies, from each other and from their environment. This worldview came to be generally accepted because the scientific discoveries of the analytical, reductionist model of thinking led to an era of dynamic technological change and inventions. It directly led to the Newtonian, mechanistic view of a world that is essentially materialistic because it seeks to understand our world by breaking things down into their component parts so that we know how they work. Once we know how things work, we can use that knowledge of the causal laws of Nature in order to improve our physical health and comfort as a path to happiness. The discovery of fundamental forces like gravity, magnetism, electricity and nuclear energy has of course led to brilliant inventions like the internal combustion engine, the airplane, electronics, computers, space travel and nuclear power. These are wonderful technological advances that have led to a wholesale re-organisation and expansion of human life on this planet. The only problem is that if our psychological and spiritual development does not keep pace with this technological development we will end up wiping out the entire human species. Our final achievement being that we found more and more efficient ways of exploiting the planet and killing each other.

It works to a certain extent, until you realise that this view of the world is always going to be dealing with parts and not wholes, dealing with symptoms rather than causes and viewing human beings as material objects rather than as spiritual beings. A doctor or a scientist who is trained in this way runs the danger of becoming overspecialised, of knowing more and more about less and less, until he or she knows everything about nothing! Scientific knowledge runs into the danger of becoming terribly specialised and fragmented. We are only just now starting to train our scientists and doctors to think how systems function as a whole, how these different holistic systems, including human beings, interact with each other and move towards their common evolutionary purpose, which gives a planetary and spiritual perspective to life.

When Descartes said, "I think therefore I am" he made the classic error of equating Being with thinking and of identifying himself with his thinking mind. This is a really basic mistake and in a sense our whole western culture, economy and education system is based on this delusion. It is what makes our whole system tick and we buy into it because it is an underlying cultural assumption that few people question – at least up till now few people have questioned it apart from the poets and the mystics, and they have never counted for very much really. Now with the findings of modern neuroscience the value of a detached, observing consciousness has been proven, and a paradigm shift in human consciousness is underway. But it is still not easy to practice meditation or mindfulness in our daily activities. It is the ego's job to keep us thinking incessantly, new ideas, new plans, new hopes and fears – all of which is hard-wired to protect us, keep us safe and to promise us happiness at some point in the future. There is a kind of compulsiveness to the thinking mind that makes it very difficult to stop and observe it and then to experience what deep interior silence is like. You are not free to make a choice until you have experienced what the alternative is.

Is it possible for you to switch off the cognitive mind and to get into grounded presence and to reach a state of pure awareness where you are the watcher of your thoughts? If not then you are still trapped in your cognitive mind and the ego with all of its hopes and fears is in the driving seat and running your life. There is a process, that will be described at some length in this book, of being able to switch to the position of the detached observer of your thoughts and gradually slowing them down until all thoughts stop and you reach a sense of deep peace and joy – without the interference of the running commentary of your mind. But first you have to have the realization that "I am not my thoughts", and secondly experience that even without my thoughts there is still a sense of your self, of your aliveness, of a consciousness that can be aware of your thoughts as they arise. But what is important is the way that you watch your thoughts – where you become the silent witness of your thoughts. When you are in grounded presence there is a new dimension to your consciousness, you feel a conscious presence, your deeper self, which is behind or underneath the thought. There is more spaciousness because you can feel your feet or your pelvic bones in contact with gravity and your body becomes the container that has enough space to contain all of these different thoughts and feelings that represent different parts of yourself. You can accept them and let them be there without feeling the compulsion to act on them. So there is no identification with your thoughts and you are not trying to force something, or fight it or fix it. There is a time for right action later on in the process, but the first stage is the ability to get into grounded presence and to become the silent watcher of your thoughts.

Many people confuse the words mind and brain. They are not interchangeable because the mind can become conscious of the way that the brain is functioning. This has at least three fundamental aspects: awareness of personal subjective experience, awareness of consciousness *with a sense of knowing that which is known,* and a regulatory function that could be defined as "an embodied and relational process that regulates the flow of energy and information" (Dan Siegel). So the brain is picking up all of this input from our senses telling us what is happening in the outer environment, from the internal sense of what is happening in the body and also from our relationships in the world, but the mind then needs to act to regulate all of this flow of energy and information in an emerging, self-organising process.

The mind can act as a filter in order to regulate the amount of information coming to our attention, so that we can survive in a dangerous situation, or concentrate on the top priority task at hand and complete the job. So in a sense this ability to narrow down and cut out unnecessary, extra information is crucial to survival. This narrowing down and cutting out is essentially a primitive survival response of the brain. It is needed for survival in a dangerous environment, and this was an essential survival skill at an earlier stage of evolution, but it is not the most relevant or creative life skill at this stage of human evolution. This survival response where there is high arousal of the limbic brain and the nervous system together with a very focused cognitive mind is actually no more than a stage in the evolution of consciousness, we need to progress onwards to the next stage now. Pure cognitive thinking, disconnected from the body is only one aspect of consciousness. Thought cannot exist without consciousness, but pure consciousness can be present without thoughts, and in pure consciousness based on a real sense of ongoing support and safety, there lies the possibility of an expanded energetic connection with and real empathy for others.

The mind also operates in such a way that even the limited amount of sensory information coming through is often not experienced freshly, but comes through the additional filter of your pre-conceived concepts from your past experiences, or is seen through the wistful rose-tinted spectacles of your hopes for the future. So you are never really living in the full experience of the present moment but always on the way to some future point of happiness or else deriving some illusory sense of self by extrapolating from the past into the present and the future. These are very subtle things I am talking about, but the only thing that really exists is the present moment and that can never be experienced fully in all its' richness and creativity unless you are in grounded presence, which means being connected to your body. Only then is it possible to shift into Embodied Thinking and become truly creative, make good decisions and become productive of good in the world.

But at the moment the analytical, reductionist thinking still dominates our education system and our western materialistic culture. Symbolically speaking, most people's heads are still separated from their bodies. This state of disembodied being and thinking is a very dangerous situation to be in. If you could really scan people's brains with an fMRI scanner you would see how disconnected most people are. They have thoughts and feelings and physical sensations of course, but these different parts are not properly integrated into a functioning whole that is at ease with themselves and others. They are effectively bodies walking around without heads and heads walking around without bodies. As a result of this disconnection many people feel alienated, unsupported and afraid unable to connect with themselves deeply, or with the world, unable to find the "right" partner, feeling overwhelmed by the complexity and the need for constant decisions of life. They are trying very hard but at the end of the day it is too much, life is too difficult – you simply cannot live life on your own as a dis-embodied cognitive being and still manage to find your way through the maze - without a sense of connection to something bigger that is supporting you.

One sad consequence of all this fragmentation and separation is that many people tend to give away their power to the so-called experts. Of course it is good to listen to a trained accountant, a smart business consultant or a good doctor at times. These are trained professionals who have specialised knowledge that can save you a lot of time and trouble with their good advice. But at the end of the day you are also the expert on your life, you have a source of wisdom deep within yourself, you also have an intuitive knowledge and insights that are valid and need to be taken into account. What happens at those moments in life when you run up against problems that seem too big to handle on your own and the "experts" are unable to help? A chronic health problem that the medical system cannot heal? Problems at work or a financial crisis that seems too overwhelming to handle? At times of looming major personal crisis such as a death in the family, divorce, redundancy, or mental health problems there are no easy pat solutions. It feels too big for you to cope with alone and yet suddenly none of the so-called experts are able to help. What do you do when you are thrown back on your own resources, how resilient and self-reliant are you at moments like these? If you are a head without a body it becomes pretty difficult because you lack the inner self-support to be able to handle it effectively. Every person comes up against these situations at one time or another in their lives. All of your familiar survival strategies, your known and previously effective techniques for dealing with life, no longer work. The harder you try the worse it seems to get, what happens now?

This is where mindfulness and the concept of neural integration come in. This is a very broad, system-based view of how the brain functions. As a WBF Trainer I like to look at the way the brain and the body function as a whole system, and then to move to an even larger perspective of looking at the ways in which signals from one brain/body interact with significant others in personal relationships, families and societies. This is what I will be doing in this book, and this is why I am a great admirer of the work of Dan Siegel at UCLA. The mind, through mindfulness, has the ability to affect the function of the brain and achieve greater neural integration. To be integrated creates optimal functioning because there is a coordination and balance of neural activation. Coordination means that you can monitor and then influence the firing pattern of different regions into a well-functioning whole. Balance means being able to regulate the activation or deactivation of these linked areas.

Many of the principles that FM Alexander developed in the AT, which are able to release excessive muscular tension, improve balance and reduce arousal in the nervous system all have close parallels with Mindfulness and play a crucial role in Embodied Thinking. Purely cognitive thinking has been accepted in this society because it has an underlying assumption that no one questions, and that is so prevalent – in our relationships, work and education system. When you are so fixated on achieving your goal or solving your problem, you are fixated on one goal, one point only. You have no sense of spaciousness and no time to enjoy the journey getting there, and you will very often tighten up and become inflexible in your thinking. When you are completely identified with your goal you are unable to relax and just be. Life becomes full of all these problems and conflicts. There is an incessant background noise in your head that prevents you from just being, you cannot reach the inner quiet and stillness, *the pure awareness without thought*, that I call being in "grounded presence". When you can find a way to stop the thoughts then you can be fully present in your body and connect with a deeper level of Being. There is such peacefulness in grounded presence. Its like you don't have to chase after anything because you have it all already, the happiness and fulfillment you have been seeking is to be found deep within yourself and not out there somewhere. There is a sense of being grounded in a deeper sense of self, the real self that is linked to all of life and the essential unity of life – and then the answers, the insights will come to you instead of you chasing after them all of the time. Then the cognitive mind can be utilized, after the deep inner knowing, to find a way of implementing those insights in the world.

This being in the present moment is of course what mindfulness is all about, so none of this is new to the Buddhists. But mindfulness can be defined in many different ways, as Dan Siegel does here:

"One way of conceptualising mindfulness is that it is intentionally focusing attention on moment-to-moment experience without being swept up by judgments or preconceived ideas and expectations...Another way of defining mindfulness is in avoiding premature closure of possibilities that often come with a "hardening of categories" by which we filter and constrain our perceptions of the world.... And even in our everyday use of the word mindful, we have the connotation of being thoughtful, considerate and aware...In each of these three ways, being mindful brings an awakened mind to focus on things as they are with care and concern, to literally be present in awareness with what is happening right now."

So bringing a quality of mindful awareness to present experiencing is what is needed, but as the mind lives so much in the future or in the past, and very little in the present moment, awareness of the present moment experiencing of body sensations plays a crucial role in all of this. It sounds simple, but actually it isn't an easy practice. The body is the key so you have to keep bringing your awareness back to what is going on inside your body right now if you want to get to the truth of the present moment. But the body also has its defenses, patterns of body armouring that are part of your survival strategy and so habitual and deeply ingrained that they usually go unnoticed. As Alexander demonstrated, you will have unreliable and distorted sensory information about what is going on inside your body as long as bad posture, muscular tension patterns and emotional dissociation is splitting you up into lots of antagonistic bits. Of course the same process of lack of consciousness is happening on an emotional level as you can be in denial of your emotional reactions and feelings about a situation. Because these emotions feel too difficult to face in the moment, people may block off from the experience and so they disappear from consciousness, but the memory and the conflicted energy of those feelings is still stored in the body. To become fully aware of what is going on inside the body/mind in a truly embodied way takes a lot of work.

But by the use of Embodied Thinking, self-inquiry and mental awareness of what's going on within the container of your body, it is possible to reintegrate with the whole of your self. Being in grounded presence gives you a sense of being linked to something bigger than yourself, to the natural order to the universe, even though you may feel chaotic, or vulnerable at times. The sense of lack, the holes within yourself that represent the vulnerability of the missing parts that you want other people or your community to fill, they can rise into consciousness and become less compulsive. You can then feel supported by the larger Life that surrounds and permeates you and less driven by inner lack.

This helps you to be more mindful and less judgmental of all your thoughts and emotions. You can start to notice how you get triggered by certain people and situations into compulsive mental & emotional reactions. These can suck you in and totally dominate your thinking process. As you refine your skill in watching the mind you will begin to see that there are lots of different voices in your head. Everybody has them, because these voices are your running commentary on your present situation. They speculate, judge and compare, they have likes and dislikes and these voices can be in agreement or disagreement within you as well as being friendly or antagonistic to the rest of the world. Its hard to escape from all this hustle and bustle of mental activity and many people never do. They end up never escaping from their thinking process because they have never learnt the technique of how to become the detached observer through the simple process of wholebody awareness, which allows all the different voices, and all the different parts of the personality that they represent, to just be there and to have the space to become even more themselves.

They need to be accepted just as they are without acting on them. Just let them be like waves that arise and then change and fall away again. This will eventually allow a state of pure, joyous "no-mind" – as it is often termed in Buddhism, to arise, which can then become embodied, creative thinking when you want to focus on something in particular. I am talking about a subtle process of self-observation that needs to take place here and I will go into all this in more detail later. Suffice to say that there is a qualitative change in consciousness that takes place here as you shift from being the victim of compulsive thoughts into a state of grounded presence, conscious of your deeper self, a sense of Being. Whilst the head is still un-integrated with the body and not in grounded presence, the thoughts will tend to be fragmented and have an antagonistic, compulsive or fearful quality to them. They also have a powerful capacity to suck you in so that you are no longer able to be detached about them.

It is very significant that the neuroscience research findings over the past decades have all demonstrated how a secure attachment in childhood will lead to neural integration and a capacity for self-regulation. All the research shows that secure attachment in early childhood with a primary care giver, is linked to an embodied sense of really being seen, heard and valued. That is why the quality of the relationship is really important in therapy. Obviously, an attuned and empathic relationship with a therapist in later life can have a really important reparative function for clients who have never felt fully seen or heard by their parents in childhood. There is no doubt at all about that now, or that some people may need to experience a secure relationship first, before they can give sustained attention to their own inner experience.

So now we are getting to the interesting bit, what neural circuits are activated when you feel that it is safe to be in your own body and you are aware of your own experience? This is the so-called "mohawk of self awareness". This circuit of Self awareness, which runs through the midline structures of the brain, starting above the eyes at the prefrontal medial cortex (our thinking, planning and decision-making part), linking with the insula – which transmits messages from the viscera (our gut) to the emotional centres, the parietal lobes, which register and integrate sensory information from the body, the anterior cingulate which coordinate emotions and thinking and the posterior cingulate, which is necessary for our basic orientation in space. All of these need to be activated and are laying the foundations for our consciousness of Self. This default state network (DSN) shows almost no activation in clients who have suffered early life trauma, but for the lucky people who have had a secure early childhood upbringing, there is an easy and natural sense of relating to their bodies, and a secure self-confidence in their relationships and communications with the world.

So these same midline structures of self-awareness can be activated by a secure attachment to parents in childhood, an empathic and safe relationship in later life (either with a partner or with a therapist) and the ability to come into a safe and non-judgmental relationship with self- through a wholebody awareness of our experience, which is the essence of Wholebody focusing or Mindfulness meditation. So looked at in terms of science and brain function, this is the first neural pathway that needs to be activated, and anything that can help to activate this "mohawk of self-awareness" is hugely important. Once you can find a way to reactivate these midline structures of the brain it opens the door to greater neural integration and self-regulation. As Dan Siegel says: " Neural integration, the coordination and balance of the brain as separate areas that are linked together to form a functional whole, seems to be promoted with the attunement of secure attachments. The proposal here is that perhaps we are gathering some preliminary data to point in the direction that mindful awareness may also promote such neural integration through a form of intrapersonal attunement". (D. Siegel, "The Mindful Brain", 2007).

So this is the first of the nine middle pre-frontal functions, these neural pathways are actually outcomes for secure, attuned attachment (the first seven) and it is also a list for the outcome of the process of Wholebody focusing, which I would propose as a form of internal attunement that leads to greater self-awareness and embodied thinking. This is just a list and I will go into these in more detail later on in the book.

> Self-awareness through body awareness, and the ability to regulate arousal of the nervous system. This actually means being able to feel your own

body and feeling safe to be in your own body. This is not a given, and most people are so stressed and hyper aroused that fairly skilled techniques like the AT, Open Focus or mindful breath awareness are needed first in order to calm the arousal of the nervous system.

Attuned communication with another human being is a resonance process that involves the medial pre-frontal cortex. How to really take on board what the other person is saying, whilst maintaining a sense of what you your truth is and what you need is a coordinated balancing act. What seems to be crucial is the ability to maintain an attitude of curiosity, open mindedness, acceptance, and love (COAL) – both to the other person and to yourself.

Emotional balance implies the ability to allow the emotional brain (the limbic area) to have enough activation so that you are in touch with the meaning and vitality of your emotions, but not so much that you are overwhelmed by them and life becomes chaotic. As Gene Gendlin used to say: "You need to be able to smell the soup but not be in it". The middle pre-frontal cortex regions have the capacity to monitor emotions and inhibit limbic firing with high levels of bidirectional flow from the subcortical limbic to the middle pre-frontal regions.

The pre-frontal cortex has the capacity to pause before launching into action. This ensures flexibility of response and the ability to choose wisely from a variety of possible options rather than just launching into a habitual reaction. Both the AT and Gendlin's

Focusing technique emphasise the idea of the radical pause.

Cultivating empathy by asking the pre-frontal cortex to pay attention to our mirror neurons in the resonance circuits. As you closely pay attention to another person's body language, facial expression and tone of voice, you actually start to feel inside your own body, in a form of empathic imagination, what might be going on for the other person. These are called mirror neurons and this functions by way of the circuits that link the insula (which picks up internal body signals, especially linked with the vagal nerve and the connection from the neck right down to the stomach and gut areas) and the medial pre-frontal cortex. Paying attention to this sort of empathic response is important in both the AT and in Focusing. Of course this then links back to attuned communication, because if there is genuine empathy, the other person will really feel heard and then something shifts for them inside.

Insight or self-knowing occurs when you really understand your life story and the way lessons learnt from the past can affect present choices and future outcomes. The pre-frontal cortex has fibers that link it to the autobiographical memory stores in the hippocampus, and limbic firing that gives emotional texture to the contents of your story. WBF can help you to work with your life story, to integrate it, maybe to get a different perspective on it and give it a different meaning, and finally to give it a different ending.

Fear modulation is carried out via the release of the GABA neurotransmitter onto the lower limbic areas mediating fear, such as the extended nuclei of the amygdala. Fear may be "unlearned" by reframing the experience and putting it in a new perspective. If the fear or the problem is approached rather than trying to escape it, then something different happens. "Its not the end of the world, I'm still alive and breathing, I can learn something here". A secure attachment and WBF would both aid this process.

Intuition seems to be linked with input from information processing neural networks surrounding the viscera, the heart, lungs and intestines, so again the neural links from the pre-frontal cortex to the insula are important. There seems to be a body wisdom in these areas that has ways of knowing about people and situations that is separate from any sensory input. Calmness and moving into high alpha and theta wave activity seem to be important here. Once this information can be reliably trusted it can then influence reasoning and emotional reactions.

Morality: the middle pre-frontal cortex seems to be important in the development of morality. If you can imagine how you wouldn't like to be on the receiving end of that behavior then why do it to somebody else? At its most essential morality means the ability to consider the bigger picture and to consider what is best for the whole and not just for yourself. The middle pre-frontal cortex when damaged seems to be associated with a deficiency in moral thinking.

As well as the nine pathways of neural integration from the pre-frontal cortex to other areas of the brain wave, this also an integration of the left brain/right brain polarity that is possible. There are structural differences between the left and the right hemispheres that have long been studied by neuroscience and these lead to some relevant and quite important differences in function between the two sides. The left hemisphere controls the physical movement and receives sensory information from the right side of the body, whereas the right hemisphere controls the physical movement and the sensory functions of the left side of the body. However, in other respects their function is asymmetrical. The left side of the brain contains regions associated with language and is more rational, logical and analytical. The right side of the brain is non-verbal, concerned with more holistic understanding, and visual/spatial perception. In addition it is concerned with: autobiographical memory, creating an integrated map of the whole body, initial non-verbal empathic responses, a dominance in the alerting aspect of attention, the expression and modulation of emotion and symbolic understanding, According to recent research up to 90% of human communication occurs in the non-verbal, right hemisphere realm. Caring, disapproval and indifference are all primarily conveyed by facial expression, tone of voice and physical movements.

The right side is thought to mediate distress and uncomfortable emotions and correlates with a withdrawal from difficult problems. The evidence for the left side is that it mediates more positive emotional states and correlates with approach behavior to try and deal with the problem. Being aware of these differences in behavior and trying to coordinate more between the left and right sides of the brain can help to change your emotional style. As Davidson has shown, mindfulness - which is any practice that can help shift you into the detached observer role – appears to lead towards an approach state, with a left-sided shift in frontal electrical activity (Davidson, 2000). Hopefully integration could include a sense of both what you are afraid of and don't want to happen (and to allow for the lessons learnt from that) as well as a sense of what you do want and the actions that you can initiate to get your needs met. When the functions are separated in this way, the brain can integrate them into a state of connection to achieve more complex and adaptive functions.

Now the Focusing process involves a crucial integration between left and right side in trying to find the right word or phrase that fits the inner emotional and physical experience of "the whole thing". So this is quite subtle because whilst the left side is linguistic and can propose certain words or phrases, the right side of the brain is concerned with getting the feel of the whole thing and checking to try and see if the words or phrases generated resonate and fit with the feeling of that whole thing. This resonating process can take some time, going back and forth between getting a sense of the whole thing and then finding the right words that fit. This is a crucial part of Wholebody focusing and we shall go into all that in more detail later on in the book.

Purely cognitive thinking is the disembodied mind running your life and leading you from one emotional drama to the next. It is also very uncreative and unoriginal thinking, very often just replaying old belief patterns or other people's ideas. Whilst embodied thinking is the integrated brain getting a sense of its own meaning and direction secure in the awareness of support from the whole body. This book is about the difference between purely cognitive thinking and embodied thinking and the advantages of embodied thinking. Everybody knows how to think in a narrow cognitive way, the problems only seem to arise when you encounter conflict and uncertainty – moving forwards into new areas in your life when the old ways of coping, the old answers no longer work so you have to try and find a different answer. That is when you need to go deep within, to let go of the cognitive mind for a moment and search for that inner spark of creativity, a guidance from an inner sense of knowing that is more than you think you know.

So, if I am thinking about a problem, I can only be open to the infinite potential of new possibilities - if I am OK with not knowing the "correct answer" immediately. I can only know what right is if I am prepared to be wrong. If I can hold apparent conflict, incongruity, not knowing what to do in that situation, and be comfortable with that because I am in grounded presence, then I can be comfortable with not knowing. There is a type of grasping for certainty, of wanting to know the solution, of needing to be right and seen to be clever, that is actually cutting me off from finding the answer that is waiting to happen, the most simple, elegant and perfect solution. Afterwards people can always look back and say "of course, that was the simple, obvious answer to the problem" – hindsight is a great teacher - but why do the mass of people not see that before, while it takes an advanced intuitive thinker, someone that we label "a genius" to find that simple, elegant truth?

The great genius Einstein had this capacity, his brain was shown to be in predominantly alpha rhythms for most of the time, so when working on complex mathematical equations he would work with this holistic sense of "the whole thing" first, reaching a felt sense of the right direction he needed to go in. Only at the end would he use his detailed mathematical knowledge to work through the problem and to demonstrate the final solution. All great thinkers have this capacity to cut through the confusion of collective opinions and false concepts to get to a sense of "the whole thing" and then to alternate and bring in the analytical mind at crucial points when needed. Your ideas concerning the nature and overall implications of any problem are in a continuous process of growth and change. It is important to get away from fixed dogmas and to allow a little bit of lightness and flexibility, each problem and situation is unique and it is by opening up to that sense of "the whole thing", that insight and clarity comes and a real forward moving life energy emerges.

Chapter 2:
Brain Basics

In the early 1990's new brain-imaging technology, like single photon emission computerized tomography (SPEC) scans and functional magnetic resonance imaging (fMRI) scans opened up new possibilities in terms of actually seeing how different parts of the brain are activated when people are engaged in certain tasks or remember events from the past. You can now actually watch the brain as it processes memories, sensations and emotions, and map the brain circuits that are activated. Earlier technology had measured the levels of certain brain chemicals like serotonin or norepinephrine, which is essentially *the fuel of neural activity.* Now it is possible to actually look at the structure of the brain itself and see what areas are responsible for which activity and the circuits involved. This has hugely increased our understanding of our brain function.

The brain is built from the bottom up and our rational cognitive brain is actually the youngest part of our brain and occupies only 30% of the area inside the skull. The neo-cortex is the manager, making executive decisions about understanding how people and things out there function, and how we can accomplish goals, manage our time and plan our actions. But beneath the rational brain are two older brains, the limbic system (which gives an emotional reaction to the situation) and the brainstem (the reptilian brain), which developed earlier in our evolution, and are concerned with more basic concerns. Like: running the physical body, taking care of comfort, identifying safety, threat, tiredness, hunger, thirst, desire, excitement, pleasure and pain.

As the child develops in the womb the different, the different levels of the brain start to develop just as they did during the course of human evolution. The most primitive part, often known as the reptilian brain, develops first. It is located in the brain stem, just at the place where the brain balances on top of the spinal cord. It is an interesting fact that no surgeon has ever been able to perform an operation on the brain stem, if they cut into it – you are dead. This is because it controls survival, all the basic body functions that a baby can already do once its born. Things like: eat, sleep, wake, cry, breath, feel temperature changes and wetness, hunger, pain, and rid the body of toxins by peeing and shitting. The brain stem and the hypothalamus (which sits directly above it) control the body's energy levels. They co-ordinate the stable functioning of the heart and lungs and also of the endocrine and immune systems. As a result all basic life-support systems, including our body temperature, are kept within a relatively stable internal balance. The body knows how to do this, without direction from our conscious minds, and this ability to bring us back to balance is called homeostasis. However, when there are deep-seated psychological problems, even though the mind may be in denial it is amazing how the body will manifest the lack of balance in terms of sleep disturbances, the bowels not working, problems with appetite, touch, breathing and arousal.

Right above the reptilian brain is the second level, the limbic system. This is also known as the mammalian brain because all mammals that live in groups and nurture their young have one. The limbic system really starts to develop after birth. It is the seat of emotions, watches out for danger, judges what is pleasurable or frightening, and does whatever is needed to ensure survival on an instinctive level. It is the command post for dealing with the challenges of a complex social world. The limbic system develops in response to our experiences and our relationships as well as being shaped by our genetic makeup and innate temperament. This is because the brain is plastic, scientists have discovered that neurons that "fire together, wire together". When a brain circuit fires repeatedly it can become a default setting, the response that is most likely to occur. If a baby feels safe and loved its brain becomes adept at exploration, play and co-operation. If a baby feels frightened and unwanted, it will develop strategies for managing feelings of fear and abandonment. These emotional experiences and our reactions to them are of course on-going and can be significantly modified by experiences later on in life, which is the great discovery and hope of neuroplasticity.

Taken together, the reptilian brain and the limbic system make up our "emotional brain". The emotional brain is at the heart of the central nervous system, and its key task is to look out for our well-being. It can detect life-threatening danger or wonderful sexual opportunities, and a whole range of opportunities in-between and when it does so it will then release hormones that give strong visceral sensations, which activate us in the desired direction. This is your Body Wisdom at work and tuning in with these subtle sensations and finding the words or phrases to make cognitive sense of them and hence make conscious decisions based on these insights, is one of the main life skills that Focusing helps us to develop. We are making these sorts of decisions all of the time. Based on our visceral body sensations we decide what we like to eat, who we feel at ease with and those people whom we get an instant aversion to, who we want to sleep with and have as a life partner or not, what type of music we like to listen to and if we like the great outdoors or prefer sitting at home drinking tea and eating cake. But if you learnt the Focusing technique it would help you to make a whole series of important life decisions by sensing into what feels right for you at an emotional level, rather than just the pro's and con's, and all the ought's and shoulds of the cognitive mind.

When a person is faced with a situation in which there is a threat to life, theirs or others, certain mechanisms in the emotional brain prepare for either fight or flight, or freeze. This is governed by brain chemistry – it is not a choice or an act of will. This is because the limbic system is organized to assess incoming information according to how it fits a rough template, and it will jump to conclusions based on approximate fit, e.g., I woke up one night and was making my way to the bathroom; I see a vague shape of a man in the hallway wearing a black leather jacket and a balaclava hat, which shocks me into total fright and rigid alertness. I immediately assume that its a burglar and get ready to either run, or defend myself if needed. Then I double-check the vague shadowy image in the hallway and realize that actually its my leather jacket and my woolen hat on the coat stand that had frightened me. Crisis over, I laugh at myself, but I could still feel my heart pounding. This is an example of how our muscular and physiological reactions are set into motion without any conscious thought or planning on our part, leaving the cognitive mind to catch up much later, after the threat is over. Its a necessary survival response that is hard-wired into our system.

Finally we reach the third layer of the brain, the most recent development in our evolution, which is the neo-cortex. Other mammals have this as well to a certain degree, but it is much thicker in humans and it really starts to develop from the second year of life onwards. The frontal lobes give us the capacity to use language and abstract thought. They give us the capacity to absorb and organize vast amounts of information and to find meaning in all of that. Only human beings have the capacity to use the words and symbols necessary to build communities, culture, and a sense of history the frontal lobes allow us to plan and reflect, to imagine scenarios and to make predictions. They make rational choice possible and artistic creativity. This knowledge can be stored and transmitted from one generation to the next so that a structure of scientific knowledge can be built up.

If this capacity for rational, linear thought becomes too abstract and divorced from any sense of emotional connection to others or empathy for them, then it becomes cold and unfeeling. It can lead to insanities such as economic exploitation of other human beings and cultures, dogmatism and all sorts of isms where the ends coldly justify the means, and can even lead to wars, mass death and genocide. Generally people who are hard and dogmatic towards others are also hard and unfeeling towards themselves, based on early childhood experiences. There is a lack of vertical integration in the brain, because the neo-cortex is not integrating with the emotional brain and other areas that connect you with physical awareness of your body.

However, the frontal lobes are also the seat of empathy, our ability to sense into somebody else's reality. This is through the function of "mirror neurons" and the discovery of how they function was one of the great breakthroughs of neuroscience. In 1994 a group of Italian scientists had attached electrodes to individual neurons in a monkey's premotor area, linked up to a computer so that they could see precisely which neurons fired when the monkey picked up a peanut or grasped a banana. At one point a scientist was placing food pellets into a box when he looked at the computer. The monkey's motor command neurons were firing – but the money wasn't eating or moving. He was simply watching the scientist and his brain was vicariously mirroring what the scientist was doing.

Soon numerous other experiments around the world repeated this finding, not just in animals but in humans too. These findings explained how we pick up not only on other people's movement, gesture and body language, but also on their emotional state and intentions as well. It explains empathy, imitation, getting in tune with another person, and even the development of language. Mirror neurons are tremendously important in terms of our developmental attunement between mother and infant, the development of social organization and our spiritual understanding. You can see them at work in everyday situations, when people are in tune with each other they will mirror each other's gestures and body language, and their voices will take on the same intonation and rhythms. We can be uplifted by someone else's enthusiasm, provoked by their anger or dragged down by their depression. Its an important skill to be able to keep strong boundaries and awareness of self in grounded presence, at the same time as being able to empathise and understand how someone else is going through it, and to feel for them without trying to make it different (because actually you can't, you can only listen and they are the only one's who can do that). Its an important life skill to be able to understand other people's motives, expectations and values, and accept that they can be different from yours and you just need to adapt to them being different without needing to change yourself, or them!

Mirror neurons and empathy is a fundamental part of being human. We pick up on another person's gesture, facial expression, body language, tone of voice and emotional expression and feel what they are feeling within our own bodies, our own selves, and as a result of knowing how they feel, we feel empathy. But, some people who have suffered severe developmental trauma early in life and who are cut off from their own body and emotions will also find it hard to feel empathy for others.

It is also important to mirror back to people in order to feel acceptance into the group or the tribe. You will feel part of a group and accepted, through tuning in with your mirror neurons and mirroring back the gestures, emotions, and tone of voice and style of dress. However, later on once the real individuation process starts, its important to be able to maintain a clear sense of self, separate from all family, cultural and group pressures. Able to maintain secure boundaries and a strong sense of self and able to sense into what feels right for you and act accordingly. That sense of self needs to be maintained against the pressure that is coming from peer groups, and family or social structures.

Danger is a part of life, and our success at surviving is due to our ability to respond quickly to any sensory information that could be dangerous. Information is gathered in the Thalamus and there are two ways of responding: one route goes down to the amygdala, two small almond-shaped structures that lie deep in the limbic, unconscious brain, which triggers an instinctive reaction; and the other goes up to the frontal lobes where this information reaches conscious awareness and we can decide on a conscious response. Joseph LeDoux, the neuroscientist, has call the pathway to the amygdala "the low road", and has termed the pathway to the frontal cortex, which takes a few milliseconds longer, "the high road".

When under threat, the thalamus passes sensory information onto the amygdala, which can process the information faster than the frontal lobes, and if it decides that the information is a threat to survival then the limbic system goes into overdrive.

The body can move instinctively even before our mind is consciously aware, like when you find yourself ducking to avoid a ball flying towards your head, or get out of the way of a car which is about to run you down. The amygdala, the part of the limbic system which Bessel van der Kolk has termed the body's "smoke detector," enables us to sense a threat and to react quickly. It triggers the release of powerful stress hormones, including cortisol and adrenaline, which increase heart rate, blood pressure and rate of breathing – which prepares the body for the fight or flight response. Once the danger is over the body returns to its normal state fairly quickly. But when action and then recovery has been blocked, the body is still triggered to defend itself so people feel constantly agitated and aroused – with no resolution.

Trauma increases the risk of misinterpreting information, confusing what is real danger with what may be just a reminder of something that occurred in the past and is now over. Because the amygdala is overreacting to the current environment and not discriminating between past and present, traumatised people react as if the danger is happening now. So its hard to judge if people are just being playful or actually being dangerous and painful misunderstandings in relationships can occur. There can be violent explosions or pained shut-downs in response to innocent comments or facial expressions. But this obviously creates psychological and social problems – not the least of which is the feeling of struggling to stay in control and get through the day.

The "high road" is when the frontal lobes, and specifically the medial prefrontal cortex (MPFC), which is located directly above our eyes, starts to operate as the "watchtower", to view the scene from on high. If you can pause and inhibit your immediate panic reactions, (which both the Alexander

Technique and Focusing make room for) then it is possible to choose a wise and responsible response to the situation that is not just a triggered response from our hardwired, automatic reactions which have been programmed into the emotional brain. This is mindfulness, being able to hover calmly over our thoughts, feelings, bodily sensations and emotions and to observe what is going on. This allows an overview of all the different options and probable consequences, as well their emotional significance without being attached to any particular outcome in advance. It is a real skill, but this capacity is essential for preserving our relationships with our fellow human beings. When this capacity breaks down we become just like conditioned animals – as soon as we detect danger we go into our default survival response, fight, flight or freeze.

The pre-frontal cortex and especially the MPFC has greatly reduced activity during highly emotional states. This is because during a traumatic event thinking would interfere with instinctual "animal defensive" responses and this would be a threat to life. So, the pre-frontal cortex shuts down in the interest of survival. Unfortunately, it often remains in that state in PTSD, as the critical balance between the amygdala (the smoke alarm) and the MPFC (the watchtower) has radically shifted, which makes it much harder to control emotions and impulses. With some brain systems shut down and others in the sub-cortical brain regions in hyper-drive, people over-generalise what represents danger and are unable to think clearly. They startle in response to loud sounds, become enraged by small frustrations, or completely misinterpret facial expressions and tone of voice. This is also why lots of people have problems post-trauma with concentration, memory, decision-making, and talking about what happened to them.

Basically, since the stress hormones are then carried in the body there are two ways of managing the situation: top-down or bottom-up regulation. Both will achieve a better balance between the watchtower and the smoke detector. Top-down regulation involves strengthening the capacity of your MPFC (watchtower) to monitor your emotions and your body's sensations. So things like Focusing, mindfulness, different meditation techniques, neurofeedback and any form of self awareness technique will all help greatly in this regard. The most effective forms of bottom-up regulation are those that can recalibrate the autonomic nervous system (ANS), which talk therapy alone cannot do (as the arousal of the ANS originates in the brain stem). Any therapies that work through the body, using breath, touch or slow movement to calm the emotions and nervous system will be helpful. So therapies like the Alexander Technique, Yoga, Pilates or Feldenkreis method are particularly good. The two keys are: slowing the breath, as breathing is one of the few body functions that is under both conscious and autonomic control, so consciously calming the breath will help to regulate arousal in the ANS; and awareness of awareness, of how you are paying attention right now.

It is important to understand that this three-part description of the brain, is not proposing that reason is opposed to emotion. That in essence is the old paradigm of the rational, logical and scientific mind. That's old school now, what the modern neuroscience is telling us is that emotions assign value to our experience and are thus the foundation of reason. There are many studies that show that awareness of emotions is a vital part of a competent decision making process. Only a fully-rounded person, who is in touch with their self awareness on all levels, who can balance the rational and emotional brains, only such a person can feel "comfortable in their own skin" and think in an embodied way.

The neuroscientist Paul MacLean, who developed the three-part description of the brain that I've described here, compared the relationship between the rational brain and the emotional brain to one between a good rider and his horse. As long as the conditions are fairly smooth and nothing unexpected happens the rider can feel safely in control and enjoy the ride. However, unexpected sounds, threats from other animals or a sudden thunderstorm with lightening can cause the horse to bolt, and suddenly the rider is just hanging on for dear life. Similarly, when people feel that they are fighting for survival, or they are seized by rages, sexual desires or great fear, they stop thinking in a rational way and it is hard to reason with them. That's because inside their own brains the limbic system has hijacked the functioning of the rational mind in the frontal lobes. When the limbic system decides that something is a matter of life or death, it takes off just like the startled horse with the rider clinging to its back.

Many psychologists, especially those from the cognitive behavioural therapy school, will try to help people to get a new perspective on their situation and to use mental insight to regulate their behaviour. Whilst this is useful in reasonably well-functioning individuals who are facing an unexpected major crisis, it is not so useful for people who are holding the experience of major trauma in their bodies or PTSD. Because the neuroscience research is showing that many psychological problems originate from pressures from the deeper areas of the brain that then drive our motivation and our attention. When the alarm bells of the emotional brain are ringing to signal that your life is in danger, no amount of cognitive reasoning will silence it. It is then that we need bottom-up regulation which involves being more aware of the body, getting more grounded, creating more space for the breath to come and go – which will then calm the breathing down as you simply observe it. Also the AT is crucial, because by freeing the neck it becomes possible for the pressure on the brainstem to be released and as a result the fight/flight reaction gets turned off and more information starts to flow in from the rest of the body.

The same goes for any situation when our rational and emotional brains are in conflict. All f these catch-22 situations, when you are enraged with someone you love, or frightened by someone you depend on, or lust after someone who is not available for a relationship, bring up huge levels of emotional arousal and feeling blocked and powerless at the same time. A tug-of-war ensues between our rational and our emotional brains, and because most people do not have the WBF skills to be able to deal with these conflicts and find a resolution, the sense of blockage and frustration is played out in the body, mostly in the areas of visceral experience in your gut, your heart and your lungs. This leads to both physical discomfort and psychological misery. In chapter 5, "Tools for staying in contact with our experience on a deeper level" and chapter 6 "A manual of WBF", I will describe in greater detail, powerful ways to deal with these deep-seated conflicts.

How you deal with emotional frustration or conflict depends on your earliest emotional memory. Professor Alan Schore from the University of California (Schore, 1994) and Bruce Perry (Perry et al., 1995) have both done extensive and significant work is on the neurobiology of emotional development. They have both proposed a similar neurological model for explaining the effects of secure or insecure mother/infant attachment as the foundation for healthy psychological development in later life – including your capacity to handle stressful experiences.

Their research findings are truly fascinating. Right from the moment of birth, the newborn infant feels overwhelmed by a flood of new sensory stimuli. The infant screams in response to this but when it is placed on its mother's belly and feels her warmth, hears her heartbeat and soothing voice, feels her loving touch – the infant is quickly soothed and made to feel secure. This is the first experience of stimulus regulation mediated by the mother. And ideally, so it goes on, the baby is upset and the presence of the mother soothes it. Gradually the mother also assists the child in regulating its emotional responses, when it feels hunger, pain or the discomfort of wet nappies. Mother and child develop an interactional pattern based on the stimulus of face-to-face contact. This enables the child to feel secure as it acclimatises to increasing degrees of stimulation and arousal. A healthy attachment between infant and mother/primary caretaker enables the infant to develop the capacity to self-regulate both positive and negative stimuli.

These interactions between mother and infant – bonding and attachment, upset and regulation, stimulus and attunement – are all right brain mediated. During infancy the right hemisphere is developing more quickly than the left, and the left-brain associated hippocampus is still immature. So it is the holistic right brain that takes in the soothing physical sensations of the presence of the mother. It is not a logical process with a narrative story line, it is the feel of the whole thing and the sense of the physical presence of the mother that soothes and regulates the child in early infancy.

Towards the end of the first year the relationship changes as the baby becomes mobile and more independent. The mother's role changes from being nurturing and soothing to sometimes setting limits and saying a clear "no". We are into the realms of limitations and possibilities and learning to deal with the inherent duality of the world. How successfully this change is dealt with depends on 3 factors: the security of the attachment bond, the capacity for the mother to display unconditional love despite the child's misbehaviour, and the ability of the mother to set and maintain fair and consistent boundaries. At the same time the hippocampus starts to develop in the limbic system, and as language begins to develop the child has a growing capacity to describe events and to make sense of his emotional and sensory experiences. The security of the childhood attachment then determines how well you are able to deal with the inevitable stress and dualities of life.

But why is it that some people are more affected by stress than others? A common assumption is that it is in their genes, which then determines their character, but is this true or not? Surely environment and training have just as much influence as our genetic make-up? There has been endless debate about this, and recently some very interesting scientific research has showed how environmental influences can penetrate into the very genes in our cells and turn them off or leave them on. In the 1990's biologist Michael Meaney began to study the stress response of rats in his lab. Some were extremely anxious and inhibited, they were a neurotic mess releasing a flood of stress hormones called glucocorticoids in response to stressful experiences, which got the heart pumping and the muscles primed for flight or fight. Others were more laid back and relaxed, they released only a trickle of glucocorticoid stress hormones when given electric shocks. Now here's the interesting bit, when they became mothers, mellow female rats regularly licked and groomed their pups, which obviously calmed and comforted the little one's, whereas the anxious mothers were too neurotic to attend to their maternal duties. So neurotic mums had neurotic pups and the tendency got passed on down the line.

The reason that the laid-back rats were less affected by stress hormones is that their brain has more receptors for them in the hippocampus. These receptors are docking stations for the hormones, and when there are more receptors in the brain, the body needs to produce less of the stress hormones. More receptors imply that you are more aware of what's going on, and because you are more aware the signals can be softer. So its like the mothers taught them to be more aware of the stress, but also to turn it off quicker – "there, there, you've had a tough day, its stressful getting all those electric shocks, but don't worry you are safe with mom now". As a direct result of more grooming and licking, the pups learnt to shrug off stressful experiences, to be curious, eager to explore new surroundings, and resilient in the face of life's set backs. There was some sort of resolution to the experience, and a moving forwards, whereas baby rats whose mother rarely licked and groomed them, grew up to be fearful and stressed out, prone to freezing in unfamiliar or unexpected situations.

Since anxious neurotic mothers gave birth to anxious neurotic babies, everyone assumed that this tendency was genetic, inherited and totally fixed. It seemed to work the other way around too, with laid-back mothers giving birth to laid-back baby rats. But Meaney decided to test this out by setting up an experiment where neurotic mothers raised baby rats born to mellow mothers, and mellow mother rats were given the task of raising baby rats born to neurotic mothers. Guess what ? Environment and training triumphed over genes, the pups with a genetic predisposition to anxiety, but brought up by caring and nurturing mothers grew up to be laid-back, frisky, curious and well-adjusted adult rats. Whereas the pups born to mellow mothers, but raised by neurotic and neglectful mothers, grew up to be jumpy, anxious and frozen with fear in unfamiliar situations. What is more, when these pups grew up and became mothers they also exhibited the behaviour that they had learnt from their adoptive mothers and not from their genetic mothers.

Meaney then went on to investigate the exact mechanism underlying this. He found that the gene that governs production of the stress hormone receptors is altered by early life experiences. This gene is twice as active in pups raised by attentive, caring mothers. All of that licking and grooming allows the glucocorticoid receptor gene to be turned on. Conversely, with a neglectful mother, the gene for the stress hormone receptor is silenced. A cluster of atoms (called a methyl group) actually sits on the gene and shuts it off. Thus, Meaney had shown that early life experiences can influence an animals DNA and amplify it or turn it down.

This was a revolutionary finding, but could this finding hold true for people as well ? As it turns out, yes it does. In his next study Meaney used samples from the Quebec Suicide Brain Bank. Using samples from the brains of suicides who had suffered abuse in childhood and comparing them to the brains of non-suicides he found significantly more methylation off switches on the gene for the glucocorticoid receptor. This is the same gene that Meaney had discovered was methylated in rats raised by un-caring mothers. When this gene is silenced there are more stress hormones in the system, making it extremely difficult to cope with adversity. It is hard to be resilient when the stress-response system is so out of balance. Meaney had joined up the dots and found the precise scientific explanation for why this happens.

Contrary to the belief that our genetic predisposition is fixed and unchanging, Meaney and other scientists have shown that our DNA is more like a CD music collection, just because you have that CD doesn't mean that you will want to play it. Just because you have a particular gene doesn't mean that it is turned on, or "expressed". In actuality whether a gene is turned on or off is strongly affected by the environment that you find yourself in. So the presence of a methyl group sitting on a piece of DNA is called an epigenetic change. It does not alter the sequence of the gene but switches it off. Depending on upbringing and experiences as we go through life, we accumulate many such changes. Our genes take on more and more of these epigenetic changes, silencing some that had previously been outspoken, and lifting the gag from others that had previously been silent. Our life's experiences will literally change the expression of our DNA.

Now for me the term "embodied thinking" would mean someone who is securely grounded in themselves and aware enough of the inter-linking process which is both mental, emotional as well as physical to be able to name and discuss what is coming up for them, even if it is fairly murky and unclear at first, and to bring it into a mature dialogue with his girlfriend. It does not mean that you need to be serene and dispassionate all the time, coming up with pearls of wisdom that show the penetrating clarity of your insight. Quite the opposite, things can be confusing and emotional and unclear, but it is only by **naming** what is happening and taking ownership of it that we are able to allow the body to readjust to the reality of the present situation in a truly wise and embodied way.

This is really an essential element in Wholebody focusing (WBF), as we shall discover later on in this book. The phenomena of state-dependent recall shows how certain moods or internal states can be spontaneously replicated by the trigger of a familiar physical sensation, like sight, sound, smell, touch or taste. It can also be set in motion by a trigger like sexual arousal of a certain body posture. Anything that is a reminder of the original trauma can cause an involuntary response. If it was a traumatic event our primitive survival responses in the limbic system is then activated which effectively hijacks the brain it bypasses the neo-cortex and no rational thought or discussion is then possible. So any body awareness techniques, like WBF – that are paying attention to the reality of our physical sensations in the present moment - are of great help in over-riding this play-back loop and focusing on the reality of the present moment which is actually not so threatening at all. If we can learn to see without projection, and to think and communicate in an honest, real and embodied way, then simple solutions that we never dreamed to be possible can appear.

Stress and trauma is a psychophysical experience, even when the traumatic event caused no physical harm. It is a well-documented conclusion that stress and trauma are a great burden to the body as well as the mind. Yet despite this wealth of study on the neurobiology of stress and trauma psychotherapy has few tools for healing the traumatised body as well as the traumatised mind. Attention is focused on some of the extreme physical symptoms that can manifest as part of a stressed or traumatised mind, the resulting problems of adaptation to normal functioning at work and in society and the possibility of pharmacological intervention as a sort of "magic bullet" to cure the problem. While it can be an effective crutch it can never be the full answer to this problem. The effects of stress and trauma triggering psycho-physical responses is acknowledged but there are very few therapies working in an integrated way using the body as a possible resource in the treatment of trauma. Somatic memory has been identified and investigated (van der Kolk, 2014) and working from extensive experience he has developed some theories of how it can be worked with in an integrated and positive way as part of the therapeutic process. Also the brilliant work of Eugene Gendlin, in his book "Focusing" (Everest House, 1978) and Babette Rothschild's insightful method of working with trauma, described in The Body Remembers (Norton & Co, 2000).

Luckily for us now neuroscience is getting even more detailed and precise and with things like brain MRI scans researchers are able to understand the brain's circuitry and see what areas of the brain are responsible for what functions and to literally see how well integrated the brain is. As I mentioned earlier, there is a polarity between the complimentary functions of the left and right sides of the brain, which need to be integrated for optimal functioning. There is also a neural integration that needs to take place between the planning and directing functions of the neocortex and our more primitive emotional reaction patterns in the limbic system, which can sometimes hijack the brain. Modern neuroscience is beginning to shed some light on the brain circuits that get activated when we are engaged in different patterns of activity and different thoughts. Its research findings are revealing intriguing links to ancient spiritual practices – such as Buddhist meditation techniques of mindfulness and awareness. These can be shown to be helpful in creating new patterns of brain circuitry and integrating different parts of the brain in a very beneficial way.

The purpose of this book is to take these ideas even further and to explore the fascinating research findings from neurobiology, which increases our understanding of how our brain works in an integrated psychophysical way. And as the key findings of neuroplasticity shows, the power of awareness and repetition can change the way our brain and our body is functioning. But this awareness needs to have the particular quality of "holding both" in an embodied way, that includes both awareness of our grounded physical presence in the moment as well as being aware of the vulnerable parts when recalling traumatic memories. Otherwise we are just thinking in a dis-embodied way, replaying old tapes, which are memories from previous situations. The Wholebody focusing technique described in detail in later chapters provides the key to all this. This can be a great tool for normal, effectively functioning people in everyday life who want to improve their quality of life experience, relationships and effectiveness at work.

So one of the key things is that the fundamental security of attachment formed from childhood depends on this right-brain ability to sense the body memory of physical presence. If things have gone seriously wrong and the child and later adult feels insecure and confused the thinking starts to get muddled and unfocused because of the overwhelming emotional reactions – then it stands to reason that this can only be repaired by the experience of a secure and unconditionally accepting relationship – within the therapeutic relationship, with a loving partner or ultimately and most securely with your own inner awareness of self. This relationship, or dialogue with the self needs to be grounded in a deep and secure sense of bodily presence in the moment.

Many people go for regular counseling or psychotherapy sessions, where they seek to understand their emotional reactions and the root causes of their psychological problems. But they often fail to see how by ignoring their bodies they may be perpetuating their problems by ignoring the way that physical sensations can trigger off intense emotional reaction patterns. This is psychological work without any physical input. So clients may learn to understand themselves better in an analytical way, but they often fail to learn how to change themselves at a fundamental level. The key point is that thinking and memory are not confined only to the brain. We have a body memory as well. A truly psychophysical therapy will help to put the client in contact with the guidance of their body wisdom so they gain a different perspective from which to view their problems.

Chapter 3.
The Neuroscience of Positive and Negative Emotions

There are numerous studies that show how mind and body are linked. One of the first such studies showed how patients with chronic depression were found to have a much higher mortality than the general population. Their health was worse and they were dying earlier. This could partly be explained by lifestyle and at-risk behaviour such as smoking, drugs and lack of exercise but it is also clear that psychological factors play a significant role. Other studies have shown that patients who are more resilient and have a more positive outlook develop better coping mechanisms and thus have better long-term disease and treatment outcomes than patients with exactly the same disease but without that sense of inner self-support and positive attitude.

It is now clear that the main link between our minds/psychological state and our bodies is through the neuroendocrine system. Brain activity can trigger the release of different hormones that can drive changes in the body's functioning. Chronic stress can trigger long-term abnormalities in the neuroendocrine system, such as a raised cortisol level. A person suffering from chronic stress is in a state of hyper-arousal, ready for fight or flight", but as neither option is particularly beneficial in this day and age, many people just live with the unresolved tension. The consequences of this can include depression, anxiety, shallow fast breathing, heart problems, high blood pressure, disturbed sleep, poor digestion and uncomfortable muscular tension patterns. There can even be involuntary twitches and movements in the body.

Other studies showed how stress could depress your immune system. Stress has been shown to depress the functioning of your immune system leaving people more vulnerable to colds and flus (Sheldon Cohen et al. 2002). So stress has been clearly shown to affect the functioning of our endocrine and immune system, as well as our blood pressure and heart function. The mind/body link is clear for all to see, but the real answer is **not** to think that the healthcare system must now provide psychological support for all people experiencing chronic pain, stress or life threatening disease in hospitals. That is again putting the answer in the hands of the experts and disempowering the patients. The real answer is to educate people, from an early age, how to work with the mind/body link at a deeper level, so that it becomes a conscious and controlled process rather than an involuntary surprise. The purpose of this book is to show how the principle of wholebody awareness could provide an understanding of how the mind/body link works, in all its subtlety. You can than learn to work with it as a two-way radio device, using the embodied mind to send conscious messages and intentions to the body and also understanding the subtle messages that our body has for our conscious mind. This will put people firmly in control of psychosomatic illnesses rather than feeling out of control and vulnerable.

Richard Davidson did some groundbreaking research into how the pre-frontal cortex, which is known to be the site of the highest order cognitive activity, the seat of judgment, planning and other executive functions, can play a key role in regulating emotional style. In a key study early in his career, with a sample group of 47 adults, he found that people with greater activation on the left side of the pre-frontal cortex (measured with an EEG machine) during baseline measurement, recovered much more quickly form the feelings of disgust, horror, anger and fear after being shown some quite upsetting images, mixed with random neutral images, on a video screen. The inference was that the left pre-frontal cortex is able to send inhibitory signals to the amygdala. (Jackson & Davidson, ("Now you feel it –now you don't" Madison University, 2004). In 2012 an fMRI study showed how the more white matter you have (axons that connect one neuron to another) lying between the pre-frontal cortex and the amygdala, the more resilient you are. (Kim & Whalen, " The Structural Integrity of an Amygdala pre-frontal pathway Predicts Trait anxiety", Journal of Neuroscience, 2009). This has very important implications for people who wish to strengthen their resilience in the face of life's periodic adversity.

But its not so simple to strengthen resilience, as it might appear to be on the surface. When you are very stressed-out at work, for example, or have just been traumatised in a serious car accident, the amygdala can go into overdrive and the emotional brain in the limbic system can hijack the executive functions of the pre-frontal cortex, because all of this is outside the window of tolerance, as Dan Siegel puts it. There is no thinking or planning possible because there is no detachment and no perspective – just a feeling of being overwhelmed in the emotions of the moment. So no top-down integration from the pre-frontal cortex is possible. Everyone has experienced this at some time, and in this situation it is very hard to stop obsessing about what went wrong, playing the role of victim in the blame game and generally falling into the grip of negative emotions.

Only after the arousal in the limbic system is calmed down and you are in the flow state of increased alpha wave activity in the pre-frontal cortex, is it possible to move into the top-down form of brain integration. This is where the large bundles of neurons running between certain areas of the pre-frontal cortex and the amygdala come into play. These neural pathways help to inhibit any negative emotional responses that get triggered in the amygdala during the course of the day, when you might feel anxious, afraid or threatened. These neural pathways will help to facilitate a rapid recovery from adversity. Then the pre-frontal cortex is acting as the watchtower, allowing for a calm overview of the whole situation and the flow of your life experiences.

So promoting vertical integration involves cultivating awareness of the inputs from lower down in the body, the brainstem and the limbic areas. It involves opening up the awareness to how everything is feeling with the container of your body, the muscles the bones, the viscera (the intestines) the lungs and heart, everything that's there. It involves tolerating input from the limbic system (the emotional brain) – like reactions of fear, feelings of distress at separation from loved ones and longings for connection, and being able to hold these in safety within the container of the body. As Dan Siegel says "With time and practice, a state of being barely tolerant of subcortical signals can transform into treasuring them for the wisdom that they bring about how we actually are feeling in the moment". (Siegel, "Pocket Guide to Interpersonal Neurobiology" 2012).

So called rational thinking very often tries to operate from just the prefrontal cortex of the brain in isolation without taking into account the subcortical regions that are profoundly important for everything that the cortex does. This is so-called pure reason, but the cortex cannot exist in isolation, it is grounded on everything that is beneath it. What is beneath it is the physical body (consisting of the muscles, bones, the connective tissues, and all the internal organs like the heart, lungs, intestines, etc.) the brainstem (which is our fight-flight-or freeze response) and the limbic area (emotion, motivation, formation of meaning, attachment and memory) - the more ancient sub-cortical regions. These subcortical inputs appear to feed more into the right-brain hemisphere, so understanding how the two hemispheres not only perform different functions but also enable different ways of "being" for the individual can help us to integrate this upward flow of information rather than just shutting down on it.

Often rational thinking will try to abstract away from the emotions as being at best a distraction and at worst an annoying disturbance. We are a left-brain dominated society and our education system reflects that. Logical, linear thinking and getting to the right answer is what the left brain is all about, but what happens when our bodies and our emotions know something more about the situation than our intellectual rational minds do? It could be that our right-brain hemisphere has a holistic sense of the bigger picture that is different from what our intellectual minds are saying. But are we comfortable with that information and do we have a methodology, a technique for integrating it? Above all it takes time because accessing physical and emotional sensations and memories happens at a different pace to our normal cognitive thinking mode. Our emotions can appear to be unclear and murky because often it requires time and patience to access them clearly. We can think 20 intellectual ideas in the time it takes us to feel an emotion and where it is carried physically in the body.

The limbic system governs our survival mechanism and emotional expression and the instinct for self-preservation runs deep. Self-preservation is even more powerful than the sexual instinct, which is also regulated by the limbic system. When confronted by an extreme survival threat it will release hormones that prepare the body for fight, flight or freeze. It has to be fast, and it has to be effective to ensure the survival of the species and when it is activated it overrides the functioning of the neo-cortex. There is no time to sit down and start negotiating with a sabre-toothed tiger! There is only time for very fast, instinctive survival responses. Perception of time changes and the brain starts functioning in a different manner. The limbic system will assess the situation very fast and the body will run if there is adequate time and space for flight. If there is no time to run but there is strength enough to fight then the body will fight. If the limbic system realises that neither fight nor flight is an option it will simply freeze, which is the state of being hyper-aroused on the inside but seemingly immobile on the outside and the victim enters an altered state of consciousness where there is no fear or pain. People who have been involved in car accidents or been mauled by wild animals and survived report this experience. Certain animals will also 'play dead' and manage to survive, like a cat will lose interest in a lifeless mouse. These limbic system responses are instantaneous, instinctive responses to perceived threat.

The danger signal is activated in the hypothalamic-pituitary-adrenal (HPA) axis and there has been lots of research into how it operates and what goes wrong with it in cases of posttraumatic stress disorder (PTSD). It is important to understand how it operates in some detail, as it is the body's instinctive response to stress and trauma. The limbic system is closely linked to the autonomic nervous system (ANS), which prepares the body for rest or for making an effort. It has two branches, the sympathetic nervous system (SNS) and the parasympathetic nervous system (PNS), which usually function in balance so that when one is activated the other is suppressed and vice versa. The SNS is aroused in states of effort and stress and the PNS is activated in states of rest and relaxation. The balance between the two is crucial and whilst it is easy to get over-stimulated, it is not so simple to switch off and relax. This takes more time, one of the main ways to stimulate the relaxation response in the PNS is by trying to slow down and deepen the rhythm of the breath. This is why simple awareness of the breath is a key meditation practice.

The amygdala in the limbic system responds to the perception of threat by releasing hormones that tell the body to prepare for action (see Figure 1.1). The amygdala signals alarm to the hypothalamus, which activates two systems, (1) it stimulates the SNS, which activates the adrenal glands to release epinephrine and norepinephrine, which mobilise the body for fight or flight. These hormones will increase respiration and heart rate, which provides more oxygen and sends blood away from the skin and into the muscles ready for quick, strong movement. The second thing that the hypothalamus does is to release corticotrophin-releasing hormone (CRH) which activates the pituitary gland to release adrenocortico-tropic hormone (ACTH) which then stimulates the adrenal gland which this time releases a hydrocortisone, which is cortisol. Cortisol is a stress hormone that can prevent inflammation in the event of injury. Now, once the traumatic experience is over and the fight is over or the escape has been successful, there is a sense of relaxing downwards and being able to breathe calmly, as a hunted animal or human would collapse onto the ground in relief, after the recognition is confirmed in the pre-frontal cortex that there is no danger anymore in the environment. The cortisol will then halt the alarm reaction, stop production of epinephrine/norepinephrine, which brings the body back to homeostasis.

Prefrontal Cortex

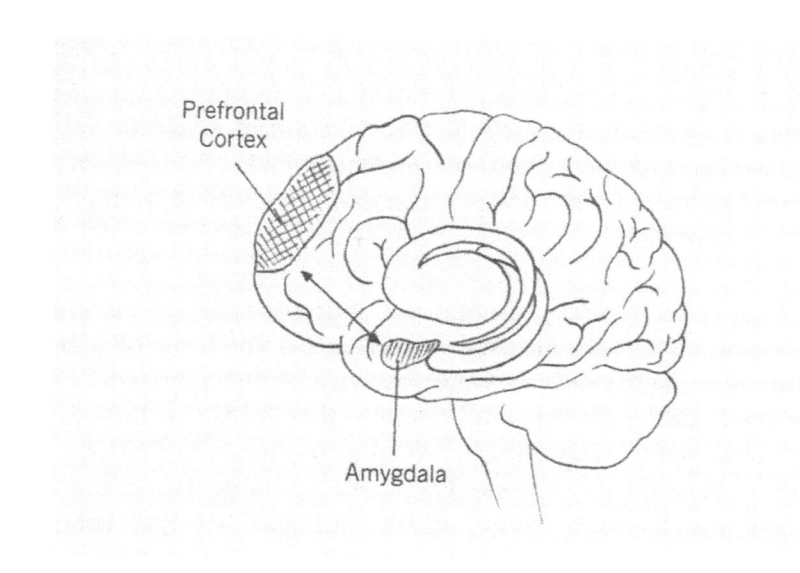

Amygdala

This system is called the HPA axis, but in chronic stress and severe trauma the system stays hyper-aroused. The sympathetic nervous system (SNS) does not get turned off and the person remains over-stimulated. It makes intuitive sense, because if a person has been very traumatised earlier in life, often that young child felt very helpless and hopeless in their situation, isolated and in a self-protective, cut-off place. My research seems to indicate that this is linked to the freeze response where neither fight nor flight is possible. The freeze response is quite complex and difficult to deal with because both the SNS and the PNS have been stimulated. The person seems calm on the surface but is actually in inner panic, and constant turmoil. The essence of the situation is that they have reached a place of supposed safety and survived the threat posed by life by cutting off and staying isolated. Isolation is safety; interaction with people poses the threat. In cases like this, it is very difficult to communicate with this part, because it doesn't want to be seen, it is very good at hiding and it needs to communication what it wants and what it is afraid of. The alarm reaction in the amygdala stays switched on and it hijacks the pre-frontal cortex, which is no longer capable of clear thinking and decision-making.

The isolated and unsupported individual is continuously activated and hyper-aroused. There is the memory of a huge traumatic event that has never been fully processed and resolved. Each new stressful event is then added to the pile of previous unresolved stress, so the mountain of pain and emotional suffering grows. There are so many situations and sensations that can trigger of the memory of that original trauma and as the full emotional intensity of that memory floods back into consciousness it is as if that event is happening now, instead of taking place at a distinct time in the past, and so the arousal never gets switched off.

However, Rachel Yehuda (Yehuda et al., 1990) has discovered that in cases of Post Traumatic Stress Disorder (PTSD) this mechanism fails to operate. She made the discovery that on a chemical level in PTSD cases the adrenal glands do not release enough cortisol to halt the arousal. Whether this is a purely biological process or influenced by a perception of the limbic system is not clear at this stage and would be an important piece of research. However, from my own experience as an Alexander Technique teacher I know that if any response is continued for a long period of time, it will gradually come to be accepted as "normal" and the body loses the sense that this is something that needs to be corrected. It is also known that the constant overstimulation of the adrenal glands in cases of ongoing stress can lead to adrenal collapse.

It is true that some people are born with a very tense, excitable nervous system and others are calmer, more grounded, less reactive and better able to handle stress. This is a genetic predisposition. But there is also the influence of stressful events during early childhood. Schore (1996), van der Kolk (1987, 1998) Siegel (1999) De Bellis et al. (1999) Perry et al. (1995) and others have shown that traumatic events in early childhood leads to a predisposition to psychological disturbance in later life. Episodes of neglect, physical, emotional or sexual abuse, insecure attachment and traumatic incidents, like going to hospital, a death in the family or serious accidents, are all stressful events. The hypothesis is that people who suffered early trauma and/or did not have the benefit of a secure attachment have a limited capacity for regulating stress or making sense of traumatic experiences later on in life. In some cases it seems likely that reduced hippocampal activity (the part of the brain where the story of what happened is processed and stored) results in a limited capacity to regulate stress and make sense of traumatic experiences later in their life (Gunnar & Barr 1998).

There is also clear evidence to support the reality of *neuroplasticity*, which means that when we focus our attention continuously and deeply in a certain direction, we are activating the brain's circuitry. This activation can strengthen the synaptic linkages in these areas and this can then alter brain structure and functioning. Neuroplasticity has both a positive and a negative side to it, in that the trauma of negative experiences can alter brain structure in long-lasting ways that make life very difficult, as they strengthen the neural pathway of this negative emotional loop. The positive potential is that it is never too late to use the focus of attention to alter the brain's structure, and understanding the positive neural pathways can make it possible to get out of a negative loop and into a positive loop.

What is clear is that the purely talking therapies do not work and in some cases it actually re-traumatizes, and just sitting and thinking about a problem or a negative situation can be counter-productive because it can trigger off the memory of the experience as if it is happening in the present moment. There is no new insight or forward moving life energy; it is just an endless repetition of the video of the old experience. This sort of negative emotional loop can leave you feeling emotionally overwhelmed and unable to cope with life effectively. Very often even just the physical sensations associated with that emotional state can be a trigger, e.g., just starting to feel short of breath and knowing that this is one of the signs of a panic attack can actually trigger a full-blown panic attack. Because of the phenomena of state-dependent recall, any specific physical sensations or memory associations that are linked to the memory of your stress or trauma can trigger you. Because this is an implicit memory and not fully conscious, it is extremely difficult to handle triggers like this. However, if this is brought into conscious awareness techniques like the Alexander Technique "directions" can be used to reduce the physical tension pattern and to create a sense of spaciousness, thus breaking the vicious circle. This creates space for a shift to happen using the WBF technique.

It is clear from understanding the neuroscience that what is needed is for the whole body/mind to come to some sort of a resting place, a place of safety and release. This cannot be just an intellectual idea suggested by your mind or by a therapist "You are safe now, this is a different situation". Affirmations of this sort, which are purely cognitive will be of no use whatsoever unless it is congruent with changes in the posture and sensations within the body, like a reduction in the levels of muscular tension in different parts of the body, the rate of breathing and the general level of arousal. If an affirmation like this is linked to a real change in the inner experiencing of the person, physically, mentally and emotionally, then it will be effective. If it is just a purely intellectual idea that is not grounded in the reality of your bodily experience, then it will not be able to calm the arousal of the nervous system

This is why the grounding exercise in WBF, which came from the Alexander Technique, was developed (see Chap. 6, "A Manual of WBF" for more details). Grounding is being in touch with the continuity of my felt experience and not allowing, pausing and putting everything else on hold – just for a few vital minutes. It can counteract the limbic hijacking of the brain, which takes place in chronic stress and trauma. It is vitally important in enabling Wholebody focusing and in helping people to cope with the everyday stress of life. It creates a safe space to rest and get back into neutral again, a safe container for all the powerful emotions that are triggered by the conflicts and frustrations of life. Rather than just being in reaction mode the whole time, it is then possible to process uncomfortable feelings through WBF, to resolve conflicts, to get a clearer perspective and to move forwards in life. This grounding exercise helps to stop the alarm response and to reduce the arousal level in the body-min, bringing back an inner harmony and balance. Then it is easier to move forwards again with renewed energy, insight, commitment and enthusiasm.

The research of Antonio Demasio has shown that effective decision-making only takes place after you integrate the reality of your emotional responses into the process. There are techniques like Wholebody focusing that can help to process your emotions that are always telling you something about the truth of your situation, and what you want or are afraid of. But it is only after these parts have been heard and given space, that they can then transform from compulsive and rigid emotional reaction patterns into reasoned emotional responses. WBF is form of mindfulness training that enables you to be more grounded in the reality of the present moment and to take the high road of positive emotional response rather than the low road of negative emotional reactions, As Dan Siegel has pointed out, we are seeking the middle way, the window of tolerance that lies between the two extremes of chaos and rigidity. Most people fall into the trap of over-rigid defensive thinking or the other extreme of being too open and influenced by outside forces, thereby losing contact with themselves and who they are. If you can find that middle ground then you open up to the plateau of infinite possibilities. There are potentially so many solutions waiting out there that you have not seen, wonderful life-changing possibilities in your work, your relationships, and in your whole life pattern, but in a sense you have to create them first by changing your thinking and opening up to the awareness of these possibilities inwardly. Modern brain research is showing how it is possible to integrate your brain by training different patterns of awareness in your brain. Most important of all is to create the sort of vertical integration that can avoid the dangers of emotional hijacking from the limbic system. It is abundantly clear that to facilitate vertical integration the brainstem needs to be relaxed. Again the AT directions help to release that vital part of the body where the head is balanced on top of the spinal column. This helps to get you fully grounded, aware, and accepting of the moment. It allows more awareness of the present moment physical sensations from the rest of your body and a calm acceptance of what is happening in your environment. Only then can you become calmly focused and turn your full creative attention to the job in hand. As the body softens and the neck releases it becomes possible to take that first step to engage with problems, to confront difficulties and move forwards into some form of activity and engagement, rather than remaining paralysed in the fear of "what if I made a terrible mistake, I feel so hopeless, and I'm not sure if I am right". Yes, you might make a mistake, but then again you might learn from that mistake and you might even make a brilliant success of it all.

So the first step in using the WBF approach is to actually acknowledge the reality of the negative emotions, and to stay with the reality of the situation for a bit. Don't beat yourself up – just hold it all within the container of your body, in a compassionate, open-minded, accepting and loving way, realizing that your emotions are actually telling you something important about your truth and what feels important to you in this situation. If you give this Wholebody Process the time it needs, which involves being able to sense where you are holding your emotions inside your body, then you will be able to start a positive internal relationship with your own wounded and vulnerable parts. This intra-personal relationship is actually an important mindfulness practice that helps you to see the bigger picture and to take responsibility for your part in the situation and also to see where responsibility lies outside of your area of influence, so you can let go and stop worrying about it. Once you can do this you are actually free from the grip of the negative emotions, because they have been transformed. It is this inner transformation and not the suppression of emotions that enables you to re-engage the pre-frontal cortex. From this new perspective, "the watchtower" as some people call it, which is actually like looking down from a vantage point on the whole scenario, you can realize how the negative emotions were only a blocked process and just behind that there was a positive energy waiting to be released.

Only after the arousal has been calmed is it possible to calmly stay in the watchtower of the pre-frontal cortex and to use cognitive thinking combined with the ease and flow of being in high alpha brain wave activity. Vertical integration leads to a feeling of calm perspective, of being in control but looking down on the whole situation from a long-term perspective. I soon learnt that this is the crucial factor in successful market trading activity. When you look at what is happening during the course of a day or a few hours, especially in a volatile market like crude oil at the moment, there is lots of movement in the market, big highs and lows, with some fairly rapid changes of position. Its a bit of a roller coaster and its hard not to get caught up in the fear or the excitement of it all. Its only when you step back and look at the monthly chart, or the 3 monthly or 6 monthly charts that is possible to get the bigger picture and to see the long-term trends unfolding. You have to know what the trend is if you are going to put money on it, its no use just going with the excitement of the moment. You have to get a calm wholebody feel of the situation, an inner knowing, and then be able to hold your position despite any contrary indications or retracements in the market position. So you need a system that you trust and the ability to make long-term decisions on the basis of that system and to hold your position in a calm and grounded way.

That's the feeling of looking down from the watchtower. It feels like being in control and making rational choices, its the ability to have long-term thinking and planning, but also the ability to delay immediate gratification in favour of holding out for long-term goals. Its also enhanced alpha wave activity in the left pre-frontal cortex, which leads to feelings of peace and calmness, and the safety of feeling supported by something bigger than you. That might literally be due to physically letting go and feeling the support of the counter-thrust from the whole planet Earth beneath you, or it might be due to the support felt through understanding & practicing some really deep religious or spiritual tradition. But the crucial thing is somehow being able to step back and see the bigger picture, whilst feeling calm and supported.

The research has shown that practicing mindfulness meditation promotes the growth of connective neurons between the pre-frontal cortex and the amygdala and increases resilience. Actually I would say that probably any form of meditation that expands your sense of peace and calmness and helps you to feel detachment would be beneficial. Because then you are getting a sense of the bigger perspective, an awareness of an expanded body container and the sense that "I feel OK, I am bigger than my problem and I feel supported in myself and by my environment". That's the crucial benefit of meditation, it stops you feeling overwhelmed by your negative emotional reactions. WBF actually continues this mindful awareness of what is going on inside the container of your body and allows you to transform the negative emotions that are there.

Linked to this, and another practice that is extremely useful is cognitive reappraisal training. This technique teaches people to reframe adversity in such a way as to believe that it is not such a total catastrophe and not as enduring as their minds would have them believe. This practice aims to challenge errors in thinking, so e.g., if you made a mistake at work its not because you are totally stupid and will be fired for that. Rather it could be due to specific circumstances on that day and by challenging your thinking it helps you to reframe the whole situation and thus your emotional reactions to it. So this form of CBT would actually fit very well with learning to take self-responsibility through the practice of Wholebody focusing, whereby you can see how to take responsibility for your part in the whole situation, and see where you responsibility lies outside your area of control. So you can learn from your mistakes and then move on from them.

Susan worked in a big post office. She worked behind a big glass screen, but everyday there were long queues of customers waiting to be served and not enough counter clerks to serve them. So when the customers arrived at her counter they were often angry and frustrated at being made to wait so long and she would apologise to them and feel responsible in some way and stressed. Susan reacted to this situation by trying to work faster, but she also noticed that her stomach was clenched and her breathing was tight and that she was physically and mentally exhausted by the end of the day. She did some WBF on this and then she suddenly realized that it wasn't her fault at all, the responsibility lay with the management for not employing enough counter clerks. So she changed her attitude and decided to only work at the speed that was right for her. When the next customer came to her counter and complained about the long delays she smiled sweetly and said, "Yes I know it is a long wait, why don't you ask to speak to the management and ask them to employ more workers"? So this carried on for a while like this, and she was a lot less stressed because she had shifted responsibility for the situation to the place where it really belonged. After a few weeks of this, the management decided to employ more counter clerks and so the problem was solved.

Chapter 4.
What is the A.T and what is Focusing?

The Alexander Technique is an integral part of WBF so it is important to understand how this technique works, which is a valid practice it in its own right that helps to open up the inner body spaces and to awaken the inner energetic body through the power of awareness. This is a doorway to be able to connect with our own Inner Body Wisdom. The Alexander story also beautifully illustrates some of the key principles of self-transformation in action, which Alexander discovered in his own way. He was one of the first people to actively work with the psychophysical unity of his self and then later on, he worked with his students. He was a pioneer in what is now a very obvious concept: that your mind and emotions influences the body and that your body posture and gesture will affect the way you are thinking and feeling.

Alexander was an Australian actor, a Shakespearean reciter who did one-man shows and had built up a successful acting practice for himself in Melbourne at the end of the last century. His story is an interesting one because it shows the power of physical and emotional habit patterns that seem to be beyond the control of the conscious, reasoning mind and how he managed to turn things around. He had studied music and drama and loved the theatre, but his promising career was ruined by a persistent soreness of the throat and a hoarseness of his voice, linked to breathing difficulties during public performances. He went to various doctors, but they were unable to help him, as there were no obvious physical reasons for his disability. Life was not working for him and he had reached a choice point, he could either give up completely or come to the inevitable conclusion that the only thing left to do was to cure him. He was thrown back on his own inner resources as the experts had failed him, so he chose to cure himself and this was the start of his journey.

Through dedicated self-observation and self-inquiry he came to realise that his problems were not just purely 'physical' problems, but were also psychological and linked to his mindset. He found that he had to find a way to put his very ambitious, goal-driven personality on hold, before he could heal his persistent physical problems. He developed the Alexander Technique, an awareness technique of the whole body, which allows the vulnerable part to open up to a sense of connection and support from the whole of the rest of the body. This creates a sustaining, energetic connection within the whole body where all the antagonistic little parts can release into a sense of connection and support from the greater whole. Then when he went on stage his voice resonated in an embodied way and he could really connect with his audience. Alexander's concept of the "psychophysical whole" and its link with voice work was a real paradigm shift for the beginning of the twentieth century. It was an amazing experience for me and when I had my first Alexander Technique lesson over 30 years ago, this inspired me to go on to train as a AT teacher and helped me to develop the concept of Wholebody focusing.

I would suggest that this happens to each and every one of us at some stage in our lives, we get derailed in the sense that we come up against some seemingly huge obstacle and all of our previous knowledge and strategies for dealing with things seem to fail. I can remember this happened to me many years ago when I was working in medical publishing, recently married with our first child. I would get terrible migraines regularly at 3 O'clock every afternoon, combined with sleepiness and an inability to concentrate. Getting up two or three times in the middle of the night to help with feeds and nappy changes was making the situation even worse but I felt compelled to do this every night because my first wife had a bad back and could not do any lifting or carrying. I felt trapped in the situation but unable to take a responsible decision. I went for my first A.T. Lessons, which I found to be absolutely amazing. The sense of lightness, release and expansion in my body and mind was such a revelation. It felt like light and life had come into a very dark place. I continued lessons and the migraines started to get better, but I also had to start facing the truth of the matter, which was that I was bored to death with medical publishing job and needed a career change but was too scared to tell my wife. I was so relieved when they eventually sacked me and that gave me the opportunity to start a three-year A.T. Training course. But that was only a partial resolution of the situation because I had not made a fully conscious choice in the matter. I had passively manipulated the situation.

Alexander had to try and work things out for himself, because there were no therapists or self help books around in the Australian outback in the 1890's. But he was persistent and resilient. He set up a system of three mirrors so that he could observe every part of his head, neck and throat when he was standing and reciting. After a period of observation he realised that he was doing three things: he was stiffening his neck, he was tightening the muscles deep inside his throat, and he gasped as he sucked in his breath.

But he was amazed to observe this because, firstly, he hadn't felt this happening within himself, and secondly, his muscular activity didn't appear to be under the direct control of his conscious reasoning mind - because when he ordered his muscles to relax and stop tensing they refused to obey. They seemed to have a mind of their own. It seemed that a direct approach wouldn't work, but what alternative was there?

Alexander had a probing mind and he analysed himself more deeply. He realised that he was over-ambitious. He wanted to get to the top as quickly as possible, to gain recognition and applause. As a result of this ambition he was trying too hard, over-tensing and getting fixed on the end result, thus effectively losing contact with the present moment and blocking his full potential. He also made one further vital observation and that was that this whole psycho-physical reaction pattern which he had observed in himself was not just something that happened when he got up on stage, it was actually present at all times (though in a milder form) a habitual way of being that he had falsely identified with so that when he got up to recite it would be triggered off in a more extreme form.

If the direct way was not going to work then Alexander had to find an indirect way. Firstly, he had objectively defined his problem: he knew what was happening in his body but he couldn't work out how to stop it happening, because every time he put himself onstage his old, instinctive, reaction pattern took over. *But if you can't stop something happening you can at least stop trying to stop it happening - stop fighting it, stop trying to fix it, create space by being non-resistant to the whole situation.* Just allow yourself to observe rather than thinking that you have to do something about the situation.

So his second step was to do absolutely nothing at all. Step back and just be aware of the situation. This moment of pause, doing nothing but keeping calm within him and observing which he termed 'inhibition', is not to be confused with the Freudian use of the term, and it proved to be the key that would unlock the door for him. Alexander reasoned that he did have one clear area of choice open to him, and that was the power to say YES or NO to the whole situation before he got involved in it: YES, I am attached to my desire to become a great actor and about to get sucked into that whole thing, or NO, right now, I do not care about it at all, I'm in a neutral space.

Now this was a very important place to have reached because it allowed his ego to step out of the picture for a moment to create a neutral space. You see, he really didn't know what the answer was. Everything that he knew came from the past, which was just the accumulated pattern of his previous thoughts, feelings and actions, and the experiences resulting from these. Every time the conscious, reasoning mind (ego) had tried to suggest a solution to him it had failed. He had not known the answer in the past - if he had he would not now be in the mess he was in - so why would the continuation of past patterns of misuse suddenly bring him liberation and success now? Impossible, Something entirely new was going to have to arise in the present, creative moment, the eternal NOW; and if it were to be truly new then by definition he would have no idea, no preconception, of what it might be. He was going to have to stop doing and start being; he was going to have to allow forces to work through him rather than thinking that he knew it all already.

So he just put a full stop to all doing, all striving and just waited in a state of heightened, creative awareness. He later said: "When you stop doing the wrong thing, the right thing will happen all by itself." Eugene Gendin, the man who discovered the Focusing Technique also said, "The right thing does itself". This is the essence of all transformation techniques and this links the Alexander Technique and Focusing: they are both essentially based on non-doing.

There is no outer activity here, but there is a state of very clear inner focus on what is - whatever it is - just accept it, look at it, and be true to it, because that is what is happening in the moment. It is not the way it will always be, but it is the way it is at the moment, and that is our starting point in the process of transformation, the raw material that we have to work with. And then a very curious thing starts to happen: by acceptance and by looking at things or people calmly and without judgment, without trying to do anything about it, we create space, and by creating space we allow things to unfold and develop in harmony with the pattern of their inner being. If we just allow enough neutral space and acceptance for things to be the way they are, even if it is blocked, there appears to be a forward moving life-energy within the blockage, a wisdom in the body that is striving towards alignment with the inner blue-print of your life and this will redress the balance.

Alexander was opening himself up to the wisdom of his own body, inwardly he was saying, "I'm not sure any more, so you show me." Rather than trying to force his neck and jaw to release he just repeated a mental invitation to his body to "allow the neck to be free...." and did nothing. But he was actually letting the answer emerge from the problem itself. Because, as is portrayed in the Yin/Yang symbol, the seed of the solution is already contained in the problem, and if you do not meet with immediate success, don't be discouraged, because it is always darkest just before the dawn. Patience, waiting, and an inner stillness become the keys to the whole situation. This is a profound truth and yet so difficult to actually be with.

To take Alexander's specific case, he had a tendency to tighten his throat and to shorten the muscles at the back of his neck, thus pulling his head back and down onto his spinal column. When he had effectively mastered *the technique of stepping back and allowing by just repeating his affirmation but not doing anything*, he found that a process of inner release could take place within his whole body. The ball of tension that had been concentrated in his neck and throat began to dissolve away and as it did so he found his jaw releasing forward and his head releasing upward (from above the atlanto-occipital joint); at the same time the whole of his vertebral column began to release and lengthen There was also a feeling of the back widening across the shoulders, ribcage and pelvis.

Once having experienced this shift by using his affirmation, "Let the neck be free, to let the jaw be free, to let the head tip forward and up (if it wants to), to let the back lengthen and widen," he realised the power of affirmations and of inviting the body to do something on its own without consciously trying. By constantly repeating these words to himself when needed was a way of reactivating his new, positive shift when under challenging conditions. It has two functions actually, one is to give the mind something positive to do rather than get caught up in its habitual negative, reactive patterns. It gives the mind something to do whilst the inner essential work of waiting and watching is in process. So Alexander was very aware that his technique was essentially a non-doing technique that could allow blockages to release from within and you cannot force this process

Needless to say each individual is unique and will have a different pattern of tension and release because they have had a different life story and so as well as using the well-known affirmation from Alexander, they can develop their own positive affirmations that are unique to themselves, but Alexander's generalised affirmation is still effective and used all over the world. His story is a wonderful example of stepping back and allowing his inner body wisdom to show him the way forwards into release and freedom.

The practice of the Alexander Technique leads to a state of grounded presence and an intense awareness of the present moment. This allows a deeply embodied thinking to develop. I first became aware of this state during my Alexander training 30 years ago and it has been repeated many times since. There is no sense of a habitual mental construction that pins the focus of attention on some point in the future and filters out the experience of the present moment. Being fully present in an embodied way requires alertness but no sense of effort. There is a sense of curiosity and aliveness that means that the present moment is experienced with freshness and an immediacy that sometimes takes my breath away. I am not experiencing life second hand through stored concepts in the mind. I am allowing forms and colours to come into my retina and to be experienced directly without any labels and concepts coming in-between me and the experience. I am allowing sounds and words to enter my ears without any judgments, tastes to enter my mouth and hit my taste buds without any likes or dislikes, tactile sensations to be felt by my finger tips without excitation or aversion. In this state there is no tension to it, no fear, just alert presence. The key to it is that I am present with every cell of my body alive and vibrant, there is an inner spaciousness to the body and present moment awareness that allows a spaciousness of the mind. There is no past or future, and the constant mental planning of the ego: defending my rights, attaining my goals. Clarity and creativity is there in abundance when the ego is out of the picture, and with the ego gone I am now more fully myself.

Eugene Gendlin, professor of psychology at Chicago University, developed the Focusing technique. He was a colleague of Carl Rogers, the well-known founder of Client-Centered Counseling, and worked with him in the 1950's to investigate the fundamental question of what made therapy effective. Rogers and his colleagues came to the conclusion that what makes therapy work has nothing to do with the content of what the client talks about, nor the theoretical orientation of the therapist but is actually dependent on the quality of the therapeutic relationship. If the therapist is genuinely non-judgmental, empathic and fully present (the 'core conditions') there is a good chance that the therapy will work. This combined with the 'actualising tendency" of the client themselves, an inner energy that is liberated once the blockages are dissolved, is what helps them to grow and to move forwards.

Eugene Gendlin was very influenced by the work of Rogers. Whilst Rogers had made ground-breaking research he had still not answered the question of why certain clients have excellent therapists but are still not able to change the way that they *relate to themselves internally*, thus remaining stuck in self-judgement or shame and seemingly unable to move forwards from that position. The inner critic is the interalised voice of all the critical authority figures that we have ever met in our life – except now it seems as if that voice is coming from inside ourselves. The key shift in therapy occurs when we are able to start internalising the non-judgmental, empathic presence of the therapist and to start relating to ourselves and to our experiences in life with that same accepting, understanding and compassionate attitude that you meet in a good therapist or counselor. Only then is change truly possible. This might seem obvious to some people but it is not easy for others and one key skill that needs to be developed is the ability to develop a little bit of a distance to yourself, a kind of internal observing presence that can just accept and let things be for a while, rather like the therapist who can sit there and allow you to be yourself, with all your hang-ups and supposed mistakes.

Gendlin was originally studying in the philosophy department at the University of Chicago. He was interested in the great philosophical question of how our lived experience of the world is related to our concepts and our understanding. What meaning do we give to our experiences and can that change as our concepts change? This might seem an abstract question but Gendlin realised that Rogers and his colleagues were actually doing this in a practical way at the Chicago Counseling Centre. They were encouraging clients to stay with their felt experience of their lives and to take the time to formulate their own meaning and language and concepts to describe this. This is taking a philosophy and living it in practical everyday situations, rather like Alexander taught a postural technique and a way of relating to his body that he wished students to apply to all their everyday life situations.

So Gendlin switched from the philosophy department to the psychology department. He started doing research with his mentor Carl Rogers into the continuing question of why psychotherapy works with some people but not with others and what the differences between the two groups are. After recording thousands of therapy cases and studying them, he found what he believed to be the causative factor, and using this he could even predict within the first few sessions who was going to benefit from therapy (and who was just going to waste their time and money). His research confirmed Roger's earlier findings that success in therapy had nothing to do with what the client talked about or even the method being used by the therapist. It was dependent on the 'core conditions being met and it appeared to be linked to something about the way that 'successful' clients talked. There was something about the way that 'successful' clients talked about themselves and their experiences that proved to be a key indicator of success or failure in therapy and this fascinated Gendlin.

By listening to the tapes Gendlin realised that clients who make effective progress in therapy would do strange things like talk and then 'um' and 'ah' and take a long pause to consider, and to reconsider, and to see what feels right. "Well its not exactly like that, its more like ......the word isn't 'annoyed' its more that I'm 'disappointed' disappointed in myself, for not taking more time before I made the decision to buy....I just wish that I hadn't rushed it so much. Also its not the end of the world either so I don't need to beat myself up about it. "

There is an ability of the client to go within and to pay attention to their own felt sense of a situation and to search for the words that fit, and also to sense the subtle physical shifts that occur at important points in their therapy. They are paying attention to their inner experiencing, what is happening within themselves, in the moment, as they are recounting a story. Paying attention to their physical sensations in their bodies and searching for the right words is embodied thinking that puts them into deep contact with their emotions and what is real. This is different from simply telling a story, intellectualising and speculating or getting caught up in the emotions of the situation and being so overwhelmed by the emotions that there is no distance and no observer anymore.

One of the most significant findings of modern neuroscience is that somatic and emotional experience are linked. This is a hugely important finding because it shows how one aspect of mind, which is our emotions, is directly linked to our physical sensations. They are experienced at the same time, so there is no emotional memory without a physical foundation to it and there are no somatic memories that exist in isolation. All emotional states, the sadness or happiness or laughter cannot exist in isolation, they need a physical body to express it and that reality is maintained in the memory. If you cry your eyes water and your chest starts heaving, something happens to your breathing and you make noises that we all recognise as crying, similar across all cultures even in very remote parts of the world.

In point of fact the neurologist Antonio Demasio developed his theory of somatic markers as a way of explaining how body sensations cue awareness of the emotions (Damasio 1994). His original work was to do with individuals who have damage to regions of the brain that are linked to emotion. Amazingly enough he discovered that emotion is necessary to rational thought. His conclusion was that in order to be able to make a rational decision, one has to be able to feel the consequences of that decision. Just attempting to think your way through in a purely cognitive way is not enough, one has to be able to feel the consequences of that decision. According to Damasio an emotion is a mixture of physical sensations that are experienced in different degrees of intensity, positive and negative. These constitute what he calls somatic markers, which are used to help us in the decision making process. So there is no such thing as a purely cognitive decision - body sensations underlie emotions and help us to weigh the consequences of different options and decide the direction that we wish to take.

Neuroscience has shown how somatic and emotional memory are both totally linked, there is no separation. In Damasio's theory of somatic markers, he proposes that the experience of emotions is comprised of body sensations that are elicited in response to various stimuli. Sensations and emotions are then encoded and stored as implicit memories. These are then triggered into recall when similar stimuli are present. So the body holds both the memory of the problem and the possibility of a deepening awareness and the ability to transform things.

Most people, even supposedly hardheaded businessmen and women, can relate to the truth of how body sensation and emotions are linked when they follow their "gut instinct". This is an example of how our bodily sensations and our thoughts and emotions are all linked, and how there is a positive aspect to this linkage that can help us to find our direction forwards. When we operate in this open and holistic manner we are able to make wise and balanced decisions and avoid hasty actions, bad decisions that we later regret that are based on false assumptions. This research finding helps us to understand the importance of emotions, which are partly experienced in our bodies, in our decision-making process.

There are degrees of awareness of your felt experience and in the early days of Focusing Gendlin and his colleagues developed a scale for measuring a client's experiencing level (Klein et al. 1969, 1986). At the low end clients speak of external events in a detached sort of way, in the middle they are more emotionally involved and at the top end the client is aware of and able to integrate of aspects of their experiencing in an alive and comfortable way. This 'Experiencing Scale' (EXP) is often used in research on the effectiveness of counselling and has direct relevance to the practice of Embodied Thinking.

In his book "Focusing" Professor Gendlin has outlined a simple six-step approach for learning to make room for the "felt sense" of a person or situation or a creative project, which shows people how they can activate this whole process on their own. Focusing is a process of paying attention inwardly to this "felt sense" which is more physical than a feeling, but not merely a bodily sensation because it has a meaning, a context and is part of a unique life history.

For example, I love to write. I could quickly list a whole series of reasons why I enjoy writing, all of them quite intellectual and coming from my head. But if I ask my body to get a whole-bodily sense of why I enjoy writing then something quite different happens. The felt sense is one of intense aliveness and a tingling energy throughout my body the phrase that comes to mind is simply "joyously alive". When I am in the full flow of writing I just feel joyously alive inside, there is no sense of effort or striving, I am intensely alive in the moment and the words just flow through me. These words that fit the felt sense feel right to me and it has got to a much deeper of truth than the list that my intellectual mind would have come up with on its own.

There is a sense of relief, an inner physical release that is combined with a new insight and an emotional shift. This is change on a psychophysical level and it seems that an inner knowing is saying – yes this is the right way to go. New options have been revealed so that choice becomes apparent and the habit pattern can be changed.

In his best-selling book "Focusing" Gendlin has outlined a simple 6-step approach to the Focusing experience. They are:

> **Clearing a Space**, which is putting all your worries aside and saying, "well if I didn't have this problem is there anything else that would stop me from feeling perfect right now. There can be several things but eventually you get a pretty clear idea of what's the main thing that's bothering you at the moment.
> **Getting** a **"felt sense"** of the situation, the whole thing, what "all of that feels like – and it may well be a very unclear sense of the problem at this stage of the process. Because this is the body and mind working together and you know more about this than just your intellectual mind could tell you at this stage.
> **Getting** a **handle** on it. This takes time, this is a word, phrase, image or feeling that comes up from the felt sense itself. You stay with the quality of the whole felt sense until something fits it just right.
> **Resonating** – you say the word, (phrase or image) and go back and forth several times and you body will give you a subtle vibrational resonance if it fits the felt sense. The felt sense may subtly change, the word or phrase may need to be refined but eventually you know that you have a fit.
> **Asking** – being with the felt sense in a special kind of non-doing way. You stay with it and ask " What is it about this whole thing that makes it so....." You are letting it be even more fully present, you don't know the answer but you stay with the freshly sensed felt sense of it. In that awareness and acceptance of it a shift will come.
> **Receiving** the sense of felt shift in a very open and

grateful way. Something has shifted and it is often surprising and deeply meaningful at the same time. It is experienced as a sense of physical shift – a slight "give" or release and a new mental insight, both at the same time. It is important to stay with this and with the sense of awe and gratitude that often accompanies the "felt shift".

That's it; those are the 6 steps of Focusing. Put simply, you could say that with the technique of Focusing you stop talking about yourself and you go within and start actually feeling the reality of what is actually happening inside of yourself. In fact, Gendlin specifically advocates the benefits of Focusing for 'normal' people in the world, not just neurotics or severely damaged patients in therapy. Its use can be viewed as an essential life skill on a day-to-day basis. I would certainly agree with Gendlin's ideas, which would be powerful enough to transform society once a majority of people accepts the view that life is a process of on going self-transformation rather than being stuck in defended positions. However, the technique of Focusing although it seems simple is actually quite subtle in practice. You have to train effective skills through regular practice with a focusing teacher or partner and it is also good to train in the subtle process of WBF with groups in training workshops.

We are at this time experiencing a period of major global, and also individual, transformation. Energy and awareness is increased, but this means that blockages and frustrations are also intensified at the same time. We can contact our higher potentialities, our inner wisdom to transform ourselves and to raise our level of consciousness. So it becomes more and more unbearable just to stand still and be stuck in the same old rut, but also easier once you take the decision to move forward along the path of growth and change.

The question is bow to change effectively. The force of habits goes deep; it is a physical, mental and emotional reality. You can recognise a bad habit yet still be powerless to change it. This is where the Paradoxical Theory of Change (Arnold Beissner) comes in. Briefly stated it is this: change occurs when one becomes what he is, not when he tries to become what he is not. "Change does not take place through a coercive attempt by the individual or by another person to change him, but it does take place if one takes the time and effort to be what he is - to be fully invested in his current positions. By rejecting the role of change agent, we make meaningful and orderly change possible" (A. Beissner). This theory, which has played a large part in my life and work, at first seems totally paradoxical. It doesn't seem to make sense. The mind rebels against this "So you're trying to tell me that if I desperately want and need to change, my best strategy is not to force anything but to just stay where I am and accept myself exactly as I am? How will that help?"

This was the dilemma that F M Alexander faced, as he struggled to change embodies habit patterns that were stronger than he was. This was the question that Gendlin researched, - what makes for effective change in therapy? Can staying with the flow of your direct inner experiencing change the way that you relate to yourself and to others and divert the mind from its habitual reaction patterns? This is also at the heart of the Buddhist practice of mindfulness, which is over a thousand years old, and also confirmed as one of the key findings of modern neuroscience - that being fully present to your internal and external thoughts, feelings and sensations can have a powerfully integrating effect on the way your brain functions.

Chapter 5.
Tools for Staying in Contact with the Flow of Our Experience at a Deeper Level

WBF is the result of combining two brilliant holistic techniques: the Alexander Technique and Focusing. The A.T. Is a powerful method of becoming aware of your deep-seated muscular tension patterns and postural imbalances that are blocking your energy flow. Alexander's brilliant insight was that if you have a problem in one particular part of the body you cannot solve that by working on that part alone. You have to involve the whole of the rest of your body, and he did this by using mental 'directions' which are in one sense invitations to the body not to tense and reactivate the old pattern and in another sense they become mental thought projections which are held in awareness and open up living connections to all the other body parts. This opens us up to a sense of spaciousness and flow within our bodies. It awakens a sensitive awareness to the flow of our life experience. It is amazing how just being gently touched by another human being can make us aware of how much muscular tension we carry in our bodies, and as we hold our attention there, the story of all the unnecessary effort or fear can begin to emerge.

The Focusing technique developed by Eugene Gendlin is also about deepening our awareness to the flow of our experiences. He was coming at it more from the psychological side and realised that rather than fighting the emotions, or feeling confused or overwhelmed, it is possible to get a sense of the whole thing and to see the bigger picture. Whatever we are dealing with: memories from the past, a frustrating relationship, or a creative project that feels blocked, there is more to it than our cognitive minds are able to understand right now. Rather than fight it or fix it or run away from it, it is possible to pause and to get a felt sense of the whole thing. The whole thing is a bodily felt sense of the situation that knows more than our little intellectual mind does, it is a broadening out into a wider understanding, a deeper wisdom and a sense of support. Through the body we are able to have a living response to the situation or the problem in the moment, rather than our reactive, habitual emotional responses, which spin us off into negative spirals. Through our bodies we can connect with a deeper understanding of ourselves and other people. In the truth and wisdom of our authentic somatic responses lies a hidden meaning, the raw sensations from which we fashion our language and our concepts. Hidden in all the frustration and the blockages, if we can but connect with it, is a positive life energy which can move us forwards. But it involves taking time, deepening our awareness and getting real with ourselves.

If you want to stay connected with the flow of your experiences you must be aware that all experiences and begin with a sensory input. It is through the senses that we perceive the world and get continual feedback on the status of our internal and external environment. So the first step is mindful, non-judgmental awareness of what is happening right now, in your body and in your environment.

Take a moment to become aware of the flow of sensory information that you are sensing right now. Firstly your posture, are you standing, sitting or lying down ? Does that feel comfortable to you and can you notice your points of contact with gravity? What is supporting you is it hard or soft? Can you feel the counter-thrust of the Earth through the soles of your feet, your sitting bones in the pelvis or your back, buttocks and back of your legs if you are lying flat? You will probably need a certain amount of hardness in order to experience the counter-thrust of the Earth properly. What sounds can you hear? Perhaps some birdsong through the open window or the sound of a clock ticking? What can you see, what forms, colours and degrees of light or shade surround you? What do your fingertips feel, what can you smell? Have you got a taste in your mouth?

What does your body feel like internally? Can you notice any aches and pains anywhere? Are some of them unusual or are some of them familiar and persistent? Is your posture straight or is your back bent or twisted in some way? How about the head, does it feel balanced or tilted forwards? Do you feel relaxed or do you feel tense? Can you maintain this posture easily or does it feel like you will have to alter your position soon? Are you too hot or too cold? Are you comfortable right now or do you feel that you will need to eat or drink soon?

All of this information is flowing through our system and this is just the raw sensory data. At this point in time you are receiving this sensory information flow to the best of your ability, but some of it may be filtered out because you are cut off from your experience for various reasons or else there may be inaccurate sensory appreciation due to the repetition of a habit which feels quite comfortable but may actually be damaging – such as smoking. In addition to this there is the question of whether you can stay in non-judgmental awareness of this flow of sensory information or whether you are having an emotional reaction of likes or dislikes to any of these experiences - which can then feed back into the system, possibly causing more relaxation or more tension.

It is important to understand that on the sensory side there are two main systems: the nerves that inform us about what is happening in the environment outside of the body by way of the five senses: eyes, ears, tongue, nose and skin; and the nerves that are located in the viscera, muscles and connective tissue and tell us what is happening inside the body. It is indicative of our present society that most of our attention is directed outwardly, where we believe that we will find satisfaction and little attention is directed inwardly to develop the skills and sensitivity necessary to explore our interior world.

As we turn our attention inwards, we can use our sense of balance in the inner ear and helps us to sustain balance, posture and a beneficial relationship with gravity. The AT can help us to be properly aligned, when we can turn gravity from an energy-sapping enemy into a friend and gain a sustaining sense of grounded support from planet Earth. This is why it is so important to make little swaying movements every now and again, to awaken our sense of aliveness, inner energy and connection with gravity. This can be done standing or sitting, so why not try it now? *If you are sitting move forwards to the front edge of your seat and find your natural balance line. Sway a little bit from side to side, feeling more weight on the left side, then on the right side of your sitting bones contacting the chair. Now put your hands on top of your thighs and rotate your upper body in a circle, to the left and then to the right, forwards and backwards, keep doing this a few times, moving very slowly and mindfully. As you do so you will be surprised to notice how much more sensory information comes into your field of awareness, including the sense of your balance line coming more alive, more energy in your body and an awareness of the counter-thrust supporting you from your sitting bones all the way up your spine to carry your head. If you want to practice the AT learn to repeat Alexander's set of "mental directions" to your self a few times to*

"Allow the neck to be free,
Allow the jaw to release forwards to the tip of the chin,
Allow more space in the mouth and between the tongue and the teeth,
Allow the head to be free to tip forwards & upwards if it wanted to,
Allow the back to lengthen from the top of your head to the base of your spine,
Allow the back to widen between the two shoulder joints and between the hip joints,

All of which is done without any sense of effort or striving.

As your balance and energy levels increase you are better enabled to locate all the different parts of your body and how they fit together in an interior spatial relationship, e.g., this sense helps you to feel if your chest is caved in and your back is bent, or the position of your head on top of your spine. You also have an internal sense of how you feel inside, in terms of heart rate, respiration, internal temperature, degree of muscular tension and visceral pressure. All of this internal sensory information is there, but it needs to be made more accessible for many people through training and the grounding in increased self-awareness that takes place during WBF.

The essence of the AT is bringing more softening and spaciousness into the body and not trying so hard, what Alexander called "non-doing". That opens you up to the reality of what is actually happening in your body now, in mindful awareness, rather than a mental construct of what you think is happening or what you think you ought to be doing.

If you want to learn to stay more in touch with the flow of your experience, then it is important to realize that much of your implicit, procedural memory of performing actions is mostly automatic and some of these habits can also be destructive and harmful. E.g., if you are in the habit of sitting and working at your computer in a slouched position with a bent back, it may feel "normal and comfortable" and yet it is actually painful and damaging. You can actually be so physically out of alignment, using so many over-tensed muscles to hold yourself upright that it is physically damaging and yet not be aware of it. So, using the Alexander Technique teaches us how to pause and then slow down the flow of certain movement patterns and postures, by pausing and repeating Alexander's mental directions to oneself, before carrying out the action slowly and mindfully. This can break the force of habit and bring a deep awareness back into the whole flow of that movement pattern, so as to make yourself more conscious and alive and it invites the body to perform that action in a natural, calm and free-flowing way. It is making implicit memory *explicit* and bringing choice and awareness back into the flow of that activity. There are many similarities in the pauses, slowing things down and the heightened awareness of many mindful movement techniques like: Tai Chi, Qi Gong, Yoga, Cranio-sacral, AT, and the Feldenkreis method.

Try changing the habitual way you perform certain activities. Its not that simple, e.g., even try folding your arms on your chest a different way around and you will see that it feels odd. When you try changing the way you sit when working on your computer it becomes even more difficult. Or try going out to a party and standing there with shoulders wide open, in a welcoming posture, balanced and flexible with your two feet spread out wide in the lunge position, rather than having your hands in your pockets, or your arms crossed. When you try deliberately to change any of your set habits, it certainly does not feel comfortable and it involves a whole process of slowing down the movement patterns to make the implicit procedural memory conscious again. This takes time and conscious effort – as in heightened awareness – to make these movements and postural sets conscious again. Only then is it actually possible to start re-educating the body and the motor sensory circuits in the brain and the nervous system. Its not easy to maintain these changes, because strongly engrained habits want to keep returning.

Why should this be? Why do people get so caught up in their automatic habits that they cannot change their habits, nor be fully present in the moment? It is clearly linked with rushing too much and trying too hard, or narrowing the attention down to focus on the immediate danger and the physical restriction and tightening that results from the fight or flight response. So another man who has studied this problem is Prof Les Fehmi, Director of the Bio-Feedback & Stress Management Clinic at Princeton Medical School. For many decades Prof Fehmi was studying the significance of different brain wave patterns, measured on an EEG machine. Basically we all have the whole range of brain wave patterns the whole time, alpha, beta, gamma, delta and theta waves, but the preponderance of the mix changes with different ways of paying attention or when engaged in different types of activities.

Brain Wave Frequencies:

Heinrich Herz, German physicist who proved the existence of electromagnetic waves. 1 Herz = 1 cycle per second.

Delta 0-4 Hz: They are associated with deep sleep and experiences of empathy.

Theta 4-8 Hz: Predominant frequency during the transition stage between wakefulness & sleep. Theta waves are noted during healing, intuition, deep meditation, and a sense of merging with the oneness of all creation.

Alpha 8-12 Hz: They are associated with meditation and creativity. This is a flow state where you can move quickly & efficiently to accomplish whatever task is at hand. Alpha appears to bridge the gap between the conscious and the sub-conscious. When alpha waves predominate most people feel calm and relaxed.

Beta 15-18 Hz: It is a very common wave form associated with the alert waking state, when you are in "get the job done" mode. Predominant when focused on one particular task or project that needs completing, or during analytical problem solving, when making judgments, decision making, processing information about the world and about us. But can also occur as a sign of anxiety or apprehension.

Gamma 26-40 Hz: Associated with perception and consciousness, often around 40 Hz., but can be 26-70 Hz. Higher level cognitive activity occurs when lower frequency gamma waves suddenly double into the 40 Hz range. Noted during higher mental activity, higher reasoning and mental insights.

Prof Fehmi came to the conclusion that a lot of the very prevalent stress and trauma in our society is associated with high beta wave activity and an aroused of the central nervous system triggered by the fight or flight response in the limbic system, which is the "emotional brain". He reasoned that if the beta could be reduced and balanced out with increased alpha wave activity then people would not only feel calmer and more relaxed but also be more creative and productive in their lives. So the question was: how to increase alpha wave activity? Prof Fehmi spent many days with EEG electrodes attached to his head and the readings coming up on his computer screen. He tried really hard to induce more alpha wave activity in his brain and failed miserably. In point of fact, the more he tried the worse it got. Finally, at the end of a long miserable day he gave up, but the electrodes were still attached to his head. At some point he glanced casually at the screen and was amazed to see that his brain had shifted into high alpha wave activity! He could only induce alpha waves when he stopped trying, which is the same thing as Alexander saying that you can only allow your directions to flow when you stop being an "end gainer". Or Gendlin saying that you can only find a way forward through life's problems when you stop feeling overwhelmed by the emotional content and are able to step back a little and get a sense of what "the whole thing" feels like in your body.

So Prof Fehmi knew that he was onto something, but how to deal with the paradox that you do want to induce alpha waves, but you are not allowed to try, because trying will only make it worse? So after much research he found the essential principle that was needed – *more space*. It all hinges on the way that you pay attention, and he developed a technique, which he called "open focus" which can be used in any situation in daily life in order to induce more alpha wave activity. Prof Fehmi discovered from his research: don't narrow your attention down, expand out to include more space, more sights (through the peripheral vision), more sounds, smells, touch, open up to the world. The sense of greater space is the key, and when you have this the brain waves slow down and become more rhythmic, the fight or flight reaction gets turned off, the breathing slows down – all because you changed the way that you pay attention to the world! He developed a series of exercises, which are simple & effective ways of increasing your sense of space and connecting with the environment surrounding you.

"Open Focus" works with the eyes a lot, and vision, as we know, takes up a lot of brain capacity. It is often said that 2/3 (60%+) of the brain is "involved" in vision. However possibly less than 20% of the brain is dedicated to "visual-only" functioning. The other 40% is doing vision+touch, or vision+motor, or vision+attention (which involves the ability to recognize objects and this takes place in the temporal lobes), or vision+spatial navigation (which involves the ability locate objects and this takes place in the parietal lobe), or vision+meaning, etc. There is generally a smooth gradation from areas fully-specialized in one thing to areas involved in many things.

This image shows the approximate area dedicated to each sensory function (smell is underneath the brain and not visible).

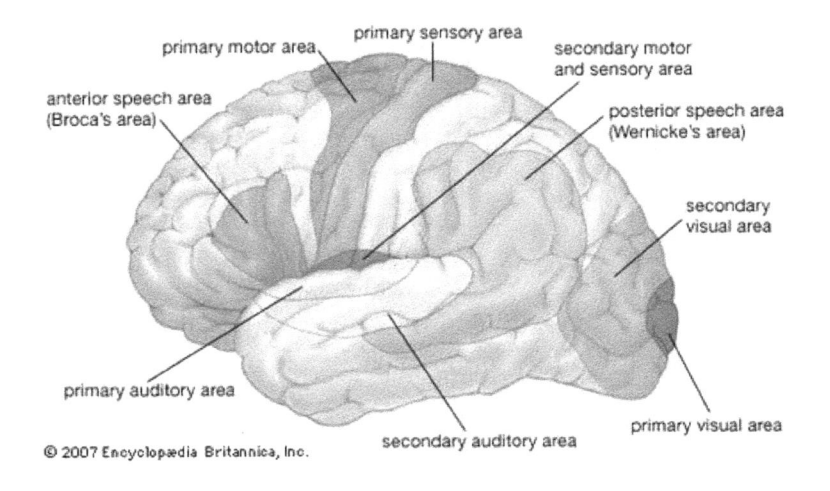

Figure: Lateral view of the brain with labeled regions: primary motor area, primary sensory area, secondary motor and sensory area, anterior speech area (Broca's area), posterior speech area (Wernicke's area), secondary visual area, primary visual area, secondary auditory area, primary auditory area. © 2007 Encyclopædia Britannica, Inc.

That is a lot of the brain that is dedicated to vision. So it stands to reason that when danger threatens and fight or flight is activated in the limbic system, the visual system will be put on hyper-alert, to look out for danger coming from any possible direction. So there is the observed response of hyper-vigilance, with the quickly moving eyes, scanning the environment for danger. On the other hand, when there is no possibility of either fight or flight the other possibility is to "freeze" and to play dead. Here the eyes can go rigid and blank off as the person retreats into themselves. These rigid eyes can often be observed in cases where the memory of a trauma is relived, and with it the feelings of helplessness and hopelessness.

So to get out of the fight/flight/freeze reaction and to calm down the arousal of the limbic system and nervous system it becomes essential to work with the eyes. Because as we all know there is a feedback loop, and due to the phenomena of "state dependent recall" just putting your eyes into a rigid forward looking stare can result in strong feelings of fear or anger. So Open Focus works with some very simple but effective techniques to restore mobility of the eyes and to get out of the stress or trauma reaction.

The first one is simply to become aware of the distance between your two eyes. Take some time to notice that you do not need to narrow down to a single point of vision, but that you have two eyes and some space in-between them. As you do that for a couple of minutes, notice how your eye balls and eye sockets soften, also your cheek bones widen and you get a sense of a softer focus in the eyes. Allow your vision to widen out now to take in more of your peripheral vision. There is always peripheral vision, and secondary areas of the visual brain cortex are devoted to that. To help activate more of that just get a sense of the wall, or an object to your left and then to your right. Be aware that there are objects there, but they are a bit blurred and not clearly in focus. Let them be just the way that they are, and be aware of the space in-between. Very often this will have the effect of calming any arousal, inducing alpha waves in the brain, and a sense of relaxation and deeper breathing in the body.

The same principle can be used again to just soften the focus of the eye balls, and look forwards to the wall in front of you, pick some area of the wall or some object in front of you and gently focus on that. Then be aware of the wall or the space behind you. Take some time to be aware of both the wall in front and the wall behind and the space in-between. As you do this it can become apparent that the space in-between becomes much more alive or vibrant in some way. With this increased awareness of space, there is a calming effect on the limbic system in the brain and the body starts to feel heavier and the breathing gets more relaxed. Congratulations! You have managed to induce more alpha waves in your brain and your brain wave pattern just got more coherent and rhythmic.

The neuroscience of this is clear, rather than rushing on with your life and all the countless jobs you need to do, you are taking some time out to *"pay attention to how you pay attention", and also how to pay attention to intention (more on this later) is crucial!* These Open Focus exercises are a mind training skill that strengthens the executive ability to sustain attention, avoid distractions, selectively change attention and then focus again, and then to allocate the resources necessary to accomplish a task. fMRI studies & other research at UCLA have shown as much executive function improvement due to these forms of mindfulness awareness practices, (MAPs) as had been achieved with the use of stimulant medication in adolescents with attention deficit challenges (ADHD). Not only that, but further research by Richard Davidson of the Mindfulness Based Stress Reduction program created by Jon Kabat-Zinn has shown an improvement in a wide range of functions, such as better immune system, the capacity for empathy, and the capacity to move towards rather than withdraw from challenges in life. This latter improvement is linked to an increase in electrical activity (registered with EEG) in the left frontal area of the brain.

Just having done these Open Focus exercises for a few minutes at regular points in the day, can keep you more relaxed, more in tune, and actually more productive in a flowing, creative way. What Alexander did with his mental directions in the AT, to soften the body, open up the interior spaces and thereby induce more relaxation and more alpha waves in the brain; so Prof Fehmi has also done with his Open Focus exercises to open up an awareness of the exterior spaces in the surrounding environment, and to reintroduce a calming of the arousal in the nervous system and sense of safety and relaxation. As I have demonstrated, the scientific principle is the same, it is asking the mind to be aware of two points and allowing the space in-between to come alive.

Curiously enough, Eugene Gendlin also demonstrated the same principle in his research whilst at the department of Psychology in the University of Chicago in the 70's & 80's. He showed how some people are cut off from the flow of their experiences whilst others have a natural ability to work with their internal sense as a way of checking out how they truly feel about a situation and using that as an internal compass. The Focusing method is a way of paying attention to the way you relate to your real emotional responses to a situation, in a curious, detached and open-minded way, rather than listening to what your head is saying about what you ought to be thinking, feeling or doing, or the opposite is getting overwhelmed by the powerful emotions of the situation. There is a big difference that happens as soon as you get into a detached and mindful relationship with the somatic expression of your emotional situation. Everybody has experienced this at some time, the most common example of this is if you experience "butterflies in the stomach", or a strong "gut instinct" which is telling you something about the situation you are in. These somatic counterparts of the emotion can be a physical sensation felt anywhere in your body, including your head and Focusing will help you to get more alive and in touch with your true self, realizing that naming the reality of your emotions and your experience does not make it any worse and ignoring and cutting off from your body and your experience does not make it go away.

Take a moment to ask your body how you feel right now. What feels comfortable and what places do not feel comfortable? Where can you notice any discomfort or muscular tension patterns? What seems to be asking for attention now? How fast is your heart beating? How deep or shallow is your breathing going. Do you feel confident and relaxed and able to take up your full body space or do you feel tight and held in some way? Take a moment to scan through your body, in a calm and grounded way, and notice what needs attention right now. This is not just a way of focusing attention on present moment experience and then letting it go again, which you would be encouraged to do in a mindfulness meditation. No, the difference here is that we are adopting a state of positive regard for self and others. This involves being curious, open-minded accepting and loving. (Dan Siegel has coined the acronym COAL for this state of being). These different body sensations are the internal sense that helps you to identify, name and to be in contact with your emotions by feeling them as bodily sensations. The Focusing process helps you to dialogue with these parts, to be curious and self-compassionate and accepting as you try to understand the story that is behind them. E.g., I can feel a ball of tension in my stomach.....I wonder what that's about, I feel curious, open-minded, accepting and loving about that........ It may feel murky and unclear at the moment, but given time and the permission to be there it will clarify into an important realization of my truth in the moment about a particular situation.

Being in connection with an internal body sensation it is a slower form of knowing and thinking than your cognitive mind, you can probably think about 20 thoughts in the time that it takes to feel one emotion-linked body sensation. Hence the long pauses that interested Gendlin in the tapes of successful therapy clients. Every emotion, - fear, anger, sadness, shame, interest, frustration, happiness, - each basic emotion and some subtle one's that do not even have a name yet, is linked to a pattern of body sensations, stimulated by patterned activity in the brain. According to Antonio Demasio's theory of somatic markers ("The Feeling of What Happens: Body, Emotion and the Making of Consciousness", 2000) emotions are first learnt in very early childhood as an experience of intense body sensations that are experienced in response to a certain situation. These sensations and the associated emotions are encoded and stored as implicit memory associated with the stimulus of the situation that originally stimulated them. The emotion has a somatic marker from then onwards. Memory of the emotion and the bodily sensation will later be triggered into recall when similar stimulation is present (state-dependent recall). This is the biology of emotion in the body and the brain. It happens in the moment and it happens when we access our memories, hence the usefulness of giving ourselves times to tune in with our 'felt sense' of the situation, our physical sensations. This will tell us more about the whole situation than our quick cognitive mind, which is good at labeling and analysing but not very good at actually feeling into and contacting the reality of emotions in the moment. The cognitive mind (the neo-cortex) is not designed for that and it cannot do it without slowing down and receiving input from the body.

Our emotions are an energy that gives us the truth of our authentic reactions to a situation. Whether or not you choose to act out on that is another question, but the emotion is the starting point, the reality of where you are right now, and if it can be named and acknowledged, without suppression through tensing the body or cutting off from it, then that is the starting point of a whole process of change and transformation. That is so much better than sitting on it in denial, or engaging with all the critical voices in your head that tell you why you shouldn't be feeling this way. As the paradoxical theory of change points out - *"Change does not take place through a coercive attempt by the individual or by another person to change him, but it does take place if one takes the time and effort to be what he is - to be fully invested in his current positions"*. That is so true.

The mind, which I will define as "a process that regulates the flow of energy and information" (Dan Siegel) operates in such a way that even the limited amount of sensory information coming through from your body is often not experienced freshly, but comes through the additional filter of your pre-conceived concepts and belief patterns from your past experiences, or is seen through the wistful rose-tinted spectacles of your hopes for the future. So it is very beneficial to periodically ask, "am I living mindlessly (on automatic pilot) or am I living mindfully?" and to renew your experience of grounded presence through the AT or Open Focus and return to the full experience of the present moment rather than always be on the way to some future point of happiness. These are very subtle things I am talking about, but the only thing that really exists is the present moment and that can never be experienced fully in all its' richness and creativity unless you really are in grounded presence, which means being fully connected to your body. Only then is it possible to stay fully in contact with the flow of your experience and become truly creative person, making ethical decisions and increasing the power of good in your community and the world.

The way to enliven the question "am I living mindlessly or am I living mindfully?" - Is to pause and periodically pay attention to your intentions. Not just the valid question of "are my intentions good and whom do they aim to benefit?" but also "am I managing to manifest my intentions today, and to achieve what I set out to achieve in the way that I set out to do so?" This is a really important practice, because when I am asking if the flow of my day's experience has matched the intentions that I had at the start of the day, or the start of the week, there is clearly a prefrontal integrative circuit being activated. Prefrontal function is integrative, because long strands of the prefrontal neurons reach out to distant and differentiated areas of the brain and body, this linkage of different elements is fundamental to the process of integration and is known to be one of the main pathways leading to a sense of well being. Let's look at this in more detail, when I examine the question "have I fulfilled my intentions for the day?" I am actually taking time out, stepping back and taking a long-term perspective. So when I do this it is fundamentally important that I pause, and make this a leisured, whole body experience, that has an integrative effect on the brain. This is not an excuse to beat myself up because I have not been more productive, or more successful, and to feel more stressed by how much I still have left to do on my to-do-list. No, that would clearly be counter productive and activate more arousal of the limbic system and the fight/flight response. Instead, I pause, enjoy and compare internal maps. *"My intention was to work on the book today, various things intervened which meant that no writing was done this morning, but I am managing to write this afternoon, and I feel happy with what I have written and that my actions are now matching my intentions. In some small way, the overall plan to write this new book is coming into manifestation. There is an actual tremor of pleasurable enjoyment in my body as I sit here at my desk, in a balanced but relaxed posture, and the thought goes through me that I am capable of achieving my aim".* So the prefrontal cortex is clearly capable of introducing a pause, stepping back a bit, so I am delaying taking premature action, like wanting to get out into the garden soon, because it is a lovely evening and I can do a bit of gardening and enjoy nature, the sunshine and the soft breeze......I am know delaying immediate gratification in favour of taking a considered course of action that will actually lead to more long-term gratification. So there has been a whole load of research that has clearly documented the benefits of being able to make this clear decision, by taking the long-term perspective. I am not only making a good decision, but I am also able to hold to my intention because I it is the right decision, and there is this curiously pleasurable wholebody sensation to it all.

In addition, there is clearly an integrative function of my brain. There is intention and awareness of intention, and this results in a sense of self-agency. This is crucial, because as studies with victims of trauma have shown, the feelings of helplessness and hopelessness are linked to feeling overwhelmed, not being able to make clear decisions, not having clear boundaries and not feeling in control of their lives. This becomes a self-fulfilling expectation. Whereas one of the results of successful therapy, that needs to be tested for, is whether the client now has a greater sense of control and self-agency? As the neuroscience shows, being aware of intentions and successfully carrying out these actions, leads to more integration and the growth of fibres in the prefrontal areas of the brain.

So there is a wholebody sense of that actually feeling right. When there is a match between my intentions for the day and what I actually managed to achieve, there is a serenity and ease to the flow of my experiences. Conversely, due to the now clearly understood link between emotional experience and somatic sensations, when your body is registering something is wrong about the situation, there is a mismatch between what your mind expects to happen and what your body actually knows about the situation, as this case study shows.

Clare was a young, attractive woman traveling alone in India. She had just visited the art museum in Delhi and was looking for a taxi to drive her back to her hotel. There was a line of cabs outside the museum, but she instinctively had a reaction to the first cab driver. He seemed shifty and she didn't like him and didn't want to go with him. She tried to go with the second cab driver, but they had a system there and you had to go with the guy who was first in line, so as she couldn't really understand it or make sense of that feeling and didn't want to make trouble, she got into the cab with the first taxi driver. They drove off and that unclear feeling got stronger and gradually clarified into a knowing: "this man is malevolent". Then she noticed that he didn't seem to be going in the right direction. He drove her to the outer suburbs of the town and she started to feel very frightened and vulnerable. When she questioned what he was doing he got aggressive and told her he was taking a shorter route. She knew he was lying and this is where she knew that she had to make a strong decision. First she prayed and asked for protection and then she strongly sent out a thought "don't do anything bad to me, you will really regret it". Then she grounded herself and organised her voice and body language not to show her panic and vulnerability. At a suitable place where there were shops and people around, in a decisive voice she asked him to drop her off. He stopped the cab, but demanded a very high price for the ride and looked threatening. At which point Clare put him on the back foot by firmly telling him that this was much more than the price they had agreed at the beginning, and she was only going to pay him the agreed amount, which she did and then got out and left him there, grateful that there were other people there to witness what was going on. She then got an honest taxi driver to take her back to her hotel, but felt quite shaken by the whole incident and regretted that she had not followed her earlier intuition, which was a bodily reaction to the whole situation.

Her body had known something more about the situation than her conscious mind had, and it had known it right from the beginning, from the first instant of meeting that taxi driver.

Clare had not been in grounded presence strongly enough at the beginning of the incident to trust her bodily intuition and absolutely refuse to get into the cab with that driver, but she did have an uncomfortable feeling in her body and questions in her mind right from the beginning. Once she knew for sure that something was wrong she did not go into panic but developed a plan of action and released her own energy and initiative into the situation. She was not powerless, implicit in that whole situation was also the possibility of her forward moving life energy that could take some measure of control and assert herself. By not panicking, but staying in grounded presence and in connection with herself, she was able to see a good possibility that had always existed from the beginning, and find a positive way forwards by asserting herself and getting out of that cab. She had not seen that possibility strongly enough when she was just listening to all the oughts and shoulds in her head and from other people.

So this is one crucial area where Focusing really comes into its own, where your body knows something more about a situation than your head and it doesn't feel quite right. There is a murky unclear feeling that has not been put into words yet. It has not yet acquired a meaning or language, but there is clearly more to that uneasy feeling inside of you than just a physical sensation. This is the creative edge where meaning is being experienced in the body. If Clare had been able to give more space and time to this feeling of unease, if she had been able to pause and not act, just not get into any taxi but instead stay with that part of her body that knew something more about that first taxi driver than her rational, conscious mind knew. That feeling of unease crystallised into the words "This man is malevolent".

That phrase summed it all up, he looked shifty, he was shifty and her body knew it, but her cognitive mind did not trust this direct, embodied knowing, so she discounted it and got into the taxi instead. She was very lucky to survive the trip without something worse happening, but in retrospect it was also a good learning experience for her. It really helped her to trust her embodied knowing about people and situations. She learnt to trust her body's sense of a situation and to ask open-ended focusing questions that helped to awaken the focusing experience and start the focusing process sooner. Such helpful questions might be: "What is going on in my body?" "Where in my body am I experiencing this right now ?", "What's happening inside ?" , , "What's the problem ?" , "How am I with this whole situation ?", "What's the meaning of this ?". This is focusing, staying with something that is unclear in the body until it gradually clarifies and meaning emerges.

Chapter 6.
A Manual of Wholebody focusing: Grounded Presence, Acceptance, Holding Both, and Allowing Change to Happen.

Grounded Presence

If you want to escape the restrictions of your conditioned mind you have to learn how to slow things down and to experience what's going on in your body and your environment fully. You have to learn how to sink below the myriad thoughts of your complex mind and to experience life in all of its simplicity and richness. Groundedness is very simple, it is all about balance: maintaining an awareness of your physical weight in relationship to gravity. It is very important for the body to be physically in balance, and by this I mean a very precise alignment of the body where the skeletal system is in balance from top of your head to soles of your feet so that the muscular system hangs loosely around the skeleton with just the right amount of muscle tone to keep the body erect but without excessive tension. Once you have this experience of the body in contact with gravity, it is then possible to get a sense of being supported by the Earth. This is a sense of being supported by something bigger than you, which leads not only to physical relaxation, but also to a psychological and spiritual assurance.

Step 1: The Swaying Exercise: This is a simple exercise that can help you to get grounded, and this replaces *Step 1: Clearing a Space* in Gendlin's 6 steps of Focusing. Allow yourself to sway gently and slowly from one side to the other. Feel the whole line of your body moving as you loosen your ankle and hip joints as you sway gently like a tree in the wind. Feel how you put more weight on one leg and then the other and you have to tense your muscles more in the weight bearing leg. Be aware also of what is happening in the soles of your feet, how the weight distribution changes. As you sway to one side more weight comes onto the balls of that foot, the sides of your foot and your heel and as you sway back to the other side more weight is shifted to the other foot. So you are playing with different possibilities, feeling the range of balance and movement that is possible. Now begin to make the movements smaller and begin to notice more the point when you actually feel that you are in your balance line with your weight more evenly distributed between both feet. For a fleeting moment you have it and then you lose it again. When you are in your balance line you may notice that there is more up-thrust from the heels, up the legs, up the pelvis, up the spine, and that because the spine feels stronger the head can balance in a different way on top of the spinal column. *It is really essential to build an awareness of your balance from the ground up, with a sense of growing awareness and relaxation.*

You will notice that the weight distribution in the soles of your feet has changed in the neutral balanced position - so that your balance line falls through the arches of your feet. As you work with this balance exercise you will gradually come to realise that not only do you have a line of balance, but you also have a centre of gravity of the body, located in the middle of the pelvis about two finger widths below the belly button. The Japanese call this the 'Hara' and attribute tremendous importance to this power centre. Certainly, if you can connect with this centre you are able to feel more "centered" which gives great resilience, calmness and emotional stability.

As you work with the swaying exercise it is also important to release any tension in the lower back, if you wish to connect fully with your centre of gravity. What is needed is for the back to lengthen and the buttocks to drop down and round so that you can then experience true grounding through your legs. Another simple exercise that can help is to bend the knees slightly, releasing the buttocks downwards and the lower back "backwards" to fill out the hollow in the lower back. This is called the "monkey position" and there is a sense of 'releasing' any excessive muscular tension in the lower back, which then allows the spine to lengthen and the pelvis to swing into its correct alignment relative to the balance line and the spine.

As you connect with your feet through this swaying exercise, keep paying attention to the soles of your feet in contact with the ground, and the way that this connects with your whole balance line from your feet to the top of your head, you will gradually become aware of how the body starts to be energised from within. There is a sense of the body becoming more alive and this awakening seems to move from the feet through the calves and knees, and up throughout the whole of the body, as though it knows where to go. The hands and the arms, everything starts to come alive as the inner energetic body awakens. In this way you are able to experience a sense of release and sustainment, which at first feels physical and energetic, but as you deepen your awareness you will realise its deeper spiritual implications.

I worked with this simple swaying exercise for many years in my Alexander and Focusing practice, when I would ask my clients to sway slowly from side to side at the start of their sessions. I will give an example of this now, taken from a session with a client and I simply ask you, the reader to experiment with doing this right now.

OK so we are just going to take a few minutes, we are going to put it all on hold, and just sway from side to side... feeling your heels, and the sides of the feet, and the balls of the feet... just let everything happen and just allowing your body to be here in your space, shifting more weight on one leg, more weight on the other... just setting your own gentle swaying rhythm... and you can feel your toes as well, you can feel your heels, you can feel the balls of your feet, you can feel the whole soles of your feet, as you pay attention to them they get bigger, they spread out more, they're getting warmer, they're getting bigger, they're contacting ... just keep bringing the mind back to the sense of your feet contacting the earth, your weight dropping down through the pelvis and the legs into the earth, and coming back up again to support you... and when you are ready you can also spread your fingers out with your palms facing down, and ground through your hands... putting your attention for a while on your hands... then on your feet... then back to your hands... then back to your feet... and when you are ready holding your attention on both your feet in contact with the floor, and grounding down through your hands.

As you do this exercise just become aware of any thoughts as they arise and then let them go again, don't get involved, just go back to an awareness of the soles of your feet in contact with the floor. The aim of the exercise is to try and attain a state that is free of thought, by continually bringing your awareness back to the soles of your feet and the palms of your hands.

The body is your natural support system. Through the startle response and other postural defense mechanisms you sometimes disconnect from your sense of being supported by the Earth. This is the body expressing fear, but paradoxically the more you pull up and away from the ground the more insecure it makes you feel. Through simple grounding exercises, like the swaying exercise which I developed many years ago (and I am sure that other practitioners have independently developed similar exercises) I found that I was able to reconnect with a sense of standing my ground, feeing my feet connecting energetically with the earth and not being afraid. It is really fundamental and I have measured and tested this on EEG machines, by this simple exercise it is possible to shift the brain from quite agitated Beta rhythms into more relaxed and creative Alpha rhythms. Psychologically and spiritually you start to feel that you are being supported and that you do not have to do it all alone.

Creating this inner balance within the body gives you the paradoxical experience that by doing less you are achieving more. By relaxing downwards you are generating an upward thrust, a new sense of vitality in the spine and skeletal system, as well as increased tone in the musculature. By doing less more happens. Often people forget that, they can start to feel insecure – thinking that they are "not getting it right" and as a result they try harder. This is counter-productive. Just relax and just pay attention to what is there then become aware how simply paying attention to what is happening within the body seems to awaken the energy and allow it to flow right through the body.

When you are in Grounded Presence there is sense of physical relaxation and psychological and spiritual connection. There is a feeling that Life is too complex to be doing it all on your own, there is too much effort and tension that way and it generally ends in disaster. There is another way, which is getting into the flow state, where there is a sense of being supported by something much bigger. There is a connection with an inner wisdom, an inner guidance and a sense of non-doing. The book writes itself, the picture paints itself, what a relief! And the quality is so much better because the intelligence and the creativity flow from an infinite source.

Step 2: What Needs Attention?

This is essentially the same as Gendlin's second step, of allowing a felt sense to form, but instead of picking one problem and deciding to focus on it, we are allowing the body to make the choice for us, an to allow the most pressing issue to come to the fore. Once you are in grounded presence it is possible to simply ask the body: what needs attention now? You can go and ask and your body in its deep wisdom will show you the place where you are carrying your most pressing issues. It starts with noticing body sensations. Maybe something doesn't feel quite right. There can be a knot of tension, or pain somewhere, the energy may be blocked. Paying attention to what is happening in the body right now and accepting it just the way that it is, making room for it to be there in that way, and then in that acceptance and awareness it can expand or release in the context of the body as a whole rather than you trying to fight it or fix it, over-ride it or get rid of it in some way.

It is hard to notice what needs attention in this wholebody way if you are in survival mode and stressed out. When you are so narrowly focused on meeting the impending threat, that there is no mental detachment to accept what is really happening and to simply observe it within the container of the body. When you are in panic mode the brain is not functioning properly. If the amygdala in the limbic system picks up on a stimulus that is similar to danger in the past it will trigger off an alarm reaction. This is the phenomenon of state-dependent recall. *This can be physical sensations within the body* as well as outer stimuli or emotional states. This can cause muscular tension to build up anywhere in the body, but often in the neck and shoulders, as part of the "startle response". This starts with a tension the neck and shoulders and in microseconds it carries on tightening up muscles all the way down the body, particularly in the stomach and then on towards the feet. The heart rate goes up, respiration increases and we are getting ready for fight or flight, or else trying to fight it or fix it, or run away from the situation. The physical posture is one of "defended against". We are certainly not in a position to accept and calmly observe what is happening in the situation and our response to it.

So it makes sense that in order to reverse this startle response we have to work in reverse order by relaxing the feet first (which we did by the swaying exercise) and then allowing the relaxation response to move back up the body. The beauty of Wholebody focusing is that it enables you to calmly and non-reactively discover where you carry your unique pattern of muscular holding and tensions and by observing from a place of groundedness and compassionate acceptance, to be able to start the process of self-transformation. This is the whole secret of self-transformation. It is only when we calmly accept ourselves as we are that we are able to change. Change does nor take place through trying to force things, but it does take place, if we take the time to be fully grounded in our current situation, our bodies and our authentic reactions and then allow the natural process of change to take place

So there is the second element – energy. As the situation begins to feel safe, because you are more grounded, the power of awareness can focus on what is calling for attention and the inner energetic body is already awakened from the swaying exercise so the energy can flow. Often people are so cut off from themselves that they are not even aware of being blocked or held in muscular tension patterns, there is just a sense of disconnect or fuzziness. This is a well-known phenomenon in Alexander work. But, as the inner energetic body comes alive from grounding there is more energy and more awareness within the body. As we all know from the flow of electrical energy, there needs to be two poles and a safe, connecting pathway to facilitate the flow of energy. So where there has been proper grounding through the soles of the feet, as a result of the swaying exercise, then the inner energetic body is awakened and there is more charge in the body.

As the inner energetic body comes alive through grounding we can become more aware of what is happening within the body as a whole, starting from the feet and moving upwards we start to notice other areas where things do not feel quite right. As the body awakens in this way it helps us to notice where there are areas of tension and holding. Each person will have a unique pattern of postural holding and tension that expresses their unique history and personality. As we begin to give these areas space and invite them into awareness, they can begin to feel more than just physical sensations, they can have an emotional charge and a story to them as well. In addition the body may remember any specific recent event or situation where there was a strong reaction and the situation feels unresolved still. This will be felt not just as physical sensation but it also has an emotional arousal, a meaning to it. So gradually the felt sense emerges from the murky discomfort from our body memory of "the whole thing" and we can start to move onto the next stage of the process.

Step 3: Getting a handle

We want to get a handle on the felt sense now, so this is the focusing process and is exactly similar to step 3 of Gendlin's 6 steps. But, just becoming aware of a simple physical sensation is not a simple thing. It can begin to feel quite emotional and overwhelming because this is your body in its wisdom saying that this is the area that has the most emotional charge at the moment and this is what needs dealing with. Actually it will not go away until it is resolved, the body will keep bringing it to your attention, through pain, anxiety or even illness, until you take the time to give it your attention and find a way to resolve it. This is where *acceptance and naming the part as it is* becomes very important, because it enables you to be in the moment without trying to fix it. Rather than trying to fight these blockages, or fix them or run away from them, trying hard to over-ride them so that we can get back to feeling "normal" again, in WBF we do the contra-intuitive thing by just staying with them in awareness. We could start by just being grateful and recognising that these blockages have served a purpose. At some point there was a choice and they represent our survival mechanisms. They may seem clumsy and inappropriate now, but these were our ways of coping with the world as a child, a way of surviving in a dangerous and confusing environment. We can start by giving them space to be even more present and respect it as a very important part of ourselves, maybe even something so familiar that it feels like its been there forever, but it can change. We can have compassion towards them and ourselves. These were successful survival strategies that have helped us to stay alive and get to where we are now. Well done, you have survived! This sense of gratitude and self-compassion can be the first step in moving away from judgments and towards true self-acceptance.

The key to an integrated personality and real change is in the WBF process is when we can respectfully name and then listen to all of these different parts of the personality and make space for them to be there just as they are. If two parts are in conflict, they need to be consciously named so that a dialogue can take place and some sort of understanding and resolution can result from this. If one part feels terribly blocked, that blockage can be held "in equal positive regard", and a forward moving life energy can be released. But what seems to be important first is the sense of being in grounded presence and supported by something much bigger than us. Then it is possible to allow all of the different parts to be there without suppression or rejection. This is really a crucial part of all therapy, allowing a sense of the whole thing and difficult emotions to be there and just becoming the detached observer that can be fully present to them.

It is only in the space created by acceptance that we can gradually become more aware of how our persistent blockages, physical patterns of protection and holding have acted as a form of body armouring. The judgements create conflict and tightness, there is the conflict between the critical voice and the part being judged, and we easily get sucked into the overwhelming emotions associated with the situation. We need to create a non-judgmental space and the observing self. This then helps to create the right distance to any bodily felt sense of the problem. We need to move to the position of detached observer, getting enough information to be able to work with what is coming to our attention in awareness, but not getting sucked into the intensity of it and not cutting off completely. As Gene Gendlin once said " You need to be able to smell the soup but not be in the soup". Finding the right distance is essential to stop you falling into the soup.

Sometimes the emotional charge is so strong that holding direct awareness of the physical tension pattern at the epicentre of the physical sensations is almost unbearable. It can be a hard thing to do when becoming aware of the felt sense in the body also unleashes a whole torrent of associated emotions You get so intensely triggered that it is no longer possible to maintain the position of detached observer. This is often the case in terms of severe trauma or sexual abuse in childhood. Here it is very useful to be working with an experienced therapist who can help the client to find a safe distance, working from around the outer edges of the epicentre of physical sensation, where it feels you are safe enough because the intensity has lessened and yet still close enough to stay in contact with what is happening and get the information that is needed as the inner process gets underway. Sometimes you even need to work from the energetic body beyond the confines of the skin in order to get a safe enough distance.

If you can keep the right distance to the tension pattern, then you can allow it to be even more present, to give it even more space to reveal itself. Then certain qualities may begin to reveal themselves, or a word, phrase or image may begin to come out of this felt sense. This is a crucial part of Gendlin's 6 steps, and indeed it often happens in the WBF process too, but it does not have to happen. The beauty of the WBF process is that the way the posture is set can become the handle (in the 6 steps of Focusing) and you can just become aware of that whole posture in grounded presence and allow that to transform itself without ever engaging the cognitive mind. But something very significant can happen with an energetic and postural release, which is really the body in its own wisdom adjusting the tensions and postural imbalances that have kept it in survival mode. Step 3, getting a handle, is where a lot of people who are new to Focusing can find it difficult and feel stuck. The beauty of WBF is that this does not need to happen at all. Usually words and phrases will come and these become the handle in the normal way, but if they don't then it is possible and highly effective as well, to carry on the process without them.

Step 4: Resonating

This is exactly the same as step 4 in Gendlin's 6-step process. Once the right word or phrase or image has emerged it is important to go back and forth between that handle and the felt sense itself. Ask yourself: is that the right fit or not? If it matches there is a sort of "resonating" that takes place in exactly that part of your body where you are holding the felt sense. This is a way of checking and confirming that you are on the right track, or perhaps it isn't exactly the right word yet and it needs some fine-tuning. E.g. Ted was feeling a headache on the top of his head. It was a vice-like grip that hurt and the words that came were "I'm tired of this all", and that fitted his life situation of feeling that he was always chasing the women, trying to make it right for them so that they would then want to be in a relationship with him. But that didn't quite resonate so instead he tried "I'm sick of this all" and that fitted, because it wasn't just draining him, it was actually making him sick and he was determined to move on from this pattern and stop making the same old mistakes.

If it matches, its important to have the sensation of matching the word and the felt sense several times because that then gives the vibrational feel of a "resonating", which is a form of 2 pointing that stimulates more alpha wave activity in the brain, as well as creating more neural integration, so important realisations and insights will start to flow in that moment.

Step 5: Holding Both and Allowing Change to Happen

This is a very different way of allowing a felt shift to happen. In Gendlin's process step 5 is where a lot of people feel stuck and then they start asking all the "Focusing questions" like: "What's the worst thing about this whole thing?"
"What does it need?"
"How would it feel if it was all perfect?"
The wait for the feelings to stir and the body to answer.
You can do all of that as well, but there is another way of doing this, which is a far easier and more effective way of allowing a felt shift to occur. The key element of Wholebody focusing, as developed by myself, is the concept of "holding both" within the container of the whole body. "Holding both in equal positive regard", when two points are held in an expanded non-judgmental awareness, this is what allows the interconnecting energy space to come alive. The energy that fills that space is intelligent, alive and knows where to go and what to do. It is our inner body wisdom in action; all we have to do is to get our ego with its preconceived ideas out of the way in order to allow the energy to flow.

Holding both is what really allows the inner body wisdom to operate and the whole release of the "felt shift" to occur. What was blocked process in the body, actions that were not performed, words that were not said, emotions that were not expressed, can slowly become free and flowing. Tiny movements can start to be felt in the body as subtle muscular releases or as more overt gestures or movements. These are not conscious movements initiated by command of the neo-cortex and executed by an act of conscious will. Rather, these are "inner directed movements", which are spontaneous movements of the whole body that knows what is needed to release the tension, complete the action and then return to a position of calm balance. It is the wisdom of the body that knows how to readjust to the present situation in a healthy and integrated way, rather than being triggered by trauma all the time. With this release a situation that seemed to be impossible a few minutes ago can suddenly seem to be manageable. Solutions appear where there were only huge problems and massive conflicts before, possibilities are suddenly seen that always existed, but you were just too stressed to be able to recognise them and work with them.

But what is essential is to stop any effort to fix it, or fight it or to force a solution. There is a period of letting go and broadening out that is really essential to this whole process of letting the answer come to you rather than getting all up-tight and trying to force a solution. But the mind will not let go of its tried and tested defense strategies until it feels safe enough to do so, and it will only feel safe enough once it is securely grounded. So having spent some time with the swaying exercise in order to get grounded and feel well-supported from the feet upwards, and having identified the part that needs attention and feels blocked, *it is now possible to hold both*. This means staying with both the wounded part and the sense of being supported by the whole Earth through an alive up-thrust of energy through your points of contact with gravity. Staying with both is a non-judgmental activity, where you can observe the whole bodily sense of the situation, staying with the body as a container, rather than looking for immediate solutions. So rather than trying to sort out the problem with your cognitive mind, or fight it, or run away from it, just be with it holding both within the container of the whole body – without trying to change anything at all.

As my colleague Kevin McEvenue has written: "Learn to be with both the part that wants attention, the wounded part, and to stand in grounded presence, grounded in the moment, feeling connected to the whole universe – holding both at the same time". It works, it may seem rather paradoxical, but it works and there is also a solid scientific reason why it works. I have done some research into this using EEG machines at the Amen Clinic in Newport Beach, Calif. What is clear from this research is that holding both, holding two points and an awareness of the energetic, connecting space in-between leads to an expansion in consciousness. Within a few minutes of doing this exercise there was a shift in the balance of brain wave activity from beta into high alpha wave activity, which is indicative of a more relaxed, intuitive and creative state of mind. This alpha wave activity was also right brain predominant, which is the more holistic, body orientated, and intuitive side of the brain.

As a result of this shift into alpha wave activity many people report a sense of being connected with something bigger than just the individual mind. There is a sense of being loved, guided and being held in a larger matrix of connected energy and consciousness. Whatever name we want to give this is actually immaterial, God, Spirit, Universe, The Buddha Mind. Call it what you will and I hope that my language and concepts do not clash with your particular view of the world, because we are all talking about the same experience - it is basically a sense of connecting with and being supported by something bigger than ourselves.

The body needs to be the container for all of this. Without the sense of the feet on the floor, getting the support of the Earth, without the sense of the energetic body coming alive and having all the space of the body to flow into and connect with - there is no safety. Often our emotional issues can feel so scary, so overwhelming, that the ego does not want to go there. Because the experience is that if you go there you get sucked in and overwhelmed by the triggered emotional content. It is not just that being in grounded presence provides safety - it is much more than that. The WBF process is essentially fluid and the fluidity needs a container - otherwise energy is dissipated and lost. The container allows the flow of different parts coming into contact with each other and the changes that result from holding these parts in connection at the edge. What felt like a blockage can melt and release, it can change into something else which is the positive expression of the blocked energy, which becomes a forward moving life energy.

Holding both also brings into manifestation the creative pause, which is common to both the Alexander Technique and the Focusing process. This period of pause allows time for a creative response rather than the knee jerk reaction of our automatic responses. Normally there is no time between the stimulus and the response and we are just on automatic pilot, reacting in a habitual way rather than in a reasoned, or an intuitive and creative way. I call this the point of freedom, in that there is a choice in life about how we wish to respond to any particular situation. It is a very small point in time that can flash past very fast or else we can deliberately choose to stop and pause for a while in order to find out what is really going on. In focusing terms we are getting a bodily sense of the whole situation at a deeper level, rather than just reacting automatically, and finding a wiser response that is grounded in a fresh perspective of the whole.

When we are holding both and in this in-between ground of the creative pause it is important that we give ourselves permission "not to know". If we are looking for something truly fresh and creative to emerge it cannot, by definition, be just a repetition of old habitual reaction habits. We have to enter this in-between ground where we do not know, we cannot know, the answer. There is something inside of us that knows more than we think we know, and we can trust that something, whilst at the same time *not knowing exactly what* that new creative vision will be. It is so important to get out of the old model of having a right or a wrong answer, or what will other people think ? There is only our unique answer that is right for us, our unique truth that we have created in the matrix of the ever-present moment.

But there can be no new creative impulse until there has been an embracing of the present moment. To be fully present to the reality of the NOW there must first be a release of all defensive posturing and habits from the past. But your body/mind will never give up its old habits until it feels safe enough to do so. It is an intensely real physical experience – you cannot negotiate or reason with someone who feels that they are hanging onto the edge of a cliff by their fingernails, with a sheer drop under their dangling legs. Only when you can guide their feet to a secure foothold, or put a strong physical support for them to stand on, only when there is this direct experience of support and groundedness, only then is it possible for physical relaxation to occur and some sort of change to take place. Until that point in time the body/mind is still caught in physical/mental trauma patterns from the past, it feels like an emergency situation and the mind and nervous system is unable to let go and fully work with the present moment. In a sense holding both is key, because it allows the trauma to become a pathway to greater awareness. By allowing the body to be the safe container for all the physical sensations, memories, thoughts and emotions that arise, it becomes safe to hold them in awareness, however uncomfortable they might be. They are only a part of you, not the whole of you. By staying with it and holding all of these different parts in the container of your body you allow your body wisdom to fully adjust to the reality of this present moment in time, without resistance or judgment. It will then find the perfect solution, in its own wisdom, without the direction of the conscious mind and without being triggered by the trauma from the past into a knee-jerk reaction.

Step 6: Giving Consent

Again this is essentially similar in both step 6 of Gendlin's process where it is called "Receiving" and in the WBF process of giving consent. When the felt shift comes it is such a relief, such a sense of physical enjoyment as well as psychological release. At some level it feels like a spiritual experience, and it is because at some level it has reconnected you with a sense of the whole. So it is natural to welcome what came and to be glad that your Body Wisdom spoke to you. There is a natural sense of gratitude and awe and a feeling of an intelligent life energy moving through the channel of your body and a wisdom guiding your life. However, old neural pathways are very persistent, there are inner critical voices that can block the new direction. This is only one small step on the way that has to be repeated many times and this is certainly not the last time that this situation will arise to test you. So there is a sense of "Actually I can't do this on my own. Life is too complex and too difficult to do alone. There seems to be an inner wisdom guiding my life, call it what you will – the unlimited potential of the human mind, or the wisdom of the Universe. I am thankful for that and I give my consent, I agree that this seems to be the best and the wisest way to go forwards, I will follow this new insight and I will return to this issue many more times, using awareness and this WBF process when needed, in order to build this new neural pathway".

So I am giving up my ego-dominated cognitive mind that wants to be in control all the time, I'm going to stop trying to figure it out with my head, because all that planning and manipulation never got me to where I wanted to be, so I am just gladly consenting to follow my inner guidance. So when I have put the ego on hold I can move beyond confining expectations that can block awareness of new possibilities. We just do not know what it is, but something within us has the wisdom to see the bigger picture and so we need to trust the process and to go with it.

Sometimes step 5: allowing change to happen will mean allowing the body to go into spontaneous movement and finding a new equilibrium through the releases that happen during these movements and stretches.
WBF & Spontaneous Movement:

Client WBF Session, with spontaneous movement.

C. I am feeling all of that sense of wanting to cry out..... But not being able to, and all of that tension in the face and the throat, back of the neck and in the chest....

T. And from your body tune in with what's happening and give permission to allow spontaneous movements to take place...

C. There are little hints of anger and some sort of rebellious energy now. The words are: "I'm not happy with the situation".

T. You are not happy with the situation, and your body is going into movement, little spiral motions with the upper body and arms swinging from side to side.

C. Yes, and my legs are shaking now....

T. Keep allowing the body to express through movement, do what feels right for your body, you don't have to understand any of this with your head.....

C. My legs have stopped shaking and my arms are making these more extreme swinging movements, forwards and backwards.....and now swinging from side to side.....and now crossing in front.
Now I've started stepping up with my knees, quite vigorously, coming up higher, as my arms are making a spiraling movement from side to side.....
Now that's clamed down and I'm swinging each alternate leg in a circular motion...

T. How does that make you feel?

C. Its easing something and I feel more loose-limbed....
But then another part is coming in and saying "Oh stop, this it feels a bit scary".....

T. So part of you feels that this is a bit scary.

C. Yes, its so different and I would like to sit down and stop all of these movements for a while.
(Client sits down).
I'll just stay with the feelings; I need a bit of time out.
(Pause)
It felt nice.
As my muscles lose some of their tension, everything feels looser and more at ease.....I'm searching for the words....
"Less controlled and less controlling", and that's also scarey.

T. "Less controlled and less controlling", and that's also scary

C. I feel like I've gone a bit too far, and now I can feel a tightness and an anxiety.....
T. I feel like you've gone a bit too far, and now you can feel a tightness and an anxiety.....

C. it feels like "a bit out of control....slightly lost .... and unfamiliar.
And now my left knee is hurting, there is an increase of tension in my chest, my facial muscles, the back of my neck...

T. That whole familiar pattern of tension is coming back again,

C. My heels are off the ground and my legs are shaking quite a lot....my feet are starting to jump and stamp.....I'm feeling quite dizzy now.

T. So just go back to your connection with gravity, your grounding and the support you are getting from that.
(Pause)

C. I'm starting to yawn, my mouth is opening wide, and then closing...its exercising, opening and releasing. I'm grimacing, trying to loosen the jaw,....
(continues)... Now I feel a bit more grounded, a bit more present.
My knee has stopped hurting, energy is working its way through....
I'm standing in a star shape now, arms outstretched, it feels safer to be in my body now. Its expansive, it feels like a stretch, it eases something.

T. You are standing in a star shape now, arms outstretched, it feels safer to be in your body now. Its expansive, it feels like a stretch, it eases something.

C. I'm taking up a bit more room, taking my space in the world.....It reminds me of an incident when my little boy got so angry that I went rigid with anger, and my parents took me to hospital, because they thought there was something wrong with me. The doctors couldn't find anything medically wrong of course.
There is part of me that has a real energy of anger and determination, the words are: "I'm not going to be beaten".

T. "I'm not going to be beaten".

These spontaneous movements from my client in this example helped him to get in contact with a lot of stuff that was underneath the wanting to cry out but not being able to. There were rigid patterns of habitual muscular tension and psychological inhibition that were preventing any release taking place, but when given the chance in a wholebody way to express itself, his body wisdom found a way to release some forward moving life energy. It is essential for his psychological health for him to be able to bring this sub-conscious material into consciousness and to integrate it.

Sometimes the somatic symptoms are so intense that a key part of the healing process involves getting the right distance to the somatic sensations and associated emotions so that they do not overwhelm the client.

Client "X": A case history of change.

Acceptance of yourself as you are is a key principle in the process of self-transformation, but it can be a very hard thing to do when becoming aware of the felt sense in the body also unleashes a whole torrent of associated emotions. When we are triggered in this way finding the right distance to the epicenter of the disturbance becomes vital. For example I had one client, Client "X", who had developed an acute self-consciousness about swallowing. He did not want to make any sound at all and got paranoid about swallowing or coughing during any group silence. This also caused him problems when speaking in public. The epicenter of tension was in his throat as the body needs to swallow occasionally and he tried to prevent himself from swallowing so as not to disturb anyone. Needless to say, this was a major life issue for him and bound up with his survival strategy in childhood – which was to be nice and non-assertive, not express his true feelings and hope that everybody liked him.

It was no good telling him that swallowing in public, in silence, is OK and does not disturb anyone else. It was hard for him to accept any of this; as just being aware of the need to swallow periodically and the tension building up in his throat as he struggled against it, would trigger him. We were working with Wholebody focusing in order to transform this whole reaction pattern, but bringing the throat area more into awareness was not helpful as this was the epicenter of an intense emotional and physical experience. We needed to get more information and get a sense of the story behind it, without being dragged into the trauma of it. Client "X" remembered that one of the worst parts of it was being put to sit next to the prettiest girl in the class for school assembly all through his teenage years. He was squirming with embarrassment and unsure how to handle his sexual energy, not sure how to be with her in the silence, and all of this was expressed as a strangulating tension in his neck and throat muscles. As he stayed with this part of his story he had more compassion and understanding for his teenage boy – but it was still too intense to get any sense of acceptance towards that part of himself. Wholebody focusing will not work; there can be no self-transformation as long as long as there is still as sense of fighting it, or fixing it, or running away from it. Client "X" was still terrified of that ball of tension in his throat, the feeling of being tapped there frozen, wanting to act but being unable to act, feeling ashamed. The emotions were all too intense, the energies turned inwards and frozen, the body paralysed in rigid tension. It all seemed hopeless.

Due to the phenomena of state-dependent recall Client "X" was being triggered merely by the physical sensations of tightness in his throat, so focusing even more on it, trying to get the bodily felt sense of it, was not helping. This is where experience and subtlety play a big role. I was able to help

Client "X" to get the right distance to the epicenter of his fear and tension in his throat. "Client "X"" I said "where are the fuzzy edges of this area of tension, how far throughout your body does it extend, where are the outer edges where it starts to feel manageable?" Client "X" stopped to consider for a while and then he pointed towards his upper chest, "probably here just behind my sternum, where my heart centre is". Then I knew it "that's where you need to work from Client "X", the fuzzy outer edges, see if you can hold both, linking this whole trauma, with all of your compassion, understanding and acceptance of the whole situation with your sense of grounded presence and the contact of your feet with the Earth. Stay with it for long enough to give your body time to readjust and to find a new way forwards".

That proved to be the key in this case, by finding the right distance to the bodily sense of trauma, Client "X" was able to find acceptance, to find a safe enough place to just stay with it, so that the power of awareness could awaken the wisdom of his living body.

As he worked with this there was a feeling of his whole body starting to come alive in a warm, comfortable way. It was like the experience of whole was supporting the painful intensity of the wounded part. In particular, Client "X" noticed that his pelvis was coming alive, there were pleasant sensations there, and rhythmic flows of energy that made him feel alive. The alignment of the pelvis changed, it seemed to straighten up and the inner space, the inner energy field opened up. In a very real way, it felt like the potency of the pelvis was now connected to a relaxation in the throat muscles. Something started to release in all of his body, a sense of vitality and connection throughout the body. Client "X" felt that it was OK to be alive, OK to be himself and within that sense of wholeness it was also OK to swallow when he was in the company of other people. The act of swallowing in a relaxed natural way could take place within a broadened field of awareness and over the next weeks and months his attitude changed. He stopped being so self-conscious; he began to be more creative and expressive. He did not allow the paranoia about swallowing to interfere with his flow of relating and releasing energy into the world through speech and action.

Client "X" wanted to contribute more to the world and he felt options opening up more both in terms of his work, his relationships and his social life. He loosened up at work and began talking and joking more and above all he started to allow himself to express the truth that his body knew inside his gut but now he noticed when he was cramping up inside and suppressing it, he stopped squeezing himself into a small space and he gave himself permission to speak his truth without worrying how other people would react to it.

The key to the WBF process of growth and change is when we can respectfully listen to all of these different parts and make space for them to be there just as they are. If two parts are in conflict dialogue and some sort of understanding and resolution can result from this. If one part is blocked, the blockage can be held "in equal positive regard", and a forward moving life energy can be released. But what seems to be important is firstly: the sense of being in grounded presence and supported by something much bigger, the sense of the whole. Secondly, allowing all of the different parts to be there without suppression or rejection. Thirdly, working at the edge of what feels important right now, where the energy is moving forwards, not some theoretical consideration of how things ought to be. Finally there is the consciousness of the container, the non-judgmental awareness that all of these different parts can fit into the larger container. The key thing is actually that the awareness can "hold" of these differing elements in the field and yet trust that the ego does not need to control, fix or direct things, because there is an intelligence and an organisational energy at work that is capable of creating meaning in a complex field. So Client "X" trusted the process, the flow of energy within a safe container. There was a new forward-moving life energy. He could not change every situation, or the outcome of it but he could change the way that he carried it, in a way that was life affirming and expressed his present truth, rather than allow himself to feel continually frustrated and angry about life.

Chapter 7.
Relationships and our Energetic Interconnectedness

"The whole is greater than the sum of the parts....and there is only the whole, which is contained in turn in each of its parts."

Wholebody focusing means that we are taking our bodies into our thinking process, as an essential part of the process. As Eugene Gendlin realized: the whole of our body is like a biological computer, registering our connection to our environment. We are not isolated human beings struggling to make our way forwards in a hostile world. In reality we are in relationship to other people and our environment the whole time and we are indissolubly linked in a process of energetic connection with the whole environment that is moving us forwards as individual human beings. There is a natural process for moving from potential to actualization, there are always possibilities waiting to be manifested in our lives. Life doesn't stand still; it is always in process and taking things in, responding in a changed direction. There is constant change that is taking place in the world a precisely ordered and yet surprisingly open way. The next step is always implicit in a fully awakened awareness and in the acceptance of what is happening right now, but that fully awakened consciousness can only take place in a field of awareness that includes all the sensory information from our bodies, as well as awareness of our thoughts and emotional reactions. This then needs to be linked to awareness of others in our personal relationships and in our communities. In that awakened awareness it suddenly becomes clear as to "what feels right" as your truth of a situation, is also right for others and if you have the courage to express that, then it will work out best for everyone involved. This will liberate a "forward moving life energy" that wants to carry the situation forwards and make the implicit an explicit manifestation. Your body can better sense that in a way that the cognitive mind cannot do so.

There is so much important information here in the body that it really would be appropriate to talk of an inner body wisdom. We can know things about other people on our first meeting with them, and the rest of our relationship with them is just a slow confirmation and revealing of what we already knew in that first contact. But of course, what we know is an unclear, bodily felt sense, and not a clearly articulated understanding. This is where Focusing can help. Then there is the whole well-documented field of body-language and the fact that no matter what you say or do, your body cannot lie and other people will only believe 25% of your verbal message and the other 75% of the information they are taking in is from your body language. So if your body language is not congruent with your verbal message people will not believe you. It's that simple and has been well documented in numerous psychological studies. The work of Eugene Gendlin and his Focusing technique is really just another way of saying that if your body cannot lie to another person then it cannot lie to you either, so if you know how to listen to it, so why not use that as a way of getting to the truth of the situation?

There are often times when a new potential relationship is just starting, or an older one is ending and things are starting to go off track, and the whole situation carries a lot of frustration and emotional charge that is confusing to the mind. What is going on? Well one thing is for sure: your mind is carrying a lot of "oughts and shoulds" about the way you should be behaving in that situation, and yet your body knows more about you and about the other person, about their intention, their integrity and about what they are really feeling. You can access all of this extra information at the inner level, by attunement and it works through mirror neurons being fired in a direct body-to-body knowing about another person. Neuroscience is now showing how the empathy circuits of the brain really do enable us to tune in with others and to feel what they are feeling. Take time out to visualize that person in your mind's eye and to just sense how your body responds to that inner image, take time to get a felt sense of what your intentions are, and then take time to get a felt sense of what the other persons intentions are (both from what they have said and from what you can sense about them inwardly). As you attend to your own intentions you create internal attunement. As you tune in with another person's intentions you are creating interpersonal attunement. There is a fundamental process of neural integration that takes place during this process that is so different from just seeing what you can get from another person in a relationship.

Cognitive thinking alone will engender conflict between my view of the situation, which I want to defend, and your view, which may well be different from mine. If I see things in very black & white and conflicted terms - my view of the situation will only engender further conflict because I believe that I have the correct solution and that you are wrong. However, when I work from a sense of my wholeness first, feeling connected to a solid sense of self, then I have a sense of my wholeness that is connecting with your wholeness so that we are both connected in "the bigger picture". When there is a sense of connection between us, then the space in-between us can come alive and in that aliveness there is a direct energetic knowing and intuitive wisdom. When I feel connected to my sense of self first of all I can be in grounded presence and express your truth directly as it is experienced in my body in the moment. I will know the right thing to say and the right thing to do. It just comes to me. There is an intuitive sense of connection that enables me to be open and receptive to the other person expressing their truth. This brings back respect and authenticity into the relationship.

In the same way, when I feel connected to you I can sense and include "your truth" of the situation in my bigger perspective as well, for it is a part of the larger field of my awareness and it can influence my thinking and help to alert me to any selfishness or rigidity in my position. Sometimes I may need to hold the sense of conflict with another person and the not knowing what to do in that situation whilst avoiding the temptation to see the world in terms of black and white separation – I am right and therefore you must be wrong. Then, at some stage in the future it may be possible to find a solution from a sense of connectedness where everybody's needs are being met. This is not an imposed solution from the cognitive mind, but is generally an answer that somehow emerges over time from a process of inner growth and a shifting of perspective.

As the inner energetic body begins to awaken through the power of awareness, I become more aware of myself and of my surrounding environment. I am not one solid massive whole, a continuous unchanging self that barges its way through life and merely negotiates with or bounces off other people like we are all solid billiard balls. No, the reality of my personality is that it is constantly evolving with age and experience and as a result of interactions with the environment and as a result of the relationships that I enter into. My sense of self is not fixed and if I am sensitive my body also feels more fluid than solid, more alive, more interpenetrating with my environment. It feels like there is fluid space within me and a recognition that the container of my whole being can contain all the different parts of me that are in a constant state of flux and change.

Any individual's personality is not fixed because everything is fluid and interactional, we are all in a constant process of change. Now, there are three essential elements to the Wholebody focusing process; firstly, there is the physical body, which contains the physical muscles, bones, organs, as well as thoughts and feelings. Then there is the sense of energy flow within that body and yet also extending beyond the boundaries of the skin to the third element, and encompassing all of that is the sense of the observing Self, which is pure consciousness.

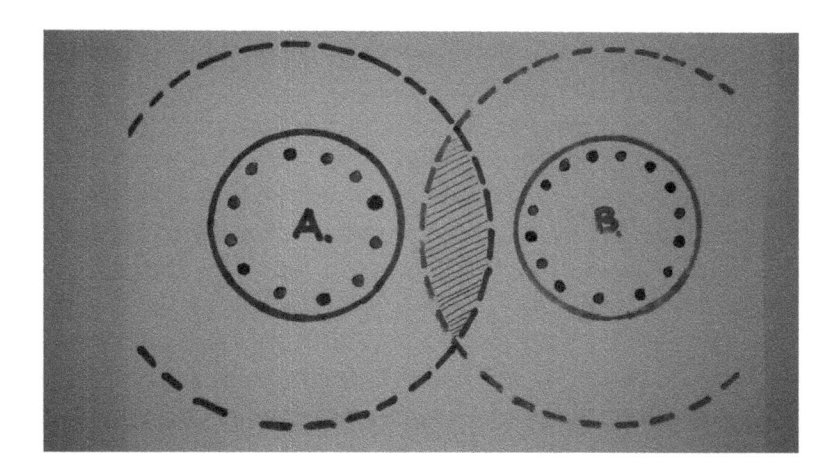

Fig. 7.1 Two person energy fields

Now the whole Focusing process is a way of seeing ourselves as essentially energy in process. We are fluid, relational, and in a constant process of becoming. We are not fixed at all but many different parts, sub-personalities that exist within the circle of the whole self (see Fig 7.1). Within the circle of "Person A" there are many different parts, which are the coloured dots within the circle. There could be a sad part, or a critical part, or an angry part, or a shy and ashamed part. One of these parts might be the dominant driver, another could be the manager that likes to be well organized, and another could be the firefighter that takes over in a real emergency situation. Two parts could be in conflict with each other, while another could be hidden and secretive, very repressed and out of awareness. There could be hundreds of these different parts, and each part is represented by a small coloured circle within the larger circle of self that represents person A and person B, e.g., red could be anger, green could be a critical voice. A first important step would be to become aware of and name these different parts within ourselves, e.g., "part of me feels "sad" right now and another part of me feels…."critical". Once we have named a part and put it out there, something is already in a process of change, because we have brought consciousness to bear on it, and as we know from Quantum mechanics – consciousness produces change. When the observing self has created a bit more space around that part and the right distance, that part has room to change rather than being fixed and constricted. Hence we could say that we are in right relationship to it. This appears paradoxical to the cognitive mind, that once a part is just allowed to be there and accepted for what it is, without any coercive attempts to force change, *it will change and transmute over time* because everything is in flux and nothing remains fixed on the material level. Just naming a part and holding it in non-judgmental awareness over time will lead to some sort of a shift. WBF is a carefully structured way of facilitating this natural process of change and transformation.

But there are certain rules, firstly, the observing self needs to be non-judgmental, a compassionate, witnessing self that is big enough to maintain the right distance to the whole issue. Then there needs to be total acceptance with no reactivity, no attempts to fight it, or fix it or run away from it – even though these are very natural, human reactions at the ego level of existence. This is not the time for the ego to get involved with all its planning and sense of effort, just let it be the way it is. This is not the sort of issue that the cognitive mind can solve easily, because the cognitive mind is based on memory, past experience, and the expectations and belief patterns that are based on that. In essence, if we stay at the ego level we are constantly recreating our past experiences and not creating any room for something new to enter into the picture. So this is the next rule, its "OK not to know" and be open to new possibilities, even though you don't know what they are at this point in time. As you just stay energetically connected in respect and love with the whole situation and all the different parts involved, there is space for these different parts within the self to unblock and to start relating to each other in a different way. This is when a sense of energetic movement, or "inner directed movement" can start to reveal itself within the body. It may seem strange and unfamiliar, but go with it because this is the body unwinding all the stress and trauma that it is holding. Allow the body to move, to stretch in unfamiliar but satisfying ways. There is an intelligence behind the energy that is guiding all of this, but it can only reveal itself as you surrender, soften and loosen up more. There may even be an intuitive sense of how this new energy expresses in a new posture, gesture or urge to express yourself in new and unfamiliar ways. Go with it, experiment, see what happens! As this process gets repeated more times a sense of trust emerges, like I often feel that I am connected to something bigger, that there is a inner wisdom that is guiding my life.

Now it is very important to connect with the body as container and the sense of the intelligent life energy within this container and extending beyond the boundaries of the physical body. The two dotted blue and red circles around person A and person B represent this symbolically. In my workshops I ask participants to experience this energy field by performing a very simple experiment to see if they can sense their life force or not.

1) Relax the shoulders and arms.
2) Cup your hands in front of you as you are holding a ball. Find the distance that feels right for you. Starting from far away slowly move the hands closer together until at a certain point you may feel that the air thickens up into a sponge-like feeling that slightly pushes the hands away from each other
3) Stay there for a while allowing the energy charge to build up until it feels like you have a warm, round ball of energy between your hands.
4) Play with it - what do you want to do with it?
5) Experiment with tensing and then releasing your shoulders, elbows or wrists; how does this affect the ball of energy between your hands?

From my experience of teaching this exercise in workshops nearly 70 per cent of students are able to sense this ball of energy between their hands. They were then able to relate to the grounding exercise and using the power of awareness to awaken the inner energetic body.

Now the observing Self, which I write with a capital 'S', is crucial. It is the Self, aware that it is aware, observing but totally without any reactions or judgments. Pure awareness cannot change over time because it has no content, so it gives the individual a sense of a core 'Self' that is ever unchanging because there are no judgments or opinions to hold onto. Pure awareness is just the awareness that you are aware, without any emotional reactions or subsequent thoughts about the object of your awareness. The quality of pure awareness is the same when you are a child or a youth or an older person. It can come when you are an adult meditating, or when you are a child playing under a tree, or when you are just out walking in a beautiful landscape. We have all had that experience of "Oh Wow, that landscape just takes my breath away" and I am just catapulted into pure awareness, filled with a sense of deep peace and bliss. So this pure, expanded awareness needs to be there to allow us to be in grounded presence and this allows the process that we call Wholebody focusing. If you look at diagram Fig 7.1 you will see the solid circle in the middle that represents the physical body, the dotted line around it that represents our energetic body and that entire dotted circle is the circle of our larger field of awareness that is in grounded presence. We are obviously aware of our bodies, we are aware of our energetic bodies and this connects us to a much larger field of awareness. How large that field of awareness is depends on our sensitivity or level of consciousness. To connect with this much larger field we need pure awareness, which is non-judgmental and inclusive, so we are just aware of "what is" in an open-minded, openhearted and compassionate way. Being in grounded presence and connected to the Earth opens us up to connect with something much bigger than our little selves. Then we start to become aware of the whole, alive, interconnected energy field in which we operate. We are energy, other people, plants, animals and objects are energy, and everything is vibration and energy.

So moving to the position of the neutral, observing Self is something that is crucial to the quality of consciousness. It is essentially a non-cognitive, pure awareness that is beyond the pull of polarities. It is innate, but may not be apparent in all people because it is something that needs to be cultivated first, and the awareness and control of the extended energetic body is an important skill that needs to be learnt, and this is why the AT is so important. The practice of mindfulness meditation helps to cultivate a sense of observing presence, whilst learning WBF helps to cultivate insight and wisdom. When you are in judgmental mode, when you are trying to figure things out so that you can fix them, or fight them or run away from them – you are in cognitive ego mode, because that is the function of the ego. The body-identified mind is always seeking to find solutions and to fix things, and this is the normal mode of functioning in our society. People are all trying to find the best answer and thus to be happy. Acceptance and the ability to observe without judgment is an ability of the observing self and the doorway to "grounded presence" – which is to be happy in the present moment. There is no preferred answer; you are no longer grasping at one polarity and rejecting the opposite pole. The paradox is that by giving up any preferred solutions there is space for a shift to take place and you allow the perfect answer to emerge.

So just as there is an energy field within each person's body, so there is also an energy field between two people in a relationship. This is the space in-between that can come alive, or be totally closed off. This became very obvious to me early on during my work as an AT teacher and later on as a WBF trainer. Each person's energetic body extends beyond their body and, so of course, it can interpenetrate with another person's energetic body. It is at the point of overlap (the shaded area in Fig. 7.1) that you can get interpenetration and an exchange of information on an energetic level. The body picks up so much energetic information, so there is a subtle sense of intuitive knowing about the other person. You can know things that you couldn't possibly know about the other, intuitive insights into character, health issues, a sense of what issues might be going on inside them or intuitive hunches about what could be the right way to approach them, whilst retaining your own integrity and clear boundaries.

As a very simple example, we all have had the experience of when people get too close into our energy field and it does not feel comfortable, so we will back off to get more distance. Or it may be the opposite thing, it feels very comfortable and then we want to get closer and desire more intimacy, but obviously you need to check with the other person first of all to see if that is OK or not. In general, psychologists have observed that certain cultures like the Japanese can tolerate being much closer to another people's energy field than, e.g., Europeans can. There is a fascinating speeded up video of a drinks party attended by Japanese and European businessmen. The Japanese want to come right-up close to the person they are talking to, but if this is a European businessman he feels uncomfortable and wants to back off. In the speeded up video version of the evening this results in a sort of a dance with the Japanese, clutching their drinks, appearing to chase their European colleagues across the floor and around the tables. No one is actually naming what is going on, because that would be considered impolite, but the body language is unmistakable. This is an example of a culturally learned difference.

To give participants an experiential sense of this in my workshops I use the approach exercise, where I line up half of the students against a wall with their eyes closed and the others approach from the opposite side of the room. When the person with their eyes closed senses that their partner has approached to what feels like the right or a comfortable distance in front of them they will raise their hands to signal them to stop. Then they will open their eyes to see where their partner is. Everyone got an energetic sense of the approach of their partner, that was due to this intuitive sixth sense of energetic awareness, but some people needed to stop the approach a long way off and others allowed the partner to come much closer in. What was interesting was how much reliable information could be picked up in this way and that the strength of the energetic signal being picked up is stronger from behind than it is from the front, when the eyes are closed.

As an AT teacher I soon discovered that I could sense the quality of a students energetic body that extended around them. Other body workers, especially craniosacral therapists have this ability as well. I could quickly tell where a student was blocked internally, what it felt like and the exact moment when the blockage released as I worked on them – and that was without having my hands anywhere near to the blockage. I could tell a client – you have just released your left calf muscle, and they would be amazed because my hands were working on their head or necks and nowhere near to their legs at all. How do you explain that? You cannot explain it by any sort of sensory input, because there was none. But if you are sensitive to our energetic inter-connection, it all becomes possible and understandable. There is so much information available, which is most accessible at the point of energetic overlapping (the shaded area in Fig 7.1).

I also carried over this energetic sensitivity into working as a Wholebody focusing trainer. When I go into grounded presence and expand my awareness, I am able to connect energetically with the person that I am working with. I can expand my awareness beyond the boundaries of my skin, beyond my physical body into a sphere where my energetic body interpenetrates with the energetic body of the person I am working with and an exchange of information and energy takes place. There is a sense of knowing more about the other person than is physically possible through my nervous system. I can get an accurate sense of their physical, mental and emotional states. *As I make more space for myself by going into grounded presence, paradoxically I make room for more of the other person.* Words or phrases come to me that seem to fit for them and if accepted, are then taken further in the process, as though they have opened doors to a whole new level of understanding.

With this combination of Alexander Technique and Focusing skills, I am able to track my client's psychophysical process. I can feel the blockages and the releases when they occur, and I know what it means in this client's life story. This level of empathic resonance and attunement creates a wonderfully fertile sense of being held and understood. It feels very safe for the client. There is an actual resonance of two energetic fields that come into attunement with each other and the end result there is a new pattern of forward moving life energy.

I had one male client who had been emotionally abused by his mother. His sexual energy had always been repressed and he was made to feel guilty about that. Even worse in a general way, his will power had been broken, in that he was not allowed to "do" anything, or "want" anything or "hold onto" any thoughts, desires or opinions of his own. His mother always made sure that he agreed with her point of view. His survival response that he developed to cope with life was *"I first have to get love and approval from another person before I can undertake any project or do anything".* If the other person disapproved and argued against an idea or a project, in some mysterious way he seemed to lose all his power and energy and be unable to proceed with the idea. In other words all of his power was projected onto the other person. If that reassurance wasn't there he had a sense of disempowerment and wanting to give up, like: he said, *"I feel like I'm floating in limbo, feeling disconnected from myself. Wheels are turning in my head but I have a feeling that I cannot focus on anything and achieve the results that I want. I don't have any energy, I never get anywhere in my life, and I never achieve the goals I set myself"*. So rather than having clear communication in relationships – "this is what I want and how are you with that?" - he reverted to manipulation instead, "let me work out how I can please you first and then you will love me and give me what I want". Of course that strategy didn't work, because his partner did not respect him as he was always giving in to her and never standing up for himself; so in the long run he felt resentful, like *"I'm being so nice and considerate, and always giving her what she wants and yet I never get what I want. This is unfair and it makes me feel angry and frustrated, (but better not say it because then she won't love me anymore and then I surely won't get what I want)"*. So this form of passive aggressive behaviour led to more overt anger from his partner and that just added another twist to the spiral. This lack of clarity in communication was rooted in developmental issues in childhood and lack of integration within the self and it caused tension between the partners and the ultimate breakup of the relationship.

Until he came to me for WBF sessions, where one of the key requirements is not to get into the blame game but to have the courage to stay fully present to the reality of your own experiences, however uncomfortable that might be. The need was to integrate the different parts within himself first of all, before engaging in outer relationships with others. Having the safety net of being in grounded presence and having a good listener enabled him to just notice what was going on and to allow a felt shift to occur. As he said later: *" I feel clear in my head, I have a clear intention. I feel grounded and full of energy. I don't care about anybody else's condemnation or approval. I'm living in the present moment and full of my own energy and enthusiasm. That energy wants to achieve something in life!"*

He felt more alive and had an abundance of energy within the container of his body, which was available to be used for work or play or sexuality. There was a spontaneous release of more energy and he had an image of himself being a surfer riding a wave, his job was to remain balanced on top of the wave and to realise that his decisions and reactions could take him sliding down one side or the other, or he could remain balanced on top of the wave in conscious awareness. It was all just his energy that could flow creatively into many different channels without any form of guilt tripping or emotional manipulation from the outside. It needed to be a conscious choice and it felt safe and good to be that way. Things started to shift within himself, and of course as he changed within, his new relationships became more successful and harmonious as well.

But, just as in intrapersonal work you need to keep the right distance to the inner wounded parts so that you can get the information needed, but do not get overwhelmed by the emotional content of it. So also in interpersonal work, you need to stay grounded in yourself with clear boundaries. This can only come from having done the hard and painstaking inner work within yourself to bring into consciousness, to understand, to love and to integrate all those different parts within the container of the body, which gives a clearly defined sense of self who you are. Being in grounded presence and doing this WBF work means that you now have effective boundaries. You know who you are and then you can also recognize what is not you, there may be toxic energy and emotions coming from another person. Then it is much easier to recognize this and to keep clear boundaries around this extra energetic information in your system. So you can stay in relationship with the other person and get the information needed, without being confused by all the emotional baggage, and conflicted patterns of information picked up from the other person. In psychotherapy the phenomena of the "counter-transference" has long been recognised, when the therapist starts to empathically pick up on the emotional state of their client, they can then start to get confused about what is their emotional stuff and what is coming from their clients and erratic behavior can result. This is why therapists need to be in supervision. Especially when your client has similar emotional issues then it's easy to get triggered and difficult to differentiate between what is your stuff and what is your client's stuff.

By the same token neuroscience has now caught up with this and provided an explanation through the phenomena of "mirror neurons". The research has shown that when we empathise the brain activates many of the same networks as when we ourselves experience pain, physical or emotional. E.g., when a mother, or father, sees their child fall over and injure an arm, they will immediately rush over to see how bad the injury is, and often as a result of deep love and concern they will start to experience real pain in their own arm, in that exact same place! The mirror neurons have activated that same brain circuitry in their own body. This is really an extraordinary capacity in the human brain, which some scientists hypothesise can only be explained as a way of developing empathy and bonding which is necessary for human development in families and communities. When I can feel your pain it can help me to see the bigger picture and to make a better decision about what to do in this situation, to find a more inclusive solution where everybody's needs are being met, rather than just shifting into the blame game.

So one of the key points that emerges from this understanding of energetic connection in relationships is that you cannot effectively interact at a higher level of energetic connection and integration if you are not integrated at the lower level first. Unless I am in a good relationship with myself, feeling clear, congruent and aligned how can I enter into a clear relationship with another person? If there are parts of myself that are denied or repressed, out of awareness and not fully present and integrated within the circle of self, how can I clearly see myself? If I am not clear within myself, then how can I see who you are and listen to your needs? How can I seek to enter into a loving respectful relationship with you if I am not an integrated and self-compassionate person within myself? It's just not going to work.

This sense of connection at the energetic level and the understanding that comes from it, leads to a totally new model of relationships and communication.

> I can try to be more transparent and seek to be as honest as possible with the other person about my motivation and how I see myself.
>
> When the other person is speaking and explaining their position, I can try to be as non-reactive as possible and just give them space to be themselves and express their side, without needing to say anything immediately to counter that statement.
>
> There can be a sense of letting it all flow right

through me, if there is no ego to resist I am just the observer of the other person expressing their point of view, this is what they are feeling, this is what they believe. So I can make statements like "I hear that you think/feel/believe that…" which do not say whether I agree or disagree. They can simply name what is happening, make it explicit, and I can let the other person know that I have heard and given space to their current position. If I am working with the energetic connection that exists between us, it also gives me the opportunity to resonate and to really experience in my body what the other person is feeling right now.

At the same time I need to be in grounded presence and to be integrated so that I have effective boundaries. This enables me to know what I am thinking and feeling, it enables me to sense into the situation whilst at the same time I have a sense my whole body container, everything that is contained within it and feel aligned with the truth my position right now. Because I am grounded and feel strong and supported, it also gives me the courage to express my truth, when it is my turn to speak.

But I am not wanting to be right, I am not letting my ego get all caught up in the situation so that "I want to be right", "I want to win the argument", "I want revenge", "I, I, I…" the whole time. There is not neutral observer, there is no self-awareness, and there is no perspective when the ego is on the rampage.

There is also a sense of holding the space and "not

knowing what the outcomes going to be, and its OK not to know". By the same token as I am not all out to win the argument, I also do not wish to just capitulate and let the other person "be right" merely for the sake of restoring some sort of harmony. This could also be powerful tendency in some people. It's OK to hold a position of "this isn't resolved yet, but things have been named and there is a process going on here".

If both sides are prepared to stay in open communication, staying energetically connected and holding both standpoints in awareness, then a shift can happen. There is some sort of softening that takes place, a sense of release and a movement towards the other person. There is some new insight, often an insight into our own behaviour patterns and how we can take responsibility for them, which brings a real sense of relief and a sense of internal relief. Often a compromise solution suggests it self which meets the needs of both parties. But that compromise can only come at the end after the whole genuine process has taken place and both sides are ready for it.

These are the basic rules for allowing an open and flowing energetic connection between 2 people in a personal relationship. As we have seen, the same rules also apply to establishing dialogue and integration between the different sub-personalities in an intrapersonal relationship. Now, as the next diagram shows (Fig 7.2) there is a hierarchy of interconnecting groups in different systems of relationships. You obviously belong to a family group, and you may then also belong to a spiritual/religious community, a professional association, or a political party. Some of these groups may overlap and interconnect in some way. In addition you belong to a country with national interests, and then to a planet with environmental concerns, and also a particular solar system and galaxy. In an infinite universe the ripples of connection go on and on, but the same basic principles of energetic interconnection still apply.

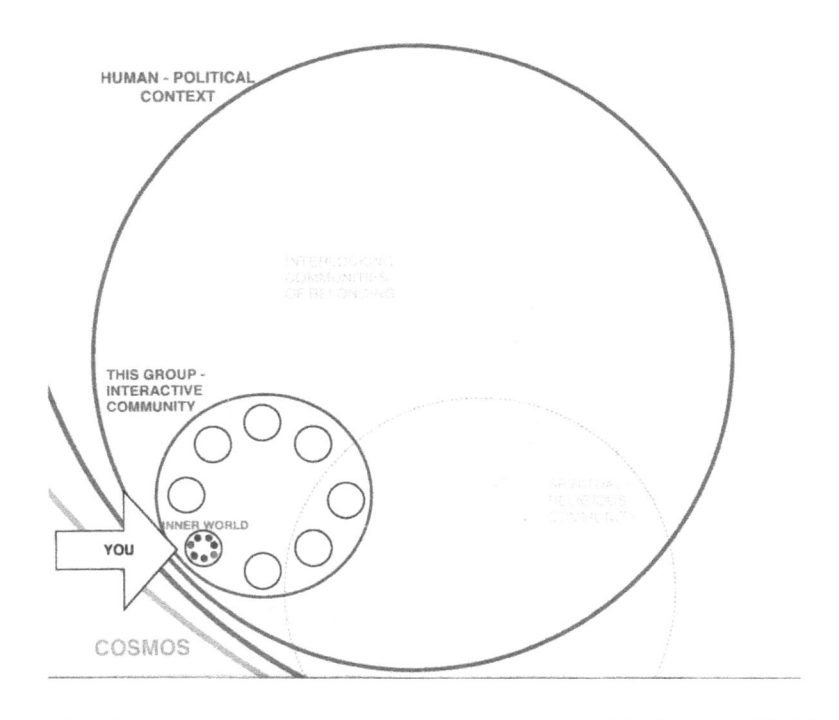

Fig 7.2, Living in an Interconnected Universe (With thanks to Sandy Gee).

Looking at the model that I have drawn, it becomes clear that there has to be good integration in each individual first of all, before personal and family relationships can function effectively, and before social and political groups can work. It is all down to the individual making the effort to integrate themselves, with techniques like WBF or other methods of self-enquiry first, before there can be world peace and harmony. If there are disowned and repressed parts of the self, there are going to be confusing messages being given at the overlap, in all the areas of energetic interpenetration.

David Bohm proposed a model for a group participatory dialogue, which allows for conscious communication within a community at a higher level of conscious relationship. Wholebody Focusing provides the tools for how to do this with an awareness of our group energetic interconnection as well. Here is model of how we can share a wholebody heartfelt conversation in a group setting (with thanks to my colleagues Kevin McEvenue & Karen Whalen).

> Identify a group facilitator who can lead the Attunement process and guide the group into Grounded Presence. He/she will allow adequate time for each participant to speak and also time to allow each offering to resonate inside, in a Wholebody listening way.
>
> Establishing Wholebody grounded presence: connecting to wholeness of self, with all the different parts of me being acknowledged and integrated. (10 mins in silence).
>
> Inviting in a felt sense of the whole living group body. Taking space and time to connect energetically with the living, breathing organism of all the members in the group (10 mins).

Taking turns sharing how it is for me to live and participate inside of this living group body.

Introducing the topic of shared interest or conversation (which arises spontaneously) and then tuning into the shared space of the "larger self" which rises up inside of this greatly expanded group energetic connection (wait here in silence for 8-10 mins).

Spontaneous sharing by group participants of what comes for them to share from this expanded experience of self inside of the living organism of the group energetic connection.
Each takes time to resonate with one another in a wholebody way and speaking when the spirit moves them to respond to previous Speaker.

At the end of group conversation there can be a sharing by participants reflecting on the process itself. The facilitator assures time keeping and turn taking throughout

One of the key abilities is to know what it means and to be able to stay in grounded presence for long periods of time. Staying in grounded presence comes from being able to practice the principles of WBF as you notice that some things within the body container are not quite right and need attention. As a result, that can be transformed and there is then an internal clarity that helps you to be able to engage with outer relationships. With this clarity you can then stand your ground and hold clear personal boundaries when needed in interpersonal relationships and also speak your truth in a group setting. This gives more space and time, a newfound ability to sense within and to speak from that place with real empathy and respect for other people at the same time. It is about speaking from your own truth first, your own felt sense of the situation, rather than trying to involve or second-guess what other people think or need. It is about being honest in "naming" things that can sometimes appear to be difficult, but having the courage to name it whilst trusting that the other people in the group have the capacity to hear it with compassion and understanding. That then contributes to the overall energy field of the group and in that freed-up space forward moving life energy can emerge that seems to have a direction and a purpose of its own. It is about the capacity to hold the balance between your truth and what you can contribute and then listening to other people with a compassionate awareness of their situation, so that there is space for the bigger picture to emerge.

What develops is a sort of non-judgmental, overall awareness of the whole group energy, holding everyone in awareness without letting one person be dominant all the time or letting others be silent. Then, at this edge of holding both self and others in awareness in the group field, without any agenda or preferred outcome, there develops a genuine compassionate appreciation of an alive group energy and consciousness, which allows new solutions to emerge from the plane of infinite possibilities. These new creative possibilities always existed, but it is just that the group as a whole was too tense of fearful to be able to see the new creative solution. Yet with the clear, open perspective of grounded presence, being connected energetically within the group and being able to see the bigger picture, some new insight or possibility can emerge that is creative, different and yet absolutely perfect. That is often the end result at the end of a WBF heartfelt group conversation.

Chapter 8.
Quantum Physics and Living in an Interconnected Universe

The findings of quantum mechanics can help to explain how we are all energetically interconnected through an underlying matrix of consciousness that some physicists like David Bohm have called the implicit order. The theories of Quantum physics all started with the original frustration encountered by researchers when they wanted to research more deeply into the properties of light. This research exposed a basic paradox, which is that a photon of light can behave both like a wave and a particle. It can have flow and rhythm just like an electro-magnetic wave form, which explains how an obstacle casts a shadow, but it can also be a particle which caries an energy charge and explains how a particle can hit a mirror and bounce off it again. This also explains why it takes a lot more energy to create blue or ultraviolet light than it does to create orange or red light. Our logical minds find this a contradiction because we want certainty and find paradoxes difficult, how can light be *both* a wave and a particle at the same time? It doesn't make sense to be both; surely one theory or the other has got to be right? But that's not the way it appears to work, so scientists got used to using one theory in one scenario and the second option in another scenario, if it worked better and gave us a workable explanation of the mechanism. So there is a contradiction here that needs to be lived with, *and this is one of the defining principles of the new consciousness in the quantum age: that we are now capable of shifting into a non-dualistic consciousness, where it is possible to tolerate paradox and ambiguity and to hold an awareness of the space in-between.*

The confusion of these early findings extended into the realm of sub-atomic particles, where it turns out that an electron can be both a wave and a particle at the same time, *and you never know where it is until you measure it.* This is just incredible stuff, because it is bringing in the role of consciousness as a pivotal factor in the whole process of how reality is created and how objects come into existence. The implications are just amazing. It begs the question posed by the old Zen question, "if there was no one there in the forest to hear it, did the tree fall?" Or as Einstein famously once said (and he didn't like quantum mechanics at all) "does that mean that if I am not looking at the moon it does not exist?" The implications are very powerful, for in some strange way it appears as though an electron can be everywhere at once with several potential wave pathways and only by looking at it and becoming conscious of it that we conjure it into existence at one specific point. Its like there is a curtain that divides our normal perceived reality from the very surreal quantum world that exists behind it and the function of the observer with human consciousness is crucial to all of this. So one of the implications of this is that we need to learn how to live with ambiguity and uncertainty, in WBF terms how to "hold both at the same time" without suffering from anxiety that we do not have a clear and definite answer, and trust the process to let the answers emerge from the connecting energy of the space in-between.

There appears to be a clear connection between the observer and the observed that affects the results of the measurements. E.g., take the energetic fluctuations of an electron spinning around the nucleus of an atom. Certain pairs of physical properties of this particle, "complimentary variables" such as it position or momentum, cannot be known simultaneously, because position refers to its place as a particle and momentum refers to its energy as a wave form, and it cannot be both at the same time. The spinning of electrons radiates energy in a discontinuous jump-like process, called a quanta of energy, and this radiation of energy is the electron's waveform function. The behaviour of this quantum waveform is discontinuous and unpredictable, showing up and manifesting in unexpected ways along many possible pathways. There is an uncertainty principle here, as formulated by Werner Heisenberg – "The more precisely its position is determined, the less precisely its momentum can be known, and vice versa." This can be expressed in a mathematical formula of statistical probability. The uncertainty in measurable quantities is due to the jolt like disturbance generated by the act of observation, so there is clearly a connection here between the human observer and the object being observed, which is not supposed to happen in classical physics, but has been verified many times in repeat experiments. So the implication clearly is that we are all energetically connected in some unified field of consciousness and the act of observation affects the outcome of the experiment.

So maybe there is also an implied relationship between consciousness, position and momentum. I can be conscious right now of the position of my whole body in this room. There is a relationship to the gravity of the Earth that increases as I slow down my thoughts. The more I slow down my individual chatter of thoughts and enter into the space of "no-mind" the more grounded I become, so that I am aware of the space inside my body container, the aliveness of my body and feeling connected to something bigger than myself by being grounded. I cannot be both the speed of my chattering mind, or the moving body, as it tries to deal with life and also have this sense of the calm observer that feels connected to other objects, people in relationships, in community and also in the bigger spiritual connection. It just doesn't work that way. The more I can calmly be in grounded presence, aware of life moving through me and around me, the more my consciousness can expand to open up to new possibilities emerging from the matrix of the present moment.

There are other fascinating findings from quantum mechanics that are helping to define the emerging consciousness of this new age. These are the amazing principles of entanglement, non-locality, and superposition that seem to form the basis for a matrix of connecting consciousness that seems to form the underlying web of life.

Let's look at these in detail. Entanglement is a very strange finding of quantum physics. When pairs of particles have been generated at the same time, or have once interacted with each other, they continue to be influenced by each other regardless of time and space. Measurement of physical properties such as position, momentum, spin and polarisation <u>are found to be linked.</u> E.g., if one particle is found to have a clockwise spin on a particular axis, the second particle will be found to have a counter-clockwise spin, this despite the fact that it is impossible to predict, according to quantum mechanics, which set of measurements will be observed. *There is thus an instantaneous knowing that takes place*, even though the second particle may now be far away. It thus appears that one particle of an entangled pair "knows" what measurement has been performed on the other one, and with what outcome, even though there is no known means for such information to be communicated between the particles, which at the time of measurement may be separated by large distances. "Non-locality" is the term used to describe how two previously connected particles can be separated across vast distances and yet continue to resonate with each other as though they were still touching, in close connection, despite there being no energy exchange between them. This knowing happens instantaneously, faster than the speed of light, which led Einstein to ridicule the whole phenomena as "spooky action at a distance". But it really happens, Einstein has been proved wrong and Neils Bohr and his Quantum mechanics has been proved right. Even though we do not know how this information is conveyed, it clearly happens. So there must be some sort of web of conscious connection that underlies the entire physical universe. Quantum mechanics can help to scientifically validate and explain some of the principles of the new world consciousness that is now emerging. So when the principles of non-duality consciousness are observed – which involves holding two points at the same time with awareness of the space in-between, being in the non-judgmental observer role, being accepting, compassionate and non-doing, without a set agenda, working to improve yourself in the awareness that there can be a transference through resonance that will influence the other person, allowing the space in-between to come alive and curious to see what happens. These are all the basic principles of WBF when we are working with a sense of energetic connectedness with the different parts of a system.

Now the crucial underlying factor in all of this is the role of human consciousness in affecting sub-atomic particles, which must also then affect molecules, cells, human beings and whole communities. E.g., there have been numerous experiments that show that prayer works, patients in the group that are being prayed for recover faster than patients in the control group who are not being prayed for. This seems to prove an energetic connection through consciousness that works across time and distance. The healing may take some time but the connection is instantaneous. The same thing is happening during a WBF session, which can take place over in person, over the phone or on Skype via the Internet. There is always a sense of a real connection between the trainer and the client, indeed as I have described elsewhere there is a very real knowing, based on felt sensing of what is going on inside the client, of what the blockage feels like and what the shift feels like when it comes. This is an energetic connection that takes place instantaneously over a distance and it works remarkably well.

Now what is crucial in WBF is the quality of consciousness, the quality of awareness or attention that we are paying to the process that is going on all by itself, if we will let it. Being the wholebody observer in grounded presence is conditional upon having a neutral, open and curious observing attitude. We wait and observe with an attitude of not-yet-knowing what could happen, and then we allow things to happen all by themselves, which is non-doing. There can be a sense of energy release leading to physical movements, or a sudden "aha" experience that comes from a sense of physical release together with some new mental insight. But implied in all of this is some sort of "two pointing" consciousness (holding both at the same time) which can be firstly the observing consciousness and then secondly the vulnerability, conflict, problem or whatever is calling for attention now And then by the laws of quantum mechanics, by staying with it in awareness, the observer will affect the vulnerable part that is being observed and allow a change to take place. Even at the very start of the process, when trying to get a felt sense of the issue - just by being able to name it, there is a sense of relief and some sort of shift takes place. There will be a larger one further down the line, but just in the observing and naming something significant takes place.

Implicit in all this is the ability to hold conflict or ambiguity without needing to find an immediate solution. As we know, in quantum physics a proton can be either a particle or a wave. Of course, the purely cognitive mind doesn't like this, as it wants certainty. The ego is geared to finding a solution that will fix the problem, so that you can get on with life as normal. What quantum physics is pointing towards is that there is also a higher level of consciousness, a wisdom that can embrace dualities, that can wait for the answer to emerge and know that this answer, when it emerges will be unusual, unexpected and totally perfect, in that all needs will be met. This corresponds to the findings of quantum mechanics that a particle can also exist as a waveform; many wave forms actually, until by the act of observation it is brought into existence as a particle and then the waveform collapses. So there are really an infinite number of possibilities in life, until some definite choice is made and then by that choice, with all of its consequences, potential is made manifest and becomes an actual event. So the "holding both" means *not* going into conditioned reaction patterns and *not* rushing to get just any solution that feels safe, but waiting and trusting to the wisdom of the universe to allow the perfect answer to emerge from all the infinite number of possibilities that are actually still open while a choice has not yet been made.

What the Quantum physics model of energetic interconnection helps explain is the sense of connection to others when I am in grounded presence. That sense of the bigger connection is linking me to what is going on all around me, at a personal, social, planetary, and universal level as well. There is a sense of a universal intelligence that can act through me, as I have a particular part to play, an important contribution to make in the evolving scheme of things. After I had evolved my understanding of how to work with this in

WBF sessions and workshops, I read some work by the Nobel prize-winning physicist and philosopher, David Bohm. From his understanding of Quantum physics he developed certain principles of human awareness that open up the energetic field and enable individuals to connect with themselves and with the group in an energetic process. I realised why his principles for group process work well, because they are an extension of the same principles that work well when two people are energetically connected and when a person is trying to integrate different parts of their self in intra-personal work. David Bohm came to the same fundamental insight that Gendlin had in focusing, that each individual person and their ego is not a separate block that functions by negotiating or fighting with other separate blocks, but that actually each self is composed of many different parts, many sub-personalities which are sometimes in conflict and sometimes in harmony, but always evolving in a constant process of interaction and change.

The same key that applies to a harmonious personality also applies to group interactions. Real growth and change occurs when we can respectfully listen to all of the different people in a group and make space for them to be there just as they are. If two people are in conflict dialogue and some sort of understanding and resolution can result from this. If one person feels blocked, that person can still be held "in equal positive regard" by the rest of the group and a forward moving life energy can be released. But what seems to be important is firstly: the sense of being in grounded presence and supported by something much bigger. Secondly, allowing all of the different people to be there without suppression or rejection. Thirdly, working at the edge of what is important right now, where is the energy going, not some theoretical consideration of how things ought to be. Finally there is the consciousness of the larger group purpose, the non-judgmental awareness that all of these different people can fit into the container of the larger group. The key thing is actually the awareness that can "hold" of these differing elements in the field and yet trust that my ego does not need to control, fix or direct things, because there is an intelligence and an organisational energy at work that is capable of creating meaning in a complex group field. So we are trusting the process, the flow of energy within a safe container. We may not be able to change the situation, the interaction, or the result but we can change the way that we carry it, in a way that is potentially life affirming rather than frustrated and life destroying.

The key point seems to be that you need to have the courage to be yourself in group interactions, to be yourself and express yourself as fully as possible within the group, but at the same time have respect for the other people and their right to be there as well. Then the rule works out that when you do and say what is right for you, it works out best for everyone else in the group, even if it isn't very comfortable at the time. It is easier to see the workings of this law with hindsight rather than in the midst of the group process, or intense personal relationships, when it can take real courage to express yourself. But know that you are needed, just as you are. The group would not function as well without you and the results of the interaction would not be as good. You need to be fully energised and present to function well, without fear and without inhibition, not forcing any particular result but making sure that your voice is heard. Then rest in the trust that there is a bigger, overarching intelligence that is guiding the whole process.

But there is a pre-condition to all of this; each individual must first be in harmony with the lower level before they can interact successfully with the next level up. So, e.g. you must have clear insight, self-understanding, harmony and integration within your own self before you can interact harmoniously within personal relationships, family systems or groups. The fact that there are so many divorces and dysfunctional families is an indication that this is not the case. How can it be when this wisdom is not handed down from our elders, or taught in schools or churches?

The same rules seem to apply right up to the progressively higher levels of connection and integration within communities, nations, our planet Earth & our whole solar system with all the 10 planets, galaxies and the spiritual centre of the whole universe, whose energy and consciousness seems to pervade everywhere. Do not think that you are ineffective! Do not hold back through fear, passivity or the erroneous belief that one person cannot possibly make any difference. You can make a big difference, but it just depends on the level of consciousness from which you are acting and also on the degree of integration and wisdom that you have achieved in your life.

The fascinating thing is how the renowned physicist David Bohm, who had a deep understanding of the implications of Quantum Physics, formulated a set of rules for creative participation in group process, which he called participatory dialogue. There are some guidelines summarised below from his books, which show an amazing similarity to the WBF process. So here is how David Bohm would formulate it:

> Know you are needed just as you are!
> Be open, curious, receptively attentive. Welcome whatever comes.
>
> Trust that a wiser, holistic intelligence can emerge.

Suspend - already known, opinions, judgments and any secret agendas, or preferred outcomes.

If judgments persist – just acknowledge them openly to yourself, or to the group.

Keep freshly sensing into the energy of the moment. Take Risks! Be willing to feel uncomfortable / vulnerable. If you are usually confident and speak easily: risk speaking less and listening more. If you are usually quiet: risk speaking out and saying what's there for you.

Include yourself. If you are feeling stuck, bored or frustrated: Ask inside - How might I be contributing to this stuckness? - Might there be something I'm withholding? And then voice it. *(It's likely to be just what is needed or missing in the group).*

Have respect for the others in the group. Allow each person to be just the way that they are. Just as you would like to be respected and allowed to be just the way that you are at this moment in time.

Keep freshly sensing what's most alive here?' or where is the energy taking the group?

This is very interesting, that these rules of participatory dialogue, coming from a completely different direction and grounded in an understanding of quantum mechanics, seem to have a very precise parallel to the WBF process. I have talked earlier in the book and especially in Chapter 6 "A Manual of Wholebody focusing" about the 6 steps of WBF and that the key to an integrated and harmonious personality is when we can respectfully listen to all of these different sub-personalities and make room for them to be there just as they are. If two parts are in conflict dialogue and some sort of understanding and resolution can result from this. If one part is blocked, the blockage can be held "in equal positive regard", and a forward moving life energy can be released. But what seems to be important is firstly: the sense of being in grounded presence and supported by something much bigger. Secondly, allowing all of the different parts to be there without suppression or rejection. Thirdly, where is the edge of feeling the energy rising up from my strong legs and my feet, like "I can stand up for myself, I can speak my truth now" and feeling that energy connecting to the wounded part that might be vulnerable and withdrawn, unable to fully be present. This is the edge where real growth and change take place, not some theoretical consideration of how things ought to be. So, whilst in intra-personal work there is the consciousness of the container of the body, the non-judgmental awareness that all of these different parts can fit into the larger container of the body, which is the whole self. The same WBF principles apply to *inter-personal work*, where the group or the community becomes the container and I need to put my antennae out in order to sense our energetic connections.

> I become the part that then needs to be fully present and accepted, just as I am.
> I need to be curious and accepting of whatever arises within myself and be able to name my truth and communicate that to the group.
> I need to be able to accept any judgments, secret agendas, preferred outcomes and critical voices.
> By the same token I need to trust that the other members of the group are capable of doing that, or at least noticing it and naming it if they are not.

> I need to keep grounding, renewing my energy and sensing into where the energy of the moment is taking the group.
>
> Notice what is going on within me in response to this group process, whatever it is: shyness, or boredom or wanting to take over the group, just be present to that and have the courage and honesty to name it, because it is also part of what is going on, named or un-named.
>
> Being open about it is a contribution to the group that allows that energy to move forwards.
>
> It's very important to keep the respect and the non-judgmental attitude towards others in the group fresh and alive.
>
> Also keep sensing into where the energy of the group process is moving or where it feels stuck.

The key thing is actually that your awareness can "hold" of these differing elements in the field and yet trust that the ego does not need to control, fix or direct things, because there is an intelligence and an organisational energy at work in the group that is capable of creating meaning in a complex field. So you can trust the process, the flow of energy within the safe container of the group. You may not be able to change certain other people or your interaction with them, but you can change the way that you carry it, in a way that is potentially life-affirming and growthful, rather than frustrated and life destroying. The key point seems to be that you need to have the courage to be yourself in group interactions, be yourself and express yourself as fully as possible within the group, but at the same time have respect for the other people and their right to be there and to be themselves.

When you do and say what is right for you, it works out best for everyone else in the group and a truly alive group intelligence can emerge, which has a mystery to it and at a certain stage there is a period of "not knowing", of giving up control, of getting yourself out of the way so that the ego can no longer interfere with the process. It is OK not to know at this stage, a necessary part of the process because there is a trusting of our inner wisdom so that the answer when it emerges, is totally new and unexpected but totally alive. It is a moving forward into new territory, which allows recognition of new possibilities that always existed within yourself but you were just too locked into old patterns of managing the situation to be able to recognise them. This is the startling insight of the new Quantum mechanics, which describes the world as being in a state of an infinite number of emerging possibilities at every level of existence. But, there has to be an observing human consciousness present to call into existence any one of these infinite number of new possibilities. What was a waveform of energy and potential can now manifest as a particle with an observable mass, but it can never be both at the same time. With the sustained power of human awareness what was only a hidden possibility can now actually pop into manifestation, and, more to the point, the power of awareness in the moment and our openness to our energetic connections calls forth the perfect answer from the greater wisdom of the whole, in response to what the individual needs at this precise moment in time. This is a key feature of Quantum mechanics and is so much part of the WBF process.

Chapter 9.
WBF & Neural Pathways to Prosperity

One of the most practical applications of WBF lies in understanding the neural pathways to prosperity. When your brain is functioning in an optimal way, you can be better motivated, have a clearer perspective and thus make better decisions in whatever profession or line of business you are operating in.

WBF gives you a key to be able to move towards feeling more positive about life. Find the happiness that is inside you first of all, regardless of the outer situation. Then you will be able to operate the law of spiritual success and magnetism, as "like attracts like". When you feel good and successful inside yourself you will then have such a positive personal magnetism and charisma that you will be able to influence all the people you meet and attract whatever you need in life. It will be attracted towards you, as a result of that optimism and positive energy that you are vibrating. You will meet the right people, somehow get the right connections, and undertake projects that you can then push forwards to a positive outcome. The things that happen to you in life are not accidental; there is a proven correlation between optimism and positive outcome. It is all the result of your positive or negative outlook, which you can change. If you need it, but at the same time you know that "I'm fine without it", then you can work towards achieving it in a balanced way and it will come to you, all the while maintaining a positive energy and a sense of lightness in your body and mind that is fundamental to all this whole process.

This is aided by the curious motto: "Don't try harder". This goes against everything that we are taught in our culture and our education system, which teaches that success takes effort, 95% perspiration and 5% inspiration, and if you just try hard enough you can make things happen. The corollary is that if you didn't succeed its because you didn't try hard enough. Whilst this may have an element of truth in certain types of physical activity like digging the garden, building a house or running a race, it certainly isn't true in meditation or creativity. Why? Because the brain needs to go into more alpha wave activity, and as has been pointed out in earlier chapters, *this can only happen when you are not trying*, when you have in essence given up all concerns about the outcome and are no longer working in a tense and anxious way. When the brain shifts into higher alpha wave activity there is a sense of trust, a feeling of ease and flow, there is a sense of the artist at work and when you are in the flow things happen easily and there is a creative flow to the situation.

When you learn how to do this and really get the feel of it and can remain in that state of flow, then you are able to fill yourself with love and a prosperity consciousness and send it back out into the world again. Then it is possible to engage with life, to move forwards into a positive life by firstly feeling good about yourself and then by undertaking positive actions. But it is important to first have a clear vision of where you want to go and what you want to achieve in life. Not just that, but if you can visualize it clearly enough in your mind, your body will start to feel what its like if that was happening right now. Neurons in your brain will start firing, hormones and neuropeptides will be released that activate different parts of your brain and travel throughout your body, and you actually get the feel of what that positive, confident state of being is like. Now the vision feels good, it has activated the nucleus accumbens in the reward circuit which keeps your dopamine levels high, so that you are feeling positive, feeling motivated, feeling good about yourself already, right now.

Now the trick in life is how to stay connected with this "feel good" factor of the original vision as you get into all of the little steps that need doing. A journey of a thousand miles starts with one step, and then the next and then all the little steps that are needed in the planning and decision making, in the writing and creative work that needs doing. This is the crucial skill in learning how to stay positive and maintain motivation as you get on with all the hard work that needs to be done. So there needs to be a sense of reward generated by connecting with a circuit that links the prefrontal cortex with the nucleus accumbens in the ventral striatum – which forms the rewards circuit of the brain. Dopamine is actually an endogenous opiate and high dopamine levels are linked to positive emotion, motivation and desire, it is also linked to feeling bliss and happiness, feeling good about yourself right now.

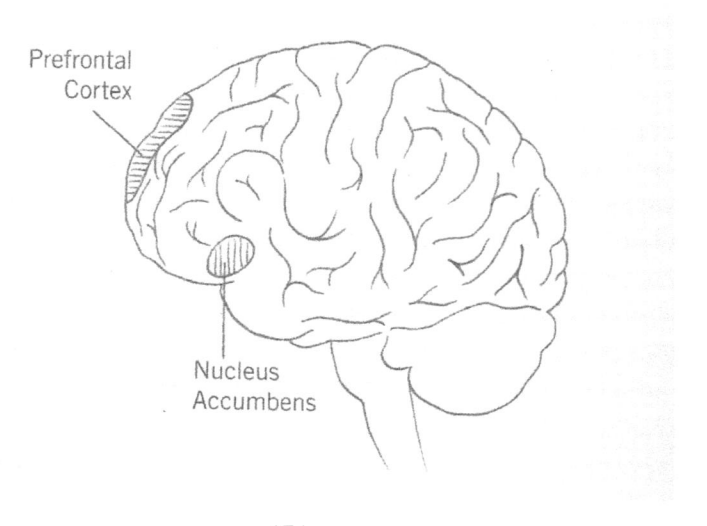

So there is that bit, which is staying connected with your long-term goal, staying positive and working with a sense of ease and flow. Then at the same time its breaking up the big vision into small attainable goals for each day, break it up into little bits, so that there is the satisfaction of having achieved your goal for the day. There is a great satisfaction in knowing that you have been able to complete that little bit today, and tomorrow is another day. It is really important to be able to keep connecting with the feelings of satisfaction that keep the dopamine levels high.

One of the major issues to be resolved is your relationship to money and whether you have a subconscious expectation of deserving prosperity or poverty, based on your character, life history and attitudes inherited from your family situation. If there is a fear and expectation of loss that will affect the outcome in one way, and if there is the opposite, sub-conscious expectation of prosperity and deserving abundance, that will lead to another outcome. There is a delicate balance line where you can be positioned between the fear and the greed and free of the pull of either emotion. WBF can help to clear blockages to action in your drive to achieve prosperity.

Martin was a struggling day trader in the commodities markets when he first came to see me. He wanted to make money, he needed to make money, he worked hard but somehow he felt blocked and he wasn't making any money. He was wondering if WBF could help him to be more successful in his career, so we arranged a couple of sessions. The most important thing was to identify the two conflicted parts that were blocking a clear flow of energy.

M: *"I feel clear in my head that I want to make money trading. My eyes are focused, my forehead feels clear. I need to make money, its got to happen, I want to try and force it. There is a lot of energy behind this desire.*

T: *OK, I hear that you want to make money and that you need to make money, but what happens when you come to place a trade?*

M: *Well there is another part that is scared of mucking up. I feel scared in my heart, scared of making a mistake and scared of loosing money.*

T: *Just stay with that feeling and try to get the felt sense of it.*

M: *I feel frozen and cold inside, cut off from my body. My mind blanks off and I cannot think. My head feels numb."*

Martin could now identify the part that wanted to make money, and that would try and force it and loose money in bad deals; and also the part that was scared stiff of making mistakes and had an absolute terror of loosing more money. Now we needed to work with holding both.

T: *"OK, so now see if you can stay with the clarity in your head, that sometimes wants to force things and also be with the part that feels scared, frozen and cold in your body. This could take a bit of time, stay with both in equal positive regard and allow the space in-between to come alive in its own way if it wants to. Let's see what happens…"*

After a couple of minutes Martin says:
M:*" I can breathe more easily, I can think more clearly. There is no pressure to trade every day. There are always fresh opportunities in the markets.*

The scared part doesn't want to make mistakes and loose money, so I can respect that and stick to my trading plan.

My brain feels capable of thinking, it can think and plan, it can pause and act, it can follow through on a decision without being driven by fear or greed.

I am aware of being strongly grounded and feeling in my power. I have energy in my body and I can look ahead and see the opportunities coming my way."

As a result of this first session, and with the help of a trading plan that we drew up afterwards, Martin was able to release a positive forward moving life energy that gave him the confidence to re-enter the trading markets and to start using his trading plan rather than making irrational, emotionally driven trading decisions on the spur of the moment, or feeling blocked out of a fear and letting opportunities pass him by.

So let's look again at some of the neural pathways of integration that can help you to be more successful in your career, whatever it is. Firstly, as we have seen in the example of Martin and his trading, lack of confidence and fear-driven decision-making can be a big stumbling block. If the fear and sense of panic is very acute it can lead to the emotional brain hijacking the pre-frontal cortex and then you become incapable of any sort of clear thinking, planning or decision making. So the first step in this situation is to get some bottom-up integration through more body awareness and getting more grounded through awareness of your points of contact with gravity. What is essential is using the radical pause, which is common to both Focusing and the Alexander Technique, so that there is no pressure to do anything at all for a period of time, whilst you give AT directions to free the neck and allow the back to lengthen & widen, or do some open focus relaxation with the eyes, or do some two-pointing awareness of the feet and the hands and the space in-between to induce more alpha brain waves. This will reduce the level of arousal in the nervous system so that you can be aware of more space in your body and start to feel safe again in your own body. As you create more space in your body you also create more space for the breath to just come and go, and the awareness of this deeper breathing pattern stimulates the parasympathetic nervous system and calms you even more.

This pause and creating more space inside is essential for anyone trading the markets, and in any line of business. It is really import for Martin to know, on any given day, that he does not need to trade anything if the conditions are not right and if the indicators are not clear to enter. In point of fact, launching into action just because you feel you have to do something is a sure recipe for disaster because it is just forward moving activity that is driven by panic. So this is one of the key neural pathways that are needed for greater integration of brain function – the ability to pause and to consider carefully. A key element of the pause is to be able to turn down the arousal in the nervous system to reach neutral, and to know that you really do not have to do anything at all until it matches your trading plan and feels right in your body. The pre-frontal cortex has the capacity to pause before acting, and this ensures flexibility of response and the ability to choose wisely from a variety of possible options.

At the same time, when the time for decision making and then action comes, there needs to be some emotional awareness as well, because as the research has proved the emotional input is crucial for good decision making. So in Martin's case he has promised the part that is scared of mucking up and losing money that he will be cautious, he will think carefully and stick to his trading plan and that he will write it all down in a journal as a way of keeping track of what is happening and avoiding sudden irrational trades. If he can stick to his plan and play the percentage game, there will inevitably be losses but the percentage of wins will be greater, so its important not to get upset, and Martin needs to avoid beating himself up about the losses when they come. At the same time, when the wins come, it's important not to get too arrogant and reckless, and not to suddenly feel infallible. So if that fearful part is bringing in an element of caution, which allows for a double-checking then it is serving a useful purpose. As Gene Gendlin used to say "you need to be able to smell the soup, but not be in it".

So what is a good trading plan? The first rule of any trading plan is *"Never trade with money that you cannot afford to lose"*. If you have kissed goodbye to the money already you are more psychologically balanced and less likely to be driven by greed or fear. So this is another neural pathway of integration, when the pre-frontal cortex can consciously modulate the amount of fear being experienced in the amygdala through the release of GABA neurotransmitters. The rest of the trading plan is whatever works for you, so you need to experiment and find out what mix of technical indicators and fundamental news analysis helps you to make profitable decisions. A good plan will help you to determine what the trend is, if you are going long or short, what your timing is - which is your entry price and exit price. It will help you to set your targets and expected profit levels, as well as your protective stops and your risk strategy. All of this boils down to experience and seeing what works for you.

The key thing is to stick to your trading plan, to learn from it and to constantly update it. *To do this you need to keep a journal and write down what worked, what didn't work and how you can learn from your mistakes and successes.* As you build up experience you will find that your intuition comes more and more into play. Intuition is a wholebody response to a situation or a decision that needs to be made. Many people talk of gut-level intuitions, but your intuitions can also be felt in your heart as well, because there is input from information processing neural networks surrounding the heart, lungs and intestines, so the neural links from the pre-frontal cortex to the insula. Calmness seems to be a key feature here, and the hallmark of intuition is a very clear sense of knowing that has bypassed all the little logical steps and got straight to the correct conclusion. It can be linked with a build up of competence from previous experience and practice, but intuition is directly accessing the truth without necessarily knowing how you got there.

One way to cultivate calmness is when you are able to shift your perspective. You need to be able to view what's been happening not just today and yesterday, but also last week, last month, during the last 3 months, or the last 6 months, you need the big historical perspective in order to be able to spot the patterns. Then you can see what is conforming to the pattern and when a new breakthrough occurs that could be profitable. Shifting to the longer perspective gives a calm overview of the situation, and it is then possible to make better decisions. Being caught up in the daily ups and downs of life is more of a roller coaster ride, the emotions are more intense, every response is heightened and it is so easy to get caught up in the drama of day-to-day events. It is also important to be looking at the markets the night before and asking "what do I think will be happening tomorrow, or in a weeks time or a months time?" You need a long-term perspective looking forwards and looking backwards. On the basis of that clearer understanding of the trend, it is then possible to plan entry points and exit points, and hold positions for a longer period rather than just rushing into trades on the day, this helps you to earn more money from your trading.

Integration of these neural pathways helps not only with trading the markets but also with the ability to achieve prosperity in any profession or line of business. Money is essentially energy; it is a paper or electronic validation of your energy levels, mental attitudes, skills and willingness to serve your family or community in some way. The flow of money is a way of regulating your energetic contribution to your community and how that is balanced by the contribution coming back to you. It is all an energy flow, so the essential point is that rather than trying to hang onto the limited amount of money in your wallet or bank account, see it as a circular flow, so that the more you give out, the more will come back to you. There is not a limited amount of wealth or resources available for you, because the universe is actually infinite. Do not limit yourself with the idea that you are in competition with others and the more they get hold of, the less wealth is available to you. Rather visualize abundance as a downpour of rain from the sky above you and the bigger the receptacle that you hold up, the greater your share of the downpour will be. There are limitless opportunities in the world, every day is a fresh opportunities, the amount of money you can earn depends fundamentally on your energy, focus, skill and *how much you think that you deserve to earn.* You are part of the circle of life, and not an isolated individual trying to fight for your share in a competition for survival.

So the WBF model works perfectly here as well. Just like what happened with the example of Martin, the more the different parts of your self can be identified and brought into consciousness, the better they can be brought into an energetic connection and then integrated through WBF. Once the internal integration has been achieved, it then opens the way for you to go out into the world and connect with the skills, the methods, the people, the communities that will be able to help you extend your sphere of influence in the world and confidence in your own abilities.

Chapter 10.
WBF and Neural Pathways to Health

Psychosomatic medicine, the study of the relationship between what's going on in your mind and what's going on in your body has been around for a long time. The ancient Greeks knew about this. In one famous story from the third century BC (as related by Plutarch) King Seleucus of Greece called the foremost doctor of the time, the anatomist Erasistratus, to examine his adult son Antiochus who was close to death with an illness that no physician could heal. Erasistratus observed that whenever the young man was close to Stratonice, the king's beautiful new teenage wife "his symptoms then became all too apparent, such as a break in the voice, blushing and downcast eyes, sudden perspiration and irregularity of the pulse". Plutarch continues: "He also became subject to swoons, doubts, fears and sudden pallor. From all these manifestations Erasistratus drew the conclusion that the king's son loved nobody but her, and that he was determined to die rather than show it." The story has a happy ending, because king Seleucus decided to give away his new wife to his son Antiochus and the illness was cured. (Nothing is said about Stratonice's wishes in this affair).

So psychosomatic medicine has been around for a long time, but because the phrase "psychosomatic" took on a derogatory slant – with the implications that whatever symptoms the person was suffering from was all in his head – it is more usually called behavioral medicine or health psychology nowadays. Whatever the name, there are many studies that all show how social isolation is associated with increased levels of cortisol and other stress hormones, raised blood pressure and a weakened immune system. This means that people who live alone and lack a robust social network tend to produce a weaker antibody response to flu vaccines. This is one of the fascinating conclusions of the latest scientific research in this field.

An interesting piece of scientific research was done many years ago to prove this point in an experiment with baby monkeys. A group of baby monkeys were given enough bottled milk for their needs but they were deprived of physical touch, love and cuddles. Pretty soon they all showed signs of trauma and depression, which is to be expected. This affected the hypothalamus, which is part of the limbic system or the emotional brain. This caused increased levels of a neuropeptide called CRF (corticotrophin releasing factor) which, when it hit the pituitary gland, stimulated the secretion of the peptide ACTH, which then travels through the bloodstream to the adrenal glands where it binds to specific receptors on the adrenal cell walls. The adrenal glands, as we know, control the production of adrenalin, which causes the fight-or-flight alarm response, which helps us to deal with conditions of extreme danger.

The adrenal glands also release the stress hormone cortisol, which is an anti-inflammatory, necessary for healing and damage control once an injury has occurred. Cortisol is released in response to stressful situations, but if the stress is ongoing large amounts will remain in the system and the feedback system will not turn off production, because the situation has not normalized itself.

This same stress-response mechanism also operates in humans. Because body and mind are linked together, you can get caught in this feedback loop, there are certain thoughts and emotions that you will get just from having large quantities of cortisol in the bloodstream. Your expectation is that you are about to get hurt; you might well say that these are the chemicals of negative expectations. In an ongoing stressful situation, there are high levels of the neuropeptide CRF (which is 10 times higher than normal in suicide cases) and also the high cortisol levels in the bloodstream; there is increased production of adrenalin in the adrenal glands and the whole nervous system is over stimulated.

Anyway, to get back to these baby monkeys who were the subjects of this cruel experiment. They were depressed and stressed at the same time, and CRF levels were getting too high. Then they brought on the 'monkey hug therapist', an older female monkey who constantly hugged and cuddled the stressed-out baby monkeys. Within a short period of time they were cured and all the chemical symptoms were reversed. The hugging broke the negative feedback loop by sending the message, "We don't need any more steroids because the trauma is over, and we feel fine." The high CRF and cortisol levels came down. This shows the value of physical contact in therapy and the reassurance of feeling safely grounded in the body again. Through hug therapy, the positive reparative message was repeated consistently over a period of time and the damage was reversed on a chemical and cellular level. Studies have actually shown that your immune system is strengthened just 20 mins after a hug. So remember – a hug a day keeps the doctor away!

This monkey hug experiment was quite an old study, but a whole series of studies have since made the same finding - that social isolation tends to increase levels of cortisol and other stress hormones, to raise blood pressure and to weaken the immune system (which can be tested by the antibody response to flu vaccines). So people who are socially engaged by doing voluntary work, singing in the church choir, raising money for charity or actively engaged in clubs and communities are all likely to have better long term health prospects than those who live alone and feel isolated. The positive emotions of self-worth, feeling a sense of meaning in life, and happiness in contributing to society all translate into better long-term health outcomes.

Behavioural medicine has also made clear the increased risk of coronary artery disease and depression. If you suffer from depression, you are more likely to do self-destructive things like smoke, drink, eat badly and not exercise, but when all of that is taken into account and ruled out as a causative factor these studies have still clearly shown, again and again, that on average the emotional state predicts the health problem. So your emotions clearly have physical consequences that need to be taken seriously. And there are underlying psychological causes of depression. As Freud once said, "Depression is aggression turned inwards on yourself" – so there is potentially a positive energy there waiting to be freed up and released into action in the world. But each person needs to do that for themselves, to find the unique causes and mechanisms and WBF provides a wonderful tool for transforming blocked energy into a forward moving life energy.

Peter was a client of mine who felt very stressed and overloaded at work. He had a domineering boss who always piled more work onto him and then gave strict deadlines. I asked him what his felt sense of the whole situation was, he took some time to sense into himself and then his hand started rubbing the front of his chest which he said felt "tight and restricted", "I can't get enough air" he replied, and sighed. I asked him what the worst thing about the whole situation was. "I can't get it all done. I feel overloaded and then I panic and it's hard to concentrate, or even get started on anything". "It's making my asthma much worse" he said, gasping for breath. We went into a WBF session where I asked him to just hold both his grounded feet and his tight and restricted lungs in compassionate awareness without any judgments or pre-conceived ideas.

As we waited patiently the space in-between started to come alive in its own way and something shifted inside. "I'm feeling calmer and more spacious inside," he said. "My feet are on the ground, and I just need to take it step by step and get started rather than getting stressed thinking about it". I could see that he was looking more empowered from his body language and his breathing had calmed down completely with no sign of the impending asthma attack. We spent the last part of the session discussing key action steps that he could undertake to improve his work situation. He knew that he would be fine after that, because he now had a technique to calm the arousal of his nervous system and to direct his energy productively rather than going into stress and worry about the situation and triggering an asthma attack.

Peter's example illustrates a fundamental point – that first of all he got back into his body, into grounded presence which gave him a sense of clarity and calmness and then some sort of action step was needed, where he could feel that he was back in control and putting his energy into doing something practical, rather than just getting stressed worrying about the situation, but not actually doing anything. The damaging health effects of being out of control, worry and negative thoughts are clearly proven now, and the neural pathways of these sorts of negative emotions are clearly understood, as opposed to the neural pathways of positive emotions, being able to think, plan and execute action steps, which are activated by higher brain wave activity in the left pre-frontal cortex and the neural pathways that link from there.

Michael Marmot, who is professor of public health at UCL, has spent a long time investigating this, in two famous studies Whitehall I and II. The original **Whitehall Study** investigated social determinants of health, specifically the cardiovascular disease prevalence and mortality rates among British male civil servants between the ages of 20 and 64. The original Whitehall I Study, examined over 18,000 male civil servants, and was conducted over a period of ten years, beginning in 1967. A second study, Whitehall II, examined the health of 10,308 civil servants aged 35 to 55, of whom two thirds were men and one-third women. Prof. Marmot was interested in investigating the effects of stress on health and life expectancy. He chose to study Whitehall civil servants because it was easy to divide people into grade levels and his expectation was that people in the higher grades, who had more responsibility, more stress and worked longer hours would be more prone to stress-related coronary diseases (like heart attacks) and would have a lower life expectancy. Well, the results of this massive study proved his expectation to be wrong and for a very interesting reason.

The Whitehall study did find a strong association between grade levels of civil servant employment and mortality rates from a range of causes, but it contradicted his expectations. After controlling for other significant risk factors, men in the lowest grade (messengers, doorkeepers, etc.) had a mortality rate 3 times higher than that of men in the highest grade (administrators). Why should this be? The interesting conclusion was that the top-level administrators certainly had more stress, but they were more in control of their working environment, how they could utilize their skills and what tasks were assigned to them – because they were the ones who were in control. All the top people were mostly from a similar social class and thus had more social support and understanding of each other. So they had a greater sense of planning and control of the work situation, they could work together, support each other and by being in charge of the projects and saying, "Yes" to the whole situation they could accept the stress rather than fight against it. It was the lower grade levels who suffered more from high blood pressure (and other health issues) at work and this was associated with a greater perception of job stress, including "lack of skill utilization," "tension in the office," and "lack of clarity" in the tasks assigned. The higher blood pressure among the lowest grade servants was found to be related to the higher job stress score.

So this was a surprising result, that underscores the importance of all workers being more involved in the planning and allocation of tasks in the office and gaining a sense of long-term perspective rather than being just a cog in the machine. As we know this will activate neural circuits that link to the left pre-frontal cortex and lead to more neural integration rather than being caught in negative feeling states of depression, stress and powerlessness. The importance of workers getting more involved in the planning of tasks has been clearly shown in this big study, to have beneficial health results in terms of longer life expectancy and reduced risk of heart disease. This actually applies to any organization and one proposal that could help would be regular weekly or monthly meetings where all employees are listened to respectfully in a brainstorming group discussion where the principles of energetic interconnection are understood and practiced. This would throw up a lot of whacky ideas that could be discarded, but also a few really good practical innovations that would be extremely efficient and profitable. Also, employees could be asked what aspects of a project they feel particularly drawn too, and take responsibility for that part of the work, rather than routine allocations based on past experience. There would be a feeling of heightened energy levels and more energy in the group as these new neural pathways are activated and the research would predict significant health benefits for the workers. It would not surprise me at all if this did not lead to increased innovation and greater profitability for the business as well.

Due to the mixture of AT and Focusing there are remarkable health benefits to WBF applicable to a whole variety of diseases. The AT gives the ability to direct energy flow within the body to any diseased or vulnerable part, and the Focusing technique allows any fundamental psychological conflicts or blockages to be released to allow that cut-off part to be re-integrated and for healing to take place.

I remember one WBF student called Peter who experienced a remarkable healing. Peter suffered from glaucoma and his eyesight was getting more blurred all the time. This condition will result in blindness eventually, and as his condition worsened the doctors eventually recommended a trabeculectomy, which involves removing a small area of eye tissue to help drain the eye ball of excess fluid. Peter was distraught at the diagnosis and he also disliked the idea of the operation, but he reluctantly agreed to go ahead with it. The operation was a success, but unfortunately his wounds got infected with MRSA, which is a very serious bacterial infection that can infect patients after hospital operations. The infection spread rapidly and Peter went completely blind, he was feeling completely depressed and panic stricken at the same time. MRSA is resistant to nearly all antibiotics, there is one last line of defense, which is a very strong antibiotic that needs a series of injections and even with this the prognosis is not good. Finally, one time they were wheeling him around the hospital on a trolley, taking him to different departments to do all sorts of tests on him. The orderlies wheeled him back to his ward and they were lifting him back onto his bed when somehow they managed to drop him. So there he was, all the tubes ripped out of him, lying on the floor, blind, vulnerable and helpless, and he just started laughing, he just laughed louder and louder rolling about with laughter on the floor. The orderlies were very concerned, "Mr McIntyre" they asked, "are you OK? what's happening ? Why are you laughing so much ?" Eventually Peter stopped laughing and he replied, "I'm laughing so much because I just realized that I cannot trust you guys to take care of me, I cannot trust you to heal me, I am going to have to heal myself". And that is exactly what he did, using WBF techniques.

Peter was not a stupid or dogmatic person, he was of course prepared to try the last possible course of antibiotics, even though the doctors said there was only a slim chance of it working. But he had made a decision to take responsibility for his own healing at a very fundamental level, and he now worked with WBF to try and heal his badly infected eyes. His felt sense of the situation was: *"I feel pressure in my eyes, my vision is blurred, it's dark. I'm retreating back into my head. I feel panicky."* After spending some time holding awareness of his intense vulnerability and his grounded presence, by being aware of his feet at the same time, something shifted for Peter. The words that fitted this felt shift were:
"I'm connected to my feet, my eyes feel more energized, they are letting in more light, and my eyes are more receptive. I'm letting things be, just the way that they are, without resistance".

Peter made this his mantra, he used it all day long, soaking his eyes in this positive affirmation, and he was also able to direct the energy flow from his feet all the way up to his eyes bathing them in a stream of directed energy flow. Also, he was not fighting the situation and making an enemy of this pain and disease in his eyes, he was letting things be just the way that they were, without any resistance and that was releasing muscular tension, stimulating blood flow and life energy to sooth and heal his infected eyes.

Well, the remarkable thing is that after a week the infection was healed, within two weeks he did begin to see some light, then some blurred shapes and within a month his eyesight was completely healed. Peter went from absolute despair to a real conviction that he could heal himself from his blindness. This is a true story and what I like about Peter is his modesty and good humor at all times, including this critical situation in his life. This story also illustrates that it is not a choice between allopathic medicine, or using so-called "alternative" methods of healing, but rather a question of making informed choices in a critical situation and allowing both methods to reinforce each other and to emerge a stronger person as a result of this.

There are many other examples that could be given of how WBF is a potent method of healing. Let's take the example of my aching shoulder joint. I could do a couple of different things with it. Firstly, I can allow myself to merge with the experience of the aching, feel tense and annoyed with it, which tends to intensify the pain and prevent the emergence of any fresh life energy and potential for movement. Or, I can step back mentally from my aching shoulder and become the observer of my shoulder. From this fluid awareness of my whole living body, that is also energetically connected to its surrounding environment, I now have a way to contain, keep company with, and accept my suffering shoulder. I can let it be just the way it is without wanting to change it. I begin to notice that the sun had just came out in my beautiful garden, that my chickens just clucked and looked hungrily at me, some birds are singing in the trees, and my other shoulder feels pretty good. I have a tension in my neck, which somehow seems connected to my achy shoulder. My aching shoulder is actually well supported by my spine and pelvis and the ground below my feet.

The final important step is to invite my shoulder to have its own direct experience of its pain within the context of the support of the whole living body in grounded presence. My aching shoulder needs me to become aware of itself, connected to my whole body and to my grounded presence down through my pelvis and feet, as one unified field of awareness so that it can reorganize its self in its own way, in its own time, from its own inner wisdom. My shoulder can do this because it is now in right relationship with the whole living body, something my shoulder knows how to do in a way that my ego cannot do through effort. It takes a couple of minutes before my shoulder begins to shift and have its own experience of aching. It is noticeably softer. The deltoid muscle has relaxed and let go of an unconscious protective holding pattern. My scapula (shoulder blade) feels flat and heavy; it starts to connect with the pelvis below it. Now, there is a warm pulsing coming from the ball and socket joint itself. I support my shoulder's own experience of itself by remaining open, curious, and accepting of all the subtle inner movements arising from the shoulder's own re-organization process. I support it through my grounded presence and my willingness to just observe the way it can awaken and enliven itself in this way. My wholebody awareness of my shoulder becomes a newer, more precise, and life-enhancing awareness of my shoulder. Most especially, I am no longer suffering any pain in my shoulder. I notice what is different about my posture, my muscular tension patterns and the way my shoulder connects with the rest of my body now. There seems to be a message there for me, something that I can learn from the pain and from the healing process.

Holding both is what really allows the inner body wisdom to operate and the whole release of the "felt shift" to occur. What was blocked process in the body, actions that were not performed, words that were not said, emotions that were not expressed, can slowly become free and flowing. Tiny movements can start to be felt in the body as subtle muscular releases or as more overt gestures or movements. These are not conscious movements initiated by command of the neo-cortex and executed by an act of conscious will. Rather, these are "inner directed movements", which are spontaneous movements of the whole body that knows what is needed to release the tension, complete the action and then return to a position of homeostasis. It is the wisdom of the body that knows how to readjust to the present situation in a healthy and integrated way now, rather than being triggered by trauma all the time. With this release a situation that seemed to be impossible a few minutes ago can suddenly seem to be manageable. Solutions appear where there were only huge problems and massive conflicts before, possibilities are suddenly seen that always existed, but you were just too stressed to be able to recognise them and work with them.

But what is essential is to stop any effort to fix it, or fight it or to force a solution. There is a period of letting go and widening out of awareness that is really essential to this whole process of letting the answer come to you rather than getting all tense and trying to force a solution. But the mind will not let go of its tried and tested defense strategies until it feels safe enough to do so, and it will only feel safe enough once it is securely grounded. So having spent some time with the swaying exercise in order to get grounded and feel well-supported from the feet upwards, and having identified the part that needs attention and feels blocked, *it is now possible to hold both and to let the body, in its own time and its own wisdom, unwind the trauma and release the blocked energy.*

I will give an example of this type of hands-on WBF therapy when working with Client "X" on the table, this is what Client "X" wrote:

I had a whole series of WBF sessions with Alex and thoroughly enjoyed each one of them. I'm going to talk about them collectively because they all worked on a familiar theme, which was connected with unwinding the trauma of repressed self-expression, but they were also profoundly safe and relaxing experiences right from the start – which my body just loved. After I knew what to expect, my body started to relax as soon as I got onto the table, and as soon as Alex put hands I quickly went into very deep relaxation.

I would get to a place of very deep calmness, very early in the sessions. Alex seemed to have an extraordinary skill in his hands, and a quiet depth of concentration, so it was not just the places that he touched but also my whole body that got heavy and relaxed, releasing downwards towards the welcome support of the table. I felt that I could stop trying so hard, I didn't need to maintain a mask and I could just be myself, in a very open and safe way. But most importantly, being myself meant that I could expose imperfections and vulnerabilities that really needed healing, but that I mostly kept hidden from others. I felt safe enough to unwind this need for self-protective secrecy, and as we all know: naming an issue is already 50% of the way towards healing it.

The two preliminary questions were always very relevant: what needs attention in my body right now? And what areas feel relaxed and comfortable and able to act as a support for me? I could notice familiar patterns of tension in my stomach, in my throat, my chest and in my shoulders – which I was able to name and describe. Also I noticed a warmth and aliveness in the tops of my thighs and in my lower pelvis. As Alex put his hands on my stomach and my upper chest everything started to relax downwards, I felt safe, but in that safety the tension in my throat became even more pronounced, it really became unbearable like it was saying " I need attention and this is my chance for healing now! After about 15 minutes into the first session I wanted to name something very important: "Alex, I need to swallow, there is a tension in my throat but I feel embarrassed to swallow in front of you". I had exposed my biggest fear, and it felt like this was my chance to heal an issue that had been troubling me all through my life – and I was going to take it!

I can remember Alex working on my throat, shoulders and neck, also times when he put his hands under my sacrum, and released my pelvis. There were periods when I wanted to talk, but also long periods of just very deep relaxation, when my body felt completely safe, I felt accepted and all my defensive patterns, physical, mental & emotional, could begin to unwind. I felt like I was in heaven, but somehow I hadn't earned it yet because there was still work to be done!

The order in which things happened is a bit fuzzy in my head, actually its not so important, because the key thing was that three major areas in my body needed unwinding, and they were all inter-related.

Firstly, I noticed how the tension seemed to intensify and to move into my shoulder blades, where the whole position of my shoulders shifted backwards. It was an incredibly powerful experience – like my whole shoulder girdle was literally being pushed backwards into a new alignment. It was quite painful at times; it disturbed my sleep pattern for a few days and also made driving difficult. But the real revelation was when I was standing and talking to people: I was "keeping my back back" to the wall behind me, and not coming forwards to meet them. I knew instantly what it meant, I have had a lifetimes' habit of wanting to please others, and this translated into quite a tense and fearful habit of tensing my shoulders and leaning forwards whilst putting all my attention on the other person and trying to make it right for them. Suddenly there was this force field that would just not allow me to do that anymore. My whole alignment & shoulder position changed over a few days and it hurt a lot, but I knew it was a good pain.

I think in the second or third session the tension started to build up in my neck muscles and there were long periods of spontaneous movement with my head and neck, with huge tension building up slowly as I moved to my left and then finally a releasing movement as my head turned to the right. I couldn't work out what was happening, and then Alex asked, "Did you have a difficult birth?" That question clarified a suspicion within me. ", My mother denies it, but I know I did, and I have brain scans that show significant damage to the left & especially the right temporal lobes of the brain". These movements lasted nearly one whole session and I felt my body had undergone a re-birthing experience. Something was different after that; I no longer felt the world to be such a difficult and terrifying place. I felt more solid, relaxed and entitled to be here.

During each session I was acutely aware of the tension in my throat and my on-going issue with swallowing. I named the issue that was behind the tension: "I know that this is to do with having a very dominant mother during my childhood and feeling that I was not allowed to express my truth". The realization came that the tension in my stomach was linked to my suppressed anger and suppressed sexuality. One session Alex gently put his hands on my stomach and my throat at the same time, and as the relaxation deepened I felt a resolution to stay awake, even though I was close to falling asleep, and to allow conscious change to take place rather than drift off into comfortable oblivion. I clearly felt my throat release forwards, rather than me pulling it inwards all the time, like there was more space for my adam's apple, and as that happened I also felt a connection to a soft warm energy in my pelvis. Alex intuitively sensed this and put his hand on my lower belly whilst keeping his other hand on my throat. It was a wonderful feeling. It felt very important to allow both places to be energetically connected and I got a strong feeling that I was OK to be the way that I was. Afterwards there was a big energy blockage that had been released, so my throat and my pelvis now felt very different. I could go back into a space of feeling safe and deeply relaxed again. At the end of that session I really noticed how my shoulders had softened, I felt more "fluid" in my body, there was more space in my chest, like my heart was filling out and there was a feeling of greater confidence and optimism.

So these were the three crucial areas, my shoulders, my throat and my pelvis, that had been released over the course of the hands-on WBF sessions and they now felt re-integrated in a different way. Not just energetically integrated in my body but also in my life. I felt more empowered. If people would ask me for favors and if it was not possible I would just say "No, I'm sorry that's just not possible at the moment, I can't help you with that". And if they would ask again I would just say "Absolutely not". I was surprised at how direct and clear I could be without feelings of guilt creeping in. Sometimes I would say yes if it was possible, but other times I would listen to my needs in the moment and just say "No". So the changes I noticed were: more feelings of self-empowerment, more self-worth and a greater capacity to speak my truth clearly, both individually and in group situations. Given the importance of these issues in my life story, this was a huge amount of change in a very short space of time. It was a really potent, life-transforming experience for me, to have these WBF sessions and then to notice the situations that Life presented to me to be able to put it all into practice.

I've talked a lot about my insights, because these are what will really remain with me and become a part of my new life, long after the blissful experiences of deep relaxation whilst lying on the table have faded in my memory. But obviously both were important, because such huge changes could not have occurred unless I felt completely contained and safe within my body".

A simple exercise that can help to make the healing potential of spontaneous movement clearer is this: when going for a walk allow your legs to just take you where they want to go. Say "I trust you, my body, you know more than I do at this moment, take me to the places where I am meant to go, to experience and see what I need to see, right now". It is an amazing experience to give up direct ego control, to trust the subtle directions of your body, to discover places that you never would have seen, to experience the world with a freshness and intensity that comes from launching yourself into the unknown, and to have the remarkable feeling of your body, your legs, just moving of their own accord. By a process of synchronicity, you will be led to meet people or to see new places and things that really give you a sharper insight and a deeper realization about your ongoing life issues.

Chapter 11.
WBF and Neural Pathways to Wisdom

Many people cannot believe in God or a Creator of this universe who would allow human suffering on such a vast scale due to wars, violence, genocide and all sorts of natural catastrophes. It is not just the guilty who seem to suffer, terrible things happen to good people and it all seems so random and pointless. Is there really a God? Is there some sort of plan? Is there any point to human existence? These are difficult questions, but instead of blaming God or the Creator of this universe, let's turn it all around and ask if human beings are not responsible for many of the terrible things that happen on this planet. Who is polluting the planet? Who starts wars? Who follows the orders from the politicians to go to war and to shoot millions of their fellow humans? These are human ideas and actions, as are greed, selfishness, murder, robbery and rape. Ultimately humans are responsible, and even the classic defense that "I was only following orders" is not a defense because there was still a decision to follow the orders and not listen to the voice of conscience. Climate change is a result of human activity and although no one likes to admit to it, we are all partly responsible for it! We all have free will and responsibility for the use of that free will, so ultimately free will is based on choice and those decisions need to be taken as a result of listening to the voice of wisdom that we all have within ourselves.

All of the great spiritual traditions speak of the necessity of thinking deeply and contacting your inner wisdom before taking making an important decision, because you are the one who will be faced with the consequences and are the one who must take responsibility for the original decision. All through our lives we are faced with many situations that demand our careful attention. There are many influences in your environment that pull or push you in a certain direction, many voices telling you what to do, but there is only one person who can make those decisions and once a decision has been made and you have acted then you must bare the consequences. Karma, to use an Indian Sanskrit term, is the inevitable law of life. What goes around comes around, and so it is worth thinking deeply about the difference between a knee-jerk reaction to a situation and a reasoned response that has come from a deep place of "felt sensing" the wisdom within. All this has been talked about at some length in the earlier chapters on the Alexander Technique and Alexander's understanding of the stimulus/reaction model and the need to slow things down, pause and create more time. This is part of every spiritual tradition and it is part of WBF as well – don't be over reactive, pause and wait to seek the deeper, slower response that comes from your higher self and a place of wisdom that can see the bigger picture.

One of the special features of the WBF process is the realization of self-responsibility that slowly dawns during the process. As I pay attention to what is happening within the container of my whole body, noticing all the thoughts, feelings and somatic sensations that arise, all the confusion begins to settle down and clear within myself. Like the debris that will settle to the bottom of a glass of muddy water, the cloudiness begins to clear and light penetrates through the bright, clear water. The realization is startling: *it is not the things that happen to me in my life that are important, it is my reaction to them that makes them appear to be what they are.* Change the reaction and I can change the entire significance of that event in my life.

The Focusing process is inviting me to go into my present experience within the container of my body, and the listener is trained to facilitate that. As I focus on myself and my inner experience I gradually begin to lose interest in the other person involved in the drama and I start to get more curious about myself and my reactions. (Remember Dan Siegel and COAL: becoming Curious, Open-minded, Accepting and Loving). Why did I feel quite so upset in that situation? That was such a big emotional reaction for such a small comment wasn't it? What am I getting so triggered about? Why am I feeling so angry/afraid/ powerless about this whole thing? As my curiosity awakens I begin to explore what that "whole thing" feels like in my body and start to discover what is behind all of this…it feels mysterious, exciting and empowering – because I can change this part, its a part of me.

I start to get it - this is my experience, stemming from my reaction to the whole situation. I have a choice here; actually there are always choices in life, in any situation. I can either choose to be reactive or I can choose how I respond from a place of wisdom, from a higher perspective looking down on the whole thing. From this bigger perspective I can choose how to respond consciously, as part of the bigger blueprint of my life I can work out where I am and where I want to get to in my life, using neural pathways from my pre-frontal cortex that can help to inform my decision making from a place of deeper wisdom and knowing. However, there is a big caveat here: none of this can happen whilst I am hyper-aroused and my nervous system is all revved up. Whilst I am in the stress response my neo-cortex has been hijacked by the amygdala and there is very little rational thinking that can take place. So it may feel like I am stuck in my head, but actually I am in emotional overwhelm, with my thoughts racing round and round, feeling very ungrounded and identified with all sorts of strong emotions and stressed out. It's impossible to maintain clarity and perspective.

This is where WBF can be priceless. First, there needs to be grounding, feeling the support and safety of Mother Earth. This allows the hyper-arousal of the central nervous system to decrease as I actually start to feel safe in my body. I am feeling supported by something much bigger than myself – by the whole of planet Earth. Then I can begin to process whatever the blockage or the vulnerability is. The blocked energy gets transformed into a positive, forward moving life energy. I start to feel empowered in my whole body, strong and supported in my feet, with a sense of aliveness and optimism in my head. I feel good, I feel motivated to change the parts in me that I can change – don't worry about anyone else, let them be the way that they are and make the decisions that they need to make. I can make the changes that I need to so that I'm ready to move forwards in my life. There is a wonderful positivity in WBF and a positive attitude is a natural part of the spiritual life. We all have a choice where we want to be on the positivity spectrum. Don't just focus on the negative things that have happened in your life, focus on the positive things that have happened or could happen, connect with your forward moving life energy and use that as a basis for performing more purposeful actions and achieving more positive goals. So when the "felt shift" comes in Focusing there is actually a change in the vibrational frequency of your energy field and it is easier to move from feelings of hopelessness, despair, & powerlessness to the higher positive emotions of gratitude, joy, love, faith and a belief in a positive outcome.

When you feel centered and grounded in your sense of expanded self, feeling safe within yourself and positive about the world - this is so fundamentally different that it's much easier to maintain a positive emotional state. Once you are securely grounded in your self, it frees you up to stop worrying about other people and what they are thinking or saying and that gives you the space and calmness to make decisions that are really authentic and congruent with your deepest inner values. When you are really empowered to live in your own energy field in this way its not only that you just have more energy and are more connected with your creativity and initiative – but also it is a fundamental shift towards feeling that the world is inherently good, a more abundant, loving and generous place and that you too are filled with an abundance of love, wisdom and resources to share.

One of the defining features of the WBF process is that a process of calming, grounding and centering starts to occur, and the crucial sense of the detached observer begins to emerge. This is a natural, innate capacity in all human beings, but we can also train it more. Making authentic decisions from a place of grounded presence means that I can change from knee-jerk reactions to a reasoned response and then I have a decision that I can live with for the rest of my life because it is congruent with my deeper values.

At crucial turning points in life, wise and effective decision-making depends on a different relationship to self and to the wider environment. This depends on the ability to move from purely narrow, egotistical thinking towards being able to see the bigger picture. This means that the pre-frontal cortex is involved at the same time as being informed by the heart and the extra information flow coming from a wholebody awareness. So this involves a pause, a radical pause, to let more information come in from the body and not rush towards the safety of an immediate decision. The fear that demands an immediate solution cannot allow anything new or creative into the picture. Some of the problems that the world is facing today are so large and fundamentally different to anything experienced up till now, that it feels overwhelming and the panic reaction dominates. What are we going to do about the situation in the Middle East? What are we going to do about global warming and the concomitant problem of mass migration? These are new problems that demand authentic and creative answers. There is a real need for authentic decision making, in politics, economics or when dealing with personal crisis. But paradoxically the first thing needed is to pause and to say that *its OK not to know*, and not rush into a series of knee-jerk reactions that could ultimately make things worse. A truly wise politician or business leader would say that.

Your body knows more than your conscious mind, because your body is like a giant biological computer that links you to many ongoing processes, you're your relationships to other people, things happening in the environment, in your community and culture and to the whole electromagnetic force field of planet Earth, and our whole planetary and galactic system. There is so much inter-connection and information being taken in and processed below the level of our conscious mind, that links us to the wisdom of the whole planet and the whole collective unconscious through the sensitive awareness of our bodies. And yet the whole educational system in western culture is geared towards the necessity of making purely rational decisions, using only the rational mind to make a list of the pros and cons, (either mentally, in discussion with others, or on a bit of paper), weighs up the different elements and then comes to a decision based on whichever appears to be the longer list. But we immediately come up against an obvious problem here, as some items will be more important than others, there could be an emotional or moral significance to one particular argument that outweighs all the other items put together.

So there is actually a lot of research showing how emotions shape the decision making process –even when we are not aware of it. Even for people who think that they are making rational, logical decisions all sorts of biases have been shown to creep in, but the research is also showing that taking your emotions into account actually helps you to make better decisions. Actually there is a wonderful resource here, because your body cannot lie and by using WBF it is possible to access the wisdom of the body, to get a bigger perspective and to make wise and far-reaching decisions.

Focusing can help the whole decision making process – something that is murky and unclear will become clear when you can get a felt sense of it and stay with it long enough for change to happen. Rather than rush into a decision the first thing to be aware of is "how you make decisions". There are many different styles of decision-making. Some people rush into a decision for the sense of security & control. Others will avoid decisions and procrastinate, but with a sense of panic and paralysis combined. Others can be frozen in indecision for "fear of making the wrong decision".

But you can start to get a little bit more conscious here and introduce some elements from Focusing. Also be a bit curious, step back a bit. It's not about getting a result and rushing in, *but about awareness of your process of how you make decisions. How are you holding your body, you posture, your breathing? What's your felt sense of the way you approach this whole thing of making decisions, regardless of the content of this particular one that's worrying you?* Stay with the not knowing, the ambiguity & the uncertainty. It is very powerful to live with the attitude of, "I don't know at the moment, and I can't make a decision, but something in me knows and I am connecting with something bigger in me that can help me to clarify and to know what the next step forward is"

So get a felt sense of the implications of the "whole thing" in your body first. Get into "grounded presence" using WBF & then ask a series of very specific questions and see how your body reacts to these specific suggestions. Hold the not knowing and allow a felt shift to come. Using a combination of factual knowledge & body wisdom the decision makes itself felt inside the body. You will know the authentic response from your body's felt shift and feel how that releases life energy into action. Break a big decision up into smaller bits if you can, smaller decisions, which you can focus with and resolve. As these different bits gradually clarify themselves, its builds like a jigsaw puzzle and the bigger picture emerges. As it does so the decision will begin to make itself. If other people are involved, be curious about them, give them room and time to express themselves and to define their position, which may also be in process. This openness to relationship will help to clarify your own position. Remember that even a bad decision, or following a compulsion or an addiction that is harmful, can turn out to be beneficial if done consciously and with a curious, open attitude. If there is learning in it, it can ultimately change you for the better. In that sense there are "no wrong decisions". Any decision is right and useful if it leads to learning and forward movement in my life. The worst is being stuck and not making any decision at all for the rest of your life.

Ultimately, real wisdom reveals that when you do what is right for you it turns out to be right for everybody else. So on an outer relationship level, real wisdom is all about you as an organism getting clear about your position in relationship to others, on a personal level, in a community, in a nation or ultimately in your relationship with the Universe. So a lot of it is about maintaining energetic connection within secure boundaries and being able to maintain boundaries free of outside influences, while you make the decisions that are right for you. When you know where you stand, then you can come into proper relationship with others.

Real wisdom demands accessing your body's intuitive knowing about a situation in a Wholebody way. Something inside you knows more about this situation than your cognitive mind alone does. Once you make space for this inner wisdom, then you can bring both the inner knowing and the outer factual situation together in order to make a decision. There needs to be enough energy and resolve in order to be able to carry the decision through. When going into new territory there will be a learning curve involved, so realize that small steps in this new and different direction will lead to big changes in the future. Do not avoid taking these small steps because they do not seem big or dramatic enough, mighty oaks can grow from tiny acorns. It's the energetic blueprint behind it plus the small steps that make things grow.

Above all, real wisdom involves taking self-responsibility for your part of any situation. WBF gives you a method whereby you can transform your inner life, so that you are actually feeling good inside, regardless of the outer circumstances. This isn't just a denial of negativity and always putting on a brave face and pretending that life is great. There is more to it than that, a deeper level of understanding that comes when you do the slow, patient inner work first. This is a real energetic and emotional experience on the inner level within your body container. Then it is possible to follow the second great spiritual law, as well as not blaming anyone for my suffering it is now possible to say that I am not seeking fulfillment out there, I am not chasing satisfaction out there, in the world, because I am already experiencing it within myself right now. It is possible to feel joy right now, within the container of the body regardless of outer conditions.

When you can feel this inner joy within yourself, you feel so loved and you also love yourself because you feel something so alive and beautiful at the core of your being. This is not egotistical self-love; this is a transpersonal mystical experience that unites you with the universal love, joy and wisdom that lies within and behind all of manifested creation. Now you can love your neighbor as yourself. This is what the great saints and mystics have written about and it is possible to experience this richness, right now, during the course of an ordinary, working daily life. This is not just theory that comes from reading about the extraordinary experiences of a few exceptional people, this is direct personal experience of that sense of connection, that inner guidance and wisdom But first you must realize that it is beyond mind, it is a direct knowing in the timeless present moment, a deepening of awareness into the NOW, as Eckhart Tolle says this is *"a knowing that does not destroy the sacredness and mystery of life but contains a deep love and reverence for all that is. A knowing of which the mind knows nothing".* There is an absence of thought here, but a fullness of love and devotion. As St Theresa of Avila said: " *The important thing is not to think much, but to love much, and so do that which best strengthens you to love".*

When you are really going with the flow, there is a sense of "I can let go of all my tension, all striving and all sense of effort. I can just sit back and tune in with all that sense of trust and support from something bigger than myself, which is the whole of planet Earth and the whole universe. I am being supported". You are then living in the flow, and learning how to put out for things on the level of consciousness and waiting for the right response to come to you, rather than you trying to figure out the clever answer all the time Rather than the ego just grabbing and fighting for things all the time, feeling that resources are scarce and that there isn't enough for everyone, there can be a sense of the interconnectedness of all life on this planet, and the abundance and generosity that permeates the whole universe. WBF enables me to say: I have a problem, I don't know what the answer is right now, but I trust that something in me, some inner wisdom knows the way forwards. I can put it out there, I can give it time, I don't know the answer, and its OK not to know, and holding that level of trusting awareness helps me to connect with the energetic matrix that is the underlying electromagnetic fabric of all creation. This then connects me with a feeling of abundance, a whole ocean of light, love, peace and wisdom. And as I patiently wait, in awareness and without any time limits, the shift and the answers start to come. It can be an inner knowing from within, the physical release of a felt shift that leads to a new perspective, a freed-up energy, and a new sense of knowing that "this is the way that I need to move forwards now". Or the answers can come from the outside, seemingly by co-incidence I may meet someone, read something, be told a new piece of information or overhear a random phrase in a conversation that is actually extremely meaningful and it helps me to find that missing piece of the jig saw puzzle. As C G Jung, the great Swiss psychologist noticed, this is synchronicity at work, and this is more than co-incidence, it is a signpost from the universal wisdom in pointing the way forwards. But you do not need to get tense chasing the answers – you create a space of not knowing and non-doing and then wait for the answers to come to you.

The important thing is to step back a little bit so that you *develop the ability to be aware of how you are paying attention*. How do you habitually pay attention to other people in relationships or conversations? How do you approach work, or problem solving? These are all pretty big questions and if you observe you will see how you tend to slip into your habitual way of doing things and paying attention that may mentally tight and also physically tense and emotionally fearful. As FM Alexander would say – you are being an "end-gainer", much too focused on achieving success and making much too much effort. Yes of course you must have an aim, a vision, have a clear intention and work within a structure, a time slot which you set aside to achieve realistic and clearly defined goals, but don't get so obsessed with your goal and trying too hard to make it happen. Instead retain a sense of ease, lightness and spaciousness in the way you pay attention. Be more aware of your body, as your body is the portal to higher states of consciousness. Move more slowly; be in the moment with more awareness, more balance and relaxation. Don't be obsessed with your goals and trying too hard. All the skills related to the Alexander Technique and Focusing, outlined earlier in this book can come to your aid. In particular building in a period of pause, where you pay attention to how you are paying attention and allow the goal to become secondary, for a moment, to your state of being. What is more important is your motivation and your state of consciousness right now in this moment, and then you can flow into activity easily and effortlessly. The amount of tension that you have in your body will give you the clue, have a heightened sense of awareness combined with aliveness and less tension in your body. Have clarity of intention, but less stiff-necked efforting.

In that inner calmness and quietness your inner Body Wisdom can be heard and you can start to follow the inner guidance.

Of course this is the ongoing training in WBF, this is what it is all about, can you stay in grounded presence for longer and longer periods of the day, just feeling grounded in your feet and pelvis, feeling your body as the container and able to accept all of your authentic experiences without trying to fight it, or fix it, or run away from it? If you can do that for long enough and stay with your own experience something special will start to happen, inner transformation will take place. You will start to feel softer and more transparent, the inner energy starts to flow and the container of your body begins to feel like one inter-connected whole, instead of many antagonistic separate parts that are full of tension and working against each other. You will start to feel whole, comfortable in your own skin, not just comfortable but actually calm, serene and joyous. It is like there is a river of energy, life and love that flows under the surface of all your fluctuating life experiences.

But you need to be aware of the energy in your body container because that will put you in touch with the sea of energy that surrounds you, and as we know from nuclear physics, everything is energy that can be converted into matter and, matter can be converted back into energy. The new quantum physics shows the link between matter, energy and consciousness, and many interesting experiments prove that the observing consciousness is responsible for bringing the energy of a quantum waveform into physical manifestation as a particle. There is an underlying, energetic matrix of creation, a fabric of potential that can only come into physical existence when the consciousness is there to bring it into manifestation. So we have these 3 factors of energy, consciousness and matter. What WBF does is to help you get into contact with the free flow of energy within your own body, as you become more aware of that you are also sensitized to flows and variations in the larger energy field in the surrounding environment.

This energy is the other crucial part, because many people in our educated, technological society are living in their heads, suffering from stress and feel cut off from their bodies and just cannot feel the energy in their bodies. Many people do not feel comfortable with having an energetic charge in their bodies, cannot be creative, independent and self-directive and prefer to live subservient lives, under the direction of authority figures like parents, therapists, marriage partners or their bosses at work. As the energetic charge builds up from time to time, they don't know what to do with it, as it feels confusing and unsafe, they start to get agitated and the energy needs to get dissipated in exercise, or working long hours, or drinking/drugs, or in futile arguments, or sexual release. These are all compulsive ways of reducing the energetic charge inside the body and the anxiety that goes with it.

WBF gives us a step up the consciousness ladder, a whole new perspective from which to view the body container and everything that is contained there in there. Most crucially it lets you feel comfortable with having an energy charge in the body and brings back freedom of choice about what you want to do with that energy. So it brings self-awareness and self-direction back into your life, this is something that is increasingly being recognized as the vital turning point in therapy – the feeling is unmistakable because it is so different. This is termed "self agency" in the psychological literature, and it is recognized as the start of healthy, independent functioning in life. Now the individual can move forwards from compulsive patterns of behavior to conscious responses and choices in life. There is the awareness of the body container and all the experiences that happen in life, the conscious responses that have been processed and also the energy to fuel these conscious decisions once they have been made. All of that energy can now be channeled into creative work, conscious loving relationships, enjoyable sports activities, and different ways of connecting and interacting with your family, community activities, national politics and international humanitarian activities.

But it really has huge spiritual implications as well, because if you are on a spiritual journey, of whatever nature, you have a path to follow, which implies a journey from where you are now, towards what you want to become, a more spiritual being. But at the same time you need to be asking yourself "why am I doing this to myself? Doesn't this imply some sort of tension and conflict between the type of person I am now, compared to the type of person I am trying to become?" The spiritual path is a journey. There needs to be clarity about what motivates you and the choices that you need to make. Once those decisions have been made, there needs to be a clear intention to carry those ideals into practice, and it shouldn't be dogmatic energy – because it is all about self-transformation, and why be hard on the way you are right now? So it isn't that you have found the answer, and that you can define it out there somewhere, it is that you are trying to become the answer and you are working on it inside here, in your body container. It needs to be a warm, soft and self-compassionate energy that fuels the spiritual search, and a real sense of transforming the blockages and hindrances within your self. WBF provides a method to be in grounded presence, so that the energy, the life force within feels contained and can be transformed and then directed. Then your spiritual search can become a journey because you have a forward-moving life energy that knows where it wants to take you. It is an intelligent energy that leads to a rich and mysterious connection with others and the larger life and consciousness that pervades the whole of the universe.

The paradox is that you can only progress spiritually and reach that deeper awareness of connection and joy, through acceptance and surrender to what IS, the reality of your situation right now. It is called raising your level of awareness of the present moment and being in the Now. Let go of all your efforting, let go of all your resentment and blaming others, let go of all your striving to make things better and you will feel the perfection of the present moment and the joy that lies permeated in everything, right now. And you can experience that joy within the container of your body. The writer and philosopher Eckhart Tolle has talked about this: *"Feel the energy of your inner body. Immediately mental noise slows down or ceases. Feel it in your hands, your feet, your abdomen, and your chest. Feel the life that you are, the life that animates the body. The body then becomes a doorway, so to speak, into a deeper sense of aliveness underneath the fluctuating emotions and underneath your thinking."* (Stillness Speaks). Eckhart Tolle knows what he is talking about; unfortunately he doesn't give a detailed methodology for how to get there. WBF is a detailed and exact method for connecting with the energy within the container of your body and being able to experience the wisdom that comes from that. Two things are important to enable you to feel your aliveness, your inner energy as a human being: the first, is to be able to sense your body as one whole connected container, and the second is to feel that you have energy in this container *and that it is safe to have energy*. Once you know how to use this technique and have confidence in it you can then apply this wisdom to transform your life experience in an embodied way.

This is the perennial philosophy, the ageless wisdom: that it is possible to raise your consciousness above the inevitable dualities of life, to stop trying to grasp only the good and reject the bad experiences in life, to accept everything just as it is without trying to hold onto only the enjoyable and to fight, fix, or to run away from all the painful suffering in life. It is what it is, and not what you would want it to be. But, of course, the thing that hooks you into attachment is your desires, and the delusion that when you finally get what you want you will be happy. Of course, you may get it for a while and be happy, but you will also lose it again, and when you can't get what you want you suffer. So you need a tool like WBF that can help you to detach yourself from your experience, to step back a little bit, and just watch all these desires and the alternating play of gain and loss that is an inevitable part of life, from a place of safety in grounded presence.

Of course when you first start watching what is going on inside, it is so intense, because you really do want it and need it all, the desire is so strong, e.g. for a relationship with that person, or to live in a house in that location, or to drive that type of car. As the Buddha said "the root of all suffering is desire", but WBF is a technique for getting to a place where part of you may want it, and part of you may need it, but the container of the self is in grounded presence and feeling safe and supported. So then the desire can be transformed into something different, maybe there is a deeper need underneath that desire that comes to light, so its OK to let go of that first desire and then surprisingly you are just balanced in the middle and it doesn't matter either way. Yes, it would be enjoyable to have that, and also not to have it would be OK, and the only reason why you can say that and mean it, is because you are actually feeling intensely joyous right now, and deeply grounded in your body, but also broadening out to connect with your wider environment. So you are not caught in incessant thinking and planning in your head, or tortuous, convoluted emotions. You can just feel clear, balanced, open and joyous right now, free of the manipulations of your desire nature and you do not need to plan and work to get your happiness in the future.

But you cannot get to that state immediately, you need to train it by becoming more aware of your daily life situation and your reactions to all of that is happening. The field of personal relationships is an especially rich area to work on. Constant awareness is needed, and not just awareness but a grounded, wholebody awareness that includes everything that is going on inside your body container and in the space in between. You will discover that as well as the good things that you can be grateful for there is also a lot of frustration, anger and suffering. But if you can just contain it all and observe it from a detached perspective that experience will change. Your relationships in life will be transformed by the practice of WBF. As you change, your relationships will change, they cannot remain the same. The value of WBF lies in being able to calmly view your life's experiences from the position of the detached observer. You will be able to transform all your expectations and experiences in relationships. The benefits are clear; it stops the manipulations, the disappointed expectations, the jealousy and possessiveness and replaces that with honest communication from a place of strength and independence. WBF provides a technique with which it is possible to train the awareness. As Eckhart Tolle has said: *"Become an alchemist. Transmute base metal into gold, suffering into consciousness…you are just one step away from something incredible: a complete alchemical transmutation of the base metal of pain and suffering into gold"* (Eckhart Tolle, "The Power of Now").

The joy of this is that you cannot actually make any mistakes. Yes, you can say the wrong thing sometimes, or make wrong decisions and yes there can be suffering as a consequence of those wrong decisions, but if you keep holding all of that, the whole thing, in conscious awareness, just watch and it will then transform itself into a felt shift and a positive realization will flow from that, its wonderful. Ultimately it is all for the good and it is possible to reach a realization of real peace, joy and calmness that underlies all problems and all the duality of all life's experiences. This is the perennial wisdom, that there is a real happiness and joy that lies deep within each person, under the outer coverings of personality, profession and relationships. There is that potential for love, peace and joy within each person, and recognizing that within myself and within others I can call all men brothers and all women sisters, and work for the good of all humanity to build a better world.

Chapter 12.
WBF and Therapy

One of the main aims of good therapy, and something that seems to occur naturally during the course of a WBF session, is the realization of self-responsibility that naturally occurs during the course of a session. As I pay attention to what is happening within the container of my whole body, noticing all the thoughts, feelings and somatic sensations that arise, gradually all the different parts of the drama seem to clarify themselves and the sense of the detached observer with a new perspective gradually emerges. The realization is clear: I cannot control people or stop things happening to me in my life, but it is my reaction to them that causes me to feel joy or sorrow, or any other emotions. If I can take responsibility for my part of the situation, that is the bit that I can actually influence, and a sense of empowerment naturally arises. Self-responsibility leads to self-empowerment.

You may start off a WBF session by blaming another person for what they have said or done that made you feel bad, maybe not even what they said but *how* they said it, and how annoyed you felt. This has triggered murky, unconscious aspects of yourself, but there is no clarity about whose stuff it is or isn't and what's going on at a deeper level. So it is an easy option to start shifting into the blame game. "I'm feeling bad and it's because he/she said this and acted in that way". Then you are reacting to something you see in the other person (which may or may not really be there) then of course the other person reacts back to what was said and your tone of voice and pretty soon everything starts to got mixed up and it escalates. There is no space, no clarity and it is impossible to shift into the position of the detached observer because there is a total merging with the part that feels angry, misunderstood, or talked down to.

This is all stuff from the past, childhood wounding that needs to be worked through before you can start to see the truth clearly. Everyone has survival strategies from the past that helped him or her to deal with life. These first need to be recognized and honored for having helped the survival of the child in a difficult and dangerous world and then they can be transformed into something different. Then there can be relationships without any projections and games and a clear seeing of the reality of what is really happening right now. All the games that people play are no longer necessary when you reach a certain level of development clarity. The intimidator, who can explode or get angry at the slightest provocation, the interrogator, who is always asking awkward questions, the aloof mysterious one, who plays hard to get, the manipulator who never speaks clearly but lets you feel how angry they are with you and the victim, who says "oh, poor me" and feels that life is too difficult and other people are too powerful to cope with. These are some of the many different types of games that people play and there can be lots of variations as we all our carry our different family dramas. But there is only one way for me to go inside and take responsibility for my life situation and for my reactions and that involves focusing on myself, and trying to change the only part of the universe that I can be responsible for – which is myself and my actions – whilst letting other people be themselves and change in their own time.

The Focusing process is inviting me to go into my present experience within the container of my body, and the listener is trained to facilitate that. As I focus on myself and my inner experience I gradually begin to lose interest in the other person involved in the drama and I start to get more curious about myself and my reactions. Why did I feel quite so upset when she said that? That was such a big emotional reaction for such a small comment wasn't it? What am I getting so triggered about? Why am I feeling so angry/afraid/ powerless about this whole thing? As my curiosity awakens I begin to explore what that "whole thing" feels like in my body and start to discover what is behind all of this…it feels mysterious, exciting and empowering – because I can change this part, its a part of me.

This is where going into grounded presence can be essential. First, there needs to be some swaying and grounding, feeling the support and safety of Mother Earth. This allows the hyper-arousal of the sympathetic nervous system to decrease and the parasympathetic nervous system to increase as I actually start to become aware of more of my body. I am feeling supported by something much bigger than myself – by the whole of planet Earth and that gives a sense of groundedness, safety and calmness.

Then I can explore whatever the blockage or the vulnerability is. This is the core WBF process that has been described earlier in the book. There will certainly be the wounded or the vulnerable part, but there may well be other parts that are coming into conflict with it. A conflict will involve two or more parts that may cancel each other out, or the person may switch from one to the other as they each become temporarily dominant, but they both need space to be just the way that they are and to be understood. Only when all the parts have been understood and integrated can the blocked energy get transformed into a positive, forward moving life energy. I start to feel empowered in my whole body, feeling strong and supported in my feet, with a sense of aliveness and optimism in my head. I have insight, it feels good, I feel motivated to change the parts in me that I can change – don't worry about anyone else, let them be the way that they are and make the decisions that they need to make. I'm ready to make the decisions that are right for me and to move forwards in my life. There is a wonderful positivity in WBF and it is essential to be positive in the spiritual life. We all have a choice where we want to be on the positivity spectrum. Don't just focus on the negative things that have happened in your life, focus on the positive things that have happened instead, connect with your forward moving life energy and use that as a basis for performing more positive actions and achieving more positive goals.

Feeling safely grounded in your sense of self, feeling good about yourself and positive about the world - this is so fundamentally different that it's hard to put into words. There is a different neural circuit here because this safe, supportive sense of self involves the default state network (DSN) being activated, the Mohawk of self-awareness, where there is a comfortable awareness of being connected with your whole body.

However, now we get to the interesting bit, what neural circuits are activated when you feel safe to be in your own body and are aware of your own experience? This is the so-called mohawk of self awareness. This circuit of Self awareness, which runs through the midline structures of the brain, starting above the eyes at the prefrontal medial cortex (our thinking, planning and decision-making part), linking with the insula – which transmits messages from the viscera to the emotional centres, the parietal lobes which register and integrate sensory information from the body, the anterior cingulate which coordinate emotions and thinking and the posterior cingulate, which is necessary for our basic orientation in space. All of these need to be activated and are laying the foundations for our consciousness of Self. This default state network (DSN) shows almost no activation in clients who have suffered early life trauma.

Now, the interesting bit is that these same midline structures of self-awareness are activated by a secure attachment to parents in childhood, an empathic and safe relationship in later life (either with a partner or with a therapist) or the ability to come into a safe and non-judgmental relationship with self, through a wholebody awareness of our experience - which is focusing. So looked at in terms of science and brain function this is the essential thing that needs to happen, and anything that can help to activate the mohawk of self-awareness is wonderful and worthy of our respect. I would say that the essential function of WBF is to reactivate these midline structures of the brain.

Then you can stop focusing on others, stop the struggle for attention as a way of drawing energy to yourself, stop the continuous struggle for power and security in a world where there seems to be scarcity and not enough resources to go around, stop the competitive urges that drive all the power and control dramas. When you are really empowered and live in your own energy field in this way its not that you just have more energy and more sense of creativity and initiative – it is a fundamental shift towards feeling that the world is full of sunshine, a more abundant and generous place.

WBF has all sorts of implications in psychotherapy, which can really be understood as a way of reworking the autobiographical story of your life so that it has a different ending. When I worked with Client "X", it was clear that he needed to work with his childhood issues, because he felt disempowered as a result of what he experienced then. WBF gave him the opportunity to work from a sense of grounded presence, the adult man that is fully present here in the room, energised and standing up for himself, but he also needed to be aware of the wounded part, his inner child that was mistreated by his mother many years ago. There was a definite sense of insecurity and abandonment. But instead of just getting sucked into feelings of powerlessness, abandonment and desperation for a relationship to fill the void, it was important to remain the detached observer that could hold both: the sense of the wounded child and the sense of the whole, in grounded presence. And both were alive and present in the room, energetically connected, even though his childhood happened a long time ago. The two-pointing connection was present, so a process of change and transformation could take place.

The important thing of course is not to try and fight it, or fix it or run away from it, but to just stay with it in awareness. So he stayed with the felt sensing and he visualised his little boy:

T: *What doe your little boy look like, can you see his expression and his body posture?*
C: *He seems like a bright boy, but sad and half asleep.*
T: *Let him be like that, just the way that he is, but you stay energetically connected to him and see what happens.*
(Long pause…………)
C: *He's getting up, he doesn't want to lie around any more doing nothing, waiting for someone else to make it better. He wants to make it better himself, he's got energy now, he wants to do something now, rather than wait for this new woman who is going to make it all perfect…*
T: *He's got energy now and he wants to use it…*
C: *Not quite, it's more like - He's got energy now and <u>he's not afraid to use it</u>!*

T: *He's got energy now and <u>he's not afraid to use it</u>!*
C: *Yes he does and that feels good. I can see it and I can feel it.*

In a later session we began using WBF, working with an energetic connection with different generations in his family. Working specifically with the relationship with his father and the men in his family.

T: *What sort of role model did your father provide for you?*
C: *He didn't, I never felt any forceful presence, deep communication, or sense of connection. I never saw him stand up to my mum. It was always "yes dear, yes dear". He would give in and let her have her own way all of the time.*
T: *So how do you visualise him?*
C: *A man without substance, a man without an opinion, a shadow of a man. He looks anxious, blinking rapidly, trying to please.*
T: *Let him be like that, just the way that he is, but you stay energetically connected to him and see what happens.*
(Long pause...)
C; *His chest is filling out, he's breathing more deeply, I can see him doing jumps on his ice skates in the ice ring, he's being brave and showing off...*
T: *So he has the qualities of being brave and showing off?*
C: *Yes brave and it seems like showing off, but it's actually more a quality of intense focus and staying deeply connected to himself that enables him to do extraordinary things.*

The key to the WBF process of self transformation and getting more empowered is when we can respectfully listen to all of these different parts of a system and make space for them to be there just as they are. If two parts are in conflict and neutralizing each other, the blockage can be held "in equal positive regard", and a forward moving life energy can be released. But what seems to be important is firstly: the sense of being in grounded presence and supported by something much bigger, the sense of the whole. Secondly, allowing all of the different parts to be there without suppression or rejection. Thirdly, working at the edge of what feels important right now, where the energy is moving forwards, not some intellectual concept of how things ought to be. Finally there is the awareness of how all of these different parts are energetically connected in the larger scheme of things, in the awareness of larger self. The key thing is that this awareness can "hold" of these differing elements in the field and yet trust that the ego does not need to control, fix or direct things, because it connects with an intelligence and an organisational energy at work that is capable of giving meaning to every situation. So you need to trust the process, the flow of energy within the safe container of the body. So this is where WBA becomes such a crucial skill, that refines and teaches the energetic sensitivity to what is going on within the self, within groups and larger communities, and even at a planetary level and beyond. From this wholebody awareness, there can then be genuine, empathic, embodied communication.

You can learn to go with the flow, live in the flow, cultivating an attitude of trust towards the inner body wisdom and the energy that is taking you forwards in life. WBF postulates that it isn't helpful to try and fight our issues, or fix it, or run away from it. Its OK not to know the answer immediately, in fact it is essential, as you hold in awareness both the mass of your physical body, and the energy that flows in it and around the container of the body. Eventually I am able to hold both and then I can feel that my consciousness clicks into something different. This is clearly postulated in Quantum mechanics, that a quanta can be either a particle or a waveform if I am trying to measure it with my cognitive mind. But through the higher human faculty of pure awareness *I am capable of holding both at the same time.* This is what allows something different to happen, a quantum leap into a new pattern of manifestation, but it needs the space of pure awareness and the "not knowing" for this to occur. So take the time to hold both and to be with the contradiction, to allow what seemed to be a problem to be there, to have the space to become fully embodied, fully present, just as it is and without any labels or expectations of the cognitive mind. This allows energetic connections to occur and change to happen by itself, which is one of the fundamental laws of Quantum mechanics, that the greater the mass the less the energy, so as you get more grounded and really feel the physical weight of your body and its connection with gravity right now in this moment, so time slows down and you begin to feel less trapped, less stuck in the old pattern. Whatever you were doing before wasn't really working because there was just too much struggle and too much restless energy. The more physically grounded you are, the more accepting you are and the less stuck you feel. You open up to the infinite number of new possibilities that were always available to you, and it is the start of the WBF process of change and transformation.

One of the most debilitating effects of stress and trauma in the early life history is a sense of loss of Self. I am using the word 'Self' in the most complete sense of the word, to encompass the body, mind, emotions and soul. Underlying this loss of 'Self' at its most basic level is a sense of the loss of awareness of the body. There is a term for this; it is called "Alexithymia" which is Greek for not having any words for your feelings. People will look furious but deny that they are angry, or they will appear to be sad and upset but insist that everything in fine, deceiving themselves first and then trying to deceive the world as well. But it doesn't work, its just a confused mess and other people pick up these mixed signals. Many traumatised adults and children cannot know what they are feeling because they are so out of touch with their physical sensations – which are the basis of emotions. So as a result they are not able to handle stress or even minor frustration. They will either space out and become very passive, or else explode with rage. There is no balanced response to the reality of the present emotional situation.

There is a reason for this, as it is a survival mechanism that was brought into play in order to survive emotionally devastating childhood experiences. The research has shown that repeated emotional abuse and neglect can be just as bad in its consequences as physical abuse or even sexual molestation. It is the impact of not being seen, of not being truly heard and having no one to turn to that is difficult at any age, but particularly destructive for young children who are still trying to work out who they are and what they stand for in the world. As a consequence of having their reality repeatedly denied or negated, children in this situation will resort to cutting off from their emotions, which means cutting off from their bodily sensations – particularly in those areas of their bodies where the emotions are most intensely present.

As one client of mine said: *" when I was a small boy at home all hell could break lose at any time. Mum and dad were constantly fighting, and then mum would get dad to beat us kids for the slightest misbehavior. Mostly it wasn't even true – it wasn't us who were misbehaving, it was her ! But we didn't dare to tell dad about what she was getting up to, because he wouldn't have believed us and we would have just got beaten even more. So I learnt to stay quiet and not draw attention to myself. Now I just feel this constant confusion and tension in my head and throat, and I feel cut off from my body from the neck downwards."* Which isn't surprising as this young boy had no one to turn to and nowhere to go during a very difficult and volatile childhood. Much of his therapy involved using Alexander Technique in order to get him to regain awareness of his physical sensations and to re-inhabit his body in order to feel safe to have energy and to express himself.

Of course this is no surprise to the Alexander world as AT teachers have long been aware that the majority of their students suffer from "faulty sensory appreciation". In trying to reeducate the posture and procedural memory in such seemingly simple movements like, standing and sitting, walking, running, lifting and carrying, etc., a lot of time and effort needs to be spent in just being aware of how the body is balanced in relationship to gravity and how the different parts can move and integrate in some very simple and basic movement patterns. What feels right may well be wrong, and what feels wrong may well be right, as a student learns to move out of their comfort zones and into an easier, more flowing and more integrated movement pattern. A re-awakened sense of balance and making simple movements, very slowly and consciously is an important part of this process of getting back into relationship with the body. The student also learns how to change procedural memory by visualising movement patterns in advance and repeating the new pattern whilst keeping the interior bodily spaces open and accessible through the use of mental 'directions' - which are connecting lines of thought maintained in awareness within the body. (Refer back to this in the section on A.T., Chap. 3).

Cutting off from the body is more extreme in cases involving trauma, PTSD, and Dissociation/Multiple Personality Disorder, but all of these diagnostic labels are pretty meaningless, because as F. M. Alexander discovered more than 100 years ago, we are all somewhere along that spectrum of not being fully aware of and in contact with our bodies during the course of our daily activities. Alexander McFarlane, the well-known neuroscientist in Australia, has done some similar research with a sample group of people suffering from PTSD when asking the simple question – how do we know what we are holding in the palm of our hands when we are not looking at it? He would put things like a car key, a coin, or a can opener into their hands and the surprising result was that many people suffering from PTSD could not guess what the object was because their sensory perceptions were not well coordinated enough. The different sensory experiences of weight, shape, temperature and position are each transmitted to a different part of the brain, but this group could not put all the pieces together into a single perception, whereas the control group could. (*A. C. McFarlane, "The Long Term Costs of Traumatic Stress: Intertwined Physical and Psychological Consequences." World Psychiatry 9, No 1, 2010; 3-10*).

The essential question is not to gather enough symptoms to be able to pin a diagnosis on someone but to see what tools are available to move further along the spectrum to where you want to be, so that you can function in a truly connected, empowered and fully aware state. Using the A.T. is one such tool and I regularly bring it into my therapeutic work. The key thing about the A.T. is that it integrates sensory experience, so that instead of having the feeling that your body is composed of many different areas of physical tension, some of which are out of full awareness and others of which are working against each other; you can move towards an experience of free-flowing integration where all of these parts are now linked up and working towards a common purpose. When you give 'mental directions' it has two functions, firstly the mind is occupied with repeating a positive affirmation and is less likely to get into its habitual negative loops. Secondly, it opens up and integrates the interior spaces of the body, so that there is time and space to experience what is happening. The body as a container is brought into awareness and this is an essential therapeutic tool, because now it is possible to feel physical sensations more clearly and to be aware of the emotions that are connected to them. The pieces start to fit together and the picture becomes clearer.

Having worked for more than 25 years as an Alexander Technique teacher I know how effective giving directions can be in terms of calming down arousal and opening up the awareness of the inner body container. As well as asking the client to visualize and repeat the directions:

"Allow the neck to be free
And allow the jaw to release forwards to the tip of the chin
So that the head could tip forwards and upwards
On top of the spinal column (if it wanted to)
To allow the back to lengthen all the way from the top of the head
to the base of the spine, (or the feet if standing)
To allow the back to lengthen and widen"

I also ask my clients to visualize their upper torso as a barrel that has a depth and a volume to it, so they add the directions:

"To allow my stomach to relax,
And my gut to expand into the bowl of the pelvis,
To allow space for my heart & lungs in the cavity of my rib cage,
And to allow ease and flow as my rib cage gently expands sideways as well as forwards as I inhale,

And gently contracts inwards and downwards as I exhale."

There are many benefits to adding these extra directions as it encourages a greater depth to the visualization, as well as length and width in the awareness of the body container. If you repeat this long enough in the correct manner you can really start to feel that your upper torso feels like a big barrel with enough space to feel whatever is happening for you right now. Whatever needs attention right now, all the physical sensations, all the emotions, everything that you might need or want to do right now, impulses that could lead to words, or gestures or movements – if they are not inhibited and held in check by some other impulses from the neo-cortex or some other critical voices from inside, or outside. The body needs to act as a container for all of these in order so that they can either lead to some sort of action and fulfillment, or be held in pure awareness and transformed into something different. But there has to be space for all of this to occur within the container, otherwise we lose our vitally important experience of Self.

The brilliant neurologist Antonio Demasio has mapped out the relationship between body states, emotions and survival in a series of articles and books. He argues that the core of our self-awareness is founded on the physical sensations that convey the inner states of the body:

Primordial feelings provide a direct experience of one's own living body, wordless, unadorned, and connected to nothing but sheer existence. These primordial feelings reflect the current state of the body along varied dimensions…along the scale that ranges from pleasure to pain, and they originate at the level of the brain stem rather than the cerebral cortex. All feelings of emotions are complex musical variations on primordial feelings." (Antonio Demasio: *"Self Comes to Mind: Constructing the conscious Brain",* Random House, 2012).

The job of the brain is to constantly monitor and re-evaluate what is going on in and around us. Normally, of course, we leave it to the subcortical regions of the brain to smoothly regulate what is happening to our breathing, heartbeat, digestion, hormone secretion and immune system, whilst the neocortex gets on with the "important business" of planning our day, earning a living and enjoying our relationships. That's if you are not stressed out or traumatised. When you are, and your body feels that it is under some sort of immanent threat these systems become overwhelmed and a wide variety of physical problems occur.

Antonio Damasio and his colleagues published a brilliant piece of research in 2000 that showed how reliving a strong negative emotion connected to an incident in past causes significant changes in the brain areas that receive nerve signals from the muscles, gut and skin – areas that are crucial for regulating basic bodily function. The brain scans showed how recalling an emotional event from the past actually causes us to re-experience the visceral sensations felt during the original experience. They had precise scans showing, e.g., how a particular part of the brain stem was "active in sadness and anger, but not in happiness or fear" (Antonio *Demasio et al., "Subcortical and Cortical Brain Activity During the Feeling of Self-Generated Emotions." Nature Neuroscience 3, vol. 10, 2000*).

All of these regions are below the limbic system, which is the so-called area of the emotional brain, but when there is a real sense of threat, with great fear or panic and we feel threatened then these areas of the brain stem are activated accompanied by intense physiological arousal. This research proved how emotions and physical sensations are inextricably linked, but we have always had it in the language, in phrases like "you make me feel sick", "my skin froze", "I couldn't say a word, something was stuck in my throat", "my heart sank". The amazing thing about this research showed how just recalling an event from the past triggered off that whole cycle of physical sensations as well as the emotions. So it shows how people who are reliving a trauma feel as if it is happening now. They relive the sense of fear or blind rage as if they are in immediate danger and stuck in a fight for survival. But even at lesser levels of stress or intense frustration the same thing is happening, people get triggered and the experience is as if it is happening now.

This then causes a big existential problem because it feels unsafe to be in your body now. Reliving negative events from the past means that it starts to feel very uncomfortable, or even unsafe to be in your body. The past is alive in the physical sensations now, being bombarded by visceral warning signals, and in an attempt to survive this process many people become expert in ignoring their gut feelings and cutting off from their bodies. The more they try to ignore them and push them away, the stronger the signals become and the more they feel confused or ashamed, or panic. The body is no longer acting as a container where they can comfortably notice what is going on, and then bring it into awareness and decide on the right course of action. Instead something else happens, they either shut down or go into a panic.

The devastating thing about panic is that it feeds off itself. The individual can feel the situation coming on and then develops a fear of the physical sensations associated with going down that particular pathway. I work a lot with clients suffering from insomnia. The sleep disturbance is actually a symptom of some other stress or deeper trauma in their lives that needs to be resolved, through dialogue, or therapy or learning the Focusing process. But many people do not have these skills and want to ignore, rather than face the issues and resolve them. Many report a similar story, of going to bed and wanting to fall asleep, needing desperately to get enough hours sleep so that they can function efficiently in their jobs the next day. However their minds are awake, the thoughts are whirling and sleep does not come. The muscles are tensed, the heart rate and the breathing are too fast and the body cannot feel comfortable or relaxed. And then in the back of the mind the panic starts: "what if I cannot get to sleep tonight, I'll be so tired in the morning and unable to concentrate properly. That job gets so hard when I'm tired and I have so much to get through". That thought alone tends to raise the anxiety levels…then after a while they check their body & mind: "Am I feeling heavy and comfortable, is my breath slowing down, is my mind calming down?" The answer is no and the conclusion is "I'm never going to fall asleep, I'm so annoyed, I feel trapped and in a total panic". The fears of the bodily sensations themselves have now escalated into a total emergency situation.

WBF is a perfect tool for breaking out of this cycle of fear stimulation and arousal. In this case my client ends up getting highly aroused and fearful just at the mere thought of trying to get to sleep. The physical sensations themselves trigger off another twist in the spiral of fear, so two things are required. (1) The mind needs to get into a neutral, observing state, where it does not mind either way what is happening right now, or what the future outcome will be. This is engaging the medial prefrontal cortex in a state of mindful awareness of the whole situation, *without any pressing agenda,* so that some top-down integration of the brain structures can take place. But this will not take place as long as the fear reaction is still being triggered by the out of control bodily sensations. As we know, there is no direct link from the neocortex to the amygdala and the emotional brain. So whilst step (1) is necessary, in order to help it, the required preliminary is actually step (2). There needs to be some bottom-up integration and calming that takes place through paying attention to the soles of the feet grounding into the Earth, some swaying movements as the centre of gravity shifts position and the breathing calms down and the creation of space in a large body container, large enough to contain all of the different physical tension patterns. Then the bodily sensations can be observed just as they are, without an agenda and the process of transformation can begin to take place.

Lucy is a client of mine in London, and this is what I taught her to do. She was suffering from insomnia and all the emotions of feeling out of control and the frustration of not being able to get to sleep when she desperately needed to. She learnt bottom-up integration of the brain through the swaying movement, awareness of balance and breath, and then went into just observing what was happening in a detached manner, going into the Focusing process in order to allow a transformation to take place. At no point was there any talk of "just calm down, you are behaving in an irrational manner, get a grip on yourself, stop panicking and look at the situation rationally, you need to go to sleep"...because *there are no brain circuits to allow that* and it does not work.

So, after about 10 mins swaying (fostering bottom-up integration) when the tension felt a bit more relaxed and the breath had calmed down quite a bit, then I could ask:
(T) "How does your body react when I mention the word **SLEEP?**"
After a pause she replied

(C) "Oh, there is this area of tension around my heart centre, it's like a constriction of fear".

(T) "OK, just let it be there, give it even more space to be there and tell us about itself".

(C) "The fear says – no matter what I do or don't do I will never be able to get to sleep".

(T) "No matter what you do you will never be able to get to sleep?"

(C) "Yes, that fits it, that's the fear".

(T) "So now I suggest that you just hold both at the same time, the awareness of your feet on the ground, and the awareness of this constriction of fear around the heart centre, and also be aware of the connecting space in between. Lets see what happens, this could take a few minutes".

We both wait in silence, in sustained awareness, allowing the process to unfold. Then I can feel something shift in my heart centre, so I know that something has shifted for her as well.

(T) "Something has shifted for you, hasn't it?"

(C) "Yes how did you know that it shifted exactly then?"

(T) "I felt it, because when we get into this WBF relationship we are energetically linked. It could be mirror neurons being activated, or it could be an energetic connection at a quantum level. It doesn't really matter, but what is important is what feels different now?"

(C) " The fear has released, my body feels heavier, my breathing is calmer and I feel very tired, I feel sleepy. I think I want to go to bed now and sleep."

(T) "OK, why don't you do that?"

So she went to bed and actually had a very good night's sleep. She texted me the next morning: "Slept brilliantly, that was wonderful, thanks!"

So you can see how powerful WBF can be in a situation like this, when the has been severe arousal of the nervous system – just at the wrong moment like when Lucy was trying to get to sleep. However, of course I suspected that there was also another deeper issue, underneath the arousal and the insomnia and after a couple of weeks we got to work with it.

One session, Lucy started to talk about the stress and unpredictability of life, which worried her.
(C) "My friend set up her own business with her husband, they are both advertising consultants and have been running their own business for the past 10 years.
(T) "Yes"
(C) "She was telling me about it. Its just been a constant stress, never a moment to relax, just running all the time. That's been my dream, and now look at the reality. I might need to reconsider my aims in life".
(T) "How did you feel listening to her talking?"
(C) "I felt stressed and unsettled just listening to her".
(T) " Where do you feel that in the body?"
Pause while she checks inside.
(C) " OK, I feel it in the heart, it feels like water and it might spread everywhere".
(T) " You feel it in the heart, it feels like water and it might spread everywhere".
(C) "Yes, that's right".
(T) "That's your image. Now do you have a word, or a phrase or an emotion that might fit it?"
(C) "Its a feeling of unpredictability, its all about the unpredictability of Life…and its scary".
(T) "So it's a feeling of unpredictability, it's all about the uncertainty of Life…and its scary".
(C) "Yes".

(She sighs deeply).

So she had the felt sense of the situation, and now we needed to move into the felt shift. I asked her to simply hold both the feeling of water in her heart that might spread everywhere, and the feeling of her feet being on the ground and supporting her and to be aware of the space in between that was connecting these two points.

(T) "Just hold both and see what happens".

There was a long pause.

(C) " I can feel something different happening in my heart. Its a subtle shift and hard to put into words. My head feels clearer; my feet are firmly on the ground.... *I feel supported*".

(T) "So we started off this session talking about stress and uncertainty and now at the close you can say *I feel supported!"*

(C) "Yes, that's right, *I feel supported!"*.

That was a significant shift and a door has opened, but there is still more work to be done, in terms of shifting the belief patterns in the sub-conscious mind that are to do with the stress and uncertainty of Life. That work can continue using the WBF tool, which is a way of using increased body awareness as a way in - gradually accessing the murky areas of the sub-conscious mind that have been out of awareness but also powerfully influencing the conscious mind and day-to-day decisions. The signals have been cut off and the circuits are dead. You have to have all the information first in order to be aware of what's happening and in order to be able to make congruent, conscious decisions.

It is easy to see why people lose touch with themselves. We are living in a left-brain, cognitive, materialistic, scientific culture. Success is defined in terms of how much money you are earning, the location of your house, what sort of car you drive and where you go for your holidays. Its all about what is happening out there and "getting it right" and not at all about what is happening inside the container of your Self, the reality of how you are feeling right now, and what sort of process you are going through. By giving up the desire to "make it happen" out there and by paying more attention inside your Self, paradoxically you allow success, happiness and fulfillment to come to you, in the most perfect of ways, rather than chasing after some illusory happiness out there, all of the time.

This whole process was illustrated by some very interesting research that was done in 2004 by Ruth Lanius in Canada on trauma survivors. She was studying what happens in the brain of trauma survivors when they are not thinking about the past. This is the "default state network" (DSN) that the brain goes back to when you are idling and not engaged with anything in particular. This research opened up new insights into how trauma affects self-awareness and specifically sensory self-awareness. She first got 16 "normal" Canadians to lie in a brain scanner, as a control group, and asked them to just relax their minds as much as possible, think of nothing in particular and just focus on their breathing. This activated a default state linking of particular brain areas, (DSN) which together will work to create your sense of self.

This activates the midline structures of the brain that some scientists, like Bessel van der Kolk, like to call the Mohawk of self-awareness, starting above the eyes at the medial prefrontal cortex, which we know is important as the watchtower, and running through the centre of the brain all the way to the back of the brain at the posterior cingulate, which give us a physical sense of where we are in terms of physical presence – our internal GPS. This sense of our interior physical space is hugely important, not just in WBF therapy but also in developing our sense of exterior spatial awareness, which makes sense that the two would be linked, and it is also linked to learning, motivation and memory. So that is really interesting isn't it? If you cannot maintain a sense of your body as a container that gives you as sense of being a person taking your rightful place on the planet, filled with your energy and maintaining a motivation that is linked to a sense of some sort of future reward, - if you cannot maintain your sense of Self in this way then learning, motivation and memory will all suffer.

So this circuit of self-awareness runs through the midline structures of the brain, linking with the insula – which transmits messages from the viscera to the emotional centres, the parietal lobes, which register and integrate sensory information from the body and the anterior cingulate which coordinate emotions and thinking. All of this is laying the foundations for our consciousness of Self.

There was a huge contrast with the brain scans of the group who had suffered early life trauma, as there was almost no activation of the self-sensing areas of the brain. The MPFC, the anterior cingulate, the parietal cortex and the insula did not show any activation at all. The only area that lit up slightly on the scans was the posterior cingulate – which is necessary for our basic orientation in space.

" In response to the trauma itself, and in coping with the dread that persisted long afterward, these patients had learned to shut down the brain areas that transmit the visceral feelings, and emotions that accompany and define terror. Yet in everyday life, those same brain areas are responsible for registering the entire range of emotions and sensations that form the foundation of our self-awareness, our sense of whom we are. What we witnessed here was a tragic adaptation: In an

effort to shut off terrifying sensations, they also deadened their capacity to feel fully alive". (Bessel van der Kolk: *"The Body keeps the Score"*, Allan Lane, 20140

This loss of contact with Self also has huge implications for a person's capacity to maintain a sense of purpose and direction. Once the medial prefrontal cortex has shut down it is really hard to make decisions and to plan and follow through with appropriate action. When you lose contact with the areas of the brain that are to do with inner self-sensing (the Mohawk of self-awareness) you lose contact with your inner body container and what's happening in there, so you lose contact with your Self, your truth, your inner reality. How can you know what you want and plan for it, and be motivated to get it, if you are out of touch with your physical sensations? These physical sensations are the basis of all emotions, and they are trying to tell you something. Focusing and Wholebody Awareness is a vital tool in helping you to feel more present, to know where your physical body container is and what is going on inside through the awareness of Self.

The consequences of being cut off from your body and of not knowing what is happening means that you are unable to relate to your environment and to regulate your Self. If you cannot read the body's messages you are *"unable to detect what is truly dangerous or harmful for you and, just as bad, what is safe or nourishing. Self-regulation depends on having a friendly relationship with your body. Without it you have to rely on external regulation – from medication, drugs like alcohol, constant reassurance, or compulsive compliance with the wishes of others".* (Bessel van der Kolk: *"The Body keeps the Score"*, Allan Lane, 20140

What Bessel van der Kolk has found in his trauma patients is so true and I have found exactly that same pattern in many of my clients as well and it is so sad. Life loses its freshness and its sparkle, the sense of adventure goes, the sense of trusting yourself as you go forward to discover new relationships, new interests, new aspects of your life and your work that fascinate and motivate you, all of that sense of having energy and trusting your Self as you move forwards in your life – that goes missing, and it is priceless. Because without that, I tell you, it doesn't matter how many houses or cars you have, or how much money in the bank – life is dead, uninteresting and full of fears and threats lurking around every corner.

It is not just the people who could be diagnosed as suffering from developmental trauma or PTSD. They are at the extreme end of this spectrum of self-awareness, feeling almost totally cut-off from their bodies. But there are so many more people, especially in our present western culture and society with its worship of the cognitive mind and academic achievement, who are also suffering the effects of being pretty much cut off from their bodies and emotions. Look at the percentage levels of people on prescribed medication! , Look at the number of people who rely on alcohol or drugs of some kind, in order to relax their arousal levels at the end of a stressful day. If you drink as an occasional celebration that's fine, but if you need it every day in order to function or to feel relaxed – then something is wrong and you need to look at your life and find out what's missing. Look at the number of relationships which function with one person being the dominant partner and the other one going along with them making all the important decisions, because they don't know what they really want and even if they did they would find it very scary to stand their ground and to express their point of view to their partner. There just wouldn't be enough energy or grounded presence to do that.

So these findings have important implications not only for people who have endured early childhood trauma, or who may be suffering from the effects of a traumatic incident in later life, but also for the many people who learn to cut off from themselves as a result of a life of constant compliance, chronic stress or severe emotional disappointment. You do get old when you give up on life. All of the Cingulate areas have been shown to be significantly smaller in cases of Alzheimer's disease, and the implication is that this behavior pattern becomes a vicious circle, because the more cut-off from self-awareness you are the more your motivation, learning skills and memory deteriorate. Conversely, by learning skills that put you back in contact with your body and Self – activities like: Wholebody Awareness, yoga, Alexander Technique, Tai Chi, movement, dance, touch, singing in a choir, being aware of your breath in mindfulness meditation, - all of these and other similar activities would reverse the decline and enlarge activation in the anterior and posterior cingulate areas of the brain.

Client X: Final Session: The Healing

In one final session with my client X the healing was completed and this session illustrates the most essential points of WBF and how it heals by creating wholeness and integration within the person.

Client X started the session by doing the swaying exercise and getting into grounded presence.
X: *"I notice that I am on the cusp, at the balance point of being fully present in my body, noticing the energy and the*

aliveness and happy to be in my body whilst at the same time with a soft focus I am able to see the beauty of the environment all around me".

T: *"You are enjoying being fully present in your body whilst at the same time you are also able to see the beauty all around you".*

X: *"It feels like every cell in my body is vibrant and alive".*

"It also feels good to have achieved my goal for the day, despite difficulties I kept going and I won through by the end of the afternoon".

T: *"So it feels like you won today and that feels good".*

X: *"Yes, I didn't allow any obstacles to defeat me, I kept my sense of purpose, I kept my energy intact and I won".*

"It also feels good to rest now, to be peaceful and aware but to have energy at the same time. My body feels alive and even my poor old brain feels alive now as well!".

T: *"Your body feels alive and even your poor old brain feels alive now as well".*

Pause...

X: *"Now that's tinged with sadness because its bringing up memories of not feeling alive, of being with my Mum and how she made me feel "dead" inside, all of my energy drained away and I felt depressed. I think I carried her depression as well inside, I don't know how or why, but when I was with her, with just a look or a word or a glance and she could switch off my energy inside – without me even knowing how!"*

Pause....

"She had a way of triggering me and I could never figure out how or why. Its beyond the cognitive level, I just feel so emotionally overwhelmed when it happens. Other people can

do it too, it's like any time I feel disapproved of and "I don't even love you anymore" – like Mum did – That's it! That's what triggers me. It's the withdrawal of love, that silent or vocal disapproval, and then I crumple!

That's it, That's the trigger!!! It's that silent disapproval, that judgmental, negative energy and I just crumple up inside. I never saw that so clearly before. It's good to bring that into consciousness".

Pause....

"But I'm still feeling the powerlessness and a part of me feels that it will never go away and I want to fight it...but I don't know how to because I have no energy! ......So, I'm going to let that be there for a while and just be with it, letting it be there just the way it is without trying to change it".

T: "Would it feel OK for you to try and reconnect with your feet, **and...** to feel that sense of crumpling up inside and feeling powerless when other people disapprove of you? Could you try to hold both parts in equal positive regard at the same time and to see what happens?

X: "Yes I will try and hold both...

Pause....

Now it's starting to shift again and I'm feeling more complete. My arms and hands are starting to make this circular gesture".

T: "Yes I can see you making this large circle, starting with your hands at the top above your head and then going out to the sides and then meeting again at the bottom in front of your naval.

X; "Yes, its important to close the circle, to complete, like I completed my goal this afternoon and I now have a feeling of satisfaction, of self-agency. I feel happier and more energized from that".

T: "I want to feed back to you that it seems like you are getting bigger energetically and that your third eye is more activated".

X: "Yes, thank you for that, its true, I feel like I'm expanding into the room and taking up more space, I feel safer and bigger....
(Pause, as he enjoys the new way of being.)

That reminds me of my old survival strategy which was to make myself thinner and smaller and I was always desperately trying to fight my mum and to keep her out of my inner space, <u>but I never could keep her out!</u> She always managed to get inside of me and she somehow drained my energy and made me feel like shit so I ended up feeling so depressed....
Oh, I'm feeling it now, its like a cloak comes over me and I feel heavy, lethargic and depressed. I don't want to do anything and its like this negative - Oh what's the use of it all – type of thinking and I can feel all the energy draining out of my body right now as we talk about it.

T: "You always seem to be switching from one state into the other, so now I'm going to suggest that you get a sense of what each state feels like in your body, try to activate both in your body container somehow, and see if you can hold both states at the same time".

Pause of some minutes...

X: *"Now I am holding both at the same time, its like I can feel this rounded thing (makes the circular gesture) and I am also imagining and feeling that there is somebody else in the room who disapproves of me and doesn't love me at all.*

I'm holding both and its OK...So I can contain her negativity, she's entitled to her opinion, her disapproval and her lack of love. But I am bigger than all that and I can contain her, and just let her be that way and love her and it feels safe to do that...

Also I can have my own needs and my own agenda and achieve my own goals and that helps me to set and maintain my own boundaries. My needs are meeting somebody else's needs and that's the boundary line and its OK...

I can contain her in love and acceptance in my bigger self and be aware of my own needs at the same time...and I am not afraid of losing her if I express those needs.

T: *"So you can contain her in love and acceptance in your sense of your bigger self and still be aware of your own needs at the same time.*

X: *"Yes, my sense of my bigger self, and that is so different from my old survival strategy which was to make myself tall and thin, feeling uptight and making myself a smaller target for attack...*

This gesture helps me to feel the full, rounded, safe, secure expanded sense of my big body container".

T: *"It would be good to remember that gesture and to practice it at different times during the day".*

X: *"Yes that will help me to remember this session and what I learnt today.*

Chapter 13. Wholebody focusing and Neuroscience Research on Client X

I have always wished that I could see into the brain of a person who is having a Focusing session. I wanted to apply modern brain scanning technology to have a look at a person's brain before, during, and after a Focusing session. I know that Wholebody focusing is an empowering method for allowing the whole body to bring presence and healing to hurts and stoppages in body and emotional process. Having felt the profound shifts that take place in consciousness during Wholebody focusing (WBF) sessions, I really wanted to try and research this and capture this magic in scientific images of some sort and to understand the fundamental principles at work. Long term, I also wanted to see if permanent changes in personality and functioning can result from Wholebody focusing sessions and to prove this in a scientific way.

In WBF we start by inviting the body to function as a whole, and we emphasize the concept of the body as a container using "the power of awareness to awaken the inner wisdom of the living body". It is only when I feel grounded and connected to something bigger than myself that I can know who I really am. In a sense WBF is making explicit what is always implicit in the Focusing process: by observing the place that does not feel right within myself, I am also implying that there must be another part of myself that does feel right and it is the interconnection and support generated by these two parts that allows the transformation and shift to take place in the whole intelligent, living organism.

One hallmark of working with WBF and the sense of the whole body as a container is that I can often connect with a part of me that feels profoundly joyous – no matter what my outer situation might be – fairly early on in the session. Call it a sense of lightness, of joy, of "Beingness" – this is experienced in the whole of the organism and it is much bigger than, and can contain, the part of me that does not feel right. In regular Focusing this wonderful sense of release and happiness is most often experienced after the felt shift has taken place. I was wondering if this would show up in some way in the brain scans and in enhanced alpha or theta wave activity in the brain.

One of the things that has often struck me are the actual physical changes in the posture, alignment and structure of the body that take place during the course of a Wholebody focusing (WBF) session. These are linked to changes in energy levels, as the Focuser comes into a deeper contact with the Self. The Focuser's face can lighten up; a serene glow can come into the eyes, as there is a shift to a more integrated and relaxed state of being. There are also changes in the tone of voice, subtle changes of resonance, and shifts of intonation. Often the Wholebody Focuser will articulate a sense of being supported by the whole of Life rather than being alone and isolated in the world. There is a deepening of contact as both Focuser and listener become more grounded in Self. At times it seems as though you can catch a thought just the instant before the other person has articulated it.

With the advent of modern high-tech brain imaging technology, like MRI scans and SPEC scans, it is now possible to look at exactly what is happening inside the brain of a

Focuser and the changes that are induced there during the course of a session. What sorts of connection are being made? What parts of the brain are being stimulated? What sorts of brain wave patterns are being induced? For the first time, these precise images of what is happening inside the brain of the Focuser during a Focusing session are available for view by professionals and the general public alike.

Because we are trying to be scientific, we also need to be testing an underlying hypothesis. What is the crucial part of the whole Focusing process? What induces this transformation of consciousness? For me the crucial part of Focusing is the experience of the "felt sense" and the "felt shift" and what induces it is the neutral observing consciousness that is able to step back into the position of the detached observer. I was wondering what sort of brain imaging or brain scanning technology would be able to capture accurate images of the WBF process and help to explain in an objective way what is actually going on inside the brain of a Focuser during the crucial stages of "felt sensing" and also the "felt shift".

So the first thing was to try and record the patterns of neural firing that take place during a WBF session on a qEEG brain scanner, and the five sets of results were recorded, which showed both the type of brain wave activity and the areas of the brain that were activated.

I set up a series of specific experiments where I asked my subject:

> Be at rest, just allowing thoughts to come and go in a random manner.
> Direct awareness to two different parts of the body *simultaneously,* e.g., be aware of both the hands resting on the upper parts of the thigh and the soles

of the feet in contact with the ground, at the same time.

Pay attention to an auditory sound, e.g. birdsong outside the window, or random sounds from within the room or from the corridor outside – while maintaining a sense of the observing self by staying grounded within the totality of the whole Self.

Be aware of "what does not feel right" within the body, where it hurts or where there is tension.

Think of the area of tension and stay "in grounded presence" at the same time by being strongly aware of the soles of the feet contacting the floor *in a neutral observing manner.*

All of these patterns of neural firing were measured on an EEG scanner, and the five sets of results were recorded, which showed both the type of brain wave activity and the areas of the brain that were activated *during* a WBF session. I am only going to show the qEEG analysis that resulted from the 5th and most powerful exercise – staying in grounded presence and allowing the felt shift to take place.

In addition, I also took SPEC scans of my client, at rest before the WBF session (baseline scan) and immediately after one WBF session. As a result of this I got beautiful clear crisp images of brain surface SPEC scans and interior brain SPEC scans, and we could compare the before and after images to show the influence of the single WBF session. All these images can be viewed at the end of this chapter.

What are we really measuring? In this research, we had a sixteen-electrode EEG machine, which is a safe non-invasive procedure that measured the client's brain wave patterns and how they had changed relative to the first baseline scan. These EEGs were then converted into quantitative EEGs, (or qEEGs) which is a mathematical and statistical analysis of EEG activity that is depicted as a brain-map graphic. These colour gradations indicate how activity changed relative to baseline, and from what we know about the different types of brain wave activity, and where it is located, it is possible to gather objective information about the clients thoughts, feelings, emotions and behaviour.

For a start we can see how the client's brain function improved and moved from a less coherent (or less orderly) state to a more coherent state by the end of the WBF session. Of course when your brain works in a healthy, integrated way you work better and when your brain is more whole and balanced you feel more whole and balanced. The really significant result that shows up in theses qEEG scans is how the brain moves into alpha wave and high theta brain wave patterns, which means that the client was able to spend a lot of time in altered states of consciousness, and the change was taking place in the parietal lobe (which indicates more body awareness), in the occipital lobe (sight) and in the temporal lobe (emotional stability, understanding & use of language, long-term memory, reading faces, picking up on verbal intonation) which is where my client had suffered earlier brain damage and was having problems.

All of the exercises are not just WBF techniques, but they also encourage a state of "mindfulness" (to use a Buddhist term) and how our awareness can be directed to function in different ways, at different times. I can be aware of just one thing, e.g., I can be aware of just my feet contacting the ground as I sit here typing, or I can be aware of just the background sound of the washing machine spinning and I can easily get merged with it. My reactions start to kick in, like the machine distracts me, and it starts to annoy me, and I start to tighten in my upper chest and stomach muscles. *Or, I can choose to be aware of myself being aware,* and something different happens, I become non-resistant and my consciousness expands to include a sense of both my whole self as an embodied being and the sound of the machine in the background and the space in-between. After a bit of time, I start to feel completely different, something shifts in my attitude towards the situation and in my brain function; the space in-between starts to come alive. Funnily enough the machine then stops spinning as well.

When we did this listening to the sound experiment something very interesting happened on the EEG scans. The brain shifted from beta wave activity in (1) into alpha wave activity in (3) which is a much calmer rhythm of brain activity associated with creativity, openness, relaxation and meditation. The awareness now encompasses two reference points simultaneously and the interconnecting space in between comes alive. There was a marked shift in the predominant type of brain wave activity from beta waves in experiment (1) Baseline (at rest), compared to all the other 4 experiments, where the brain went into alpha and even theta wave activity (the super-calm relaxed state) during the WBF experiment at the end. You can replicate experiment (2) for yourself right now, if you want to. Sit upright on a chair with the palms of your hands resting on the top of your thighs, or flat on the table top in front of you. Be aware of your hands resting there in a relaxed manner and at the same time be aware of the soles of your feet contacting the floor. Hold both points in awareness "in equal positive regard" (in a neutral detached way) and also be aware of the interconnecting space in between for a couple of minutes and see what happens. If the attention wanders, keep bringing it back.

Gradually, after a period of time, what seems to happen for most people is that the breathing starts to calm down, the body starts to feel grounded and more relaxed but more supported at the same time. The space in between the two points starts to come alive in its own way and to expand. There is an inward drawing and concentration of the energy and awareness in the brain and in the spinal column and a rising and expansion of consciousness as the brain goes into alpha wave brain rhythms. There naturally arises a feeling of calmness, relaxation and openness. This is the start of a meditation session or it could be the right state of physical and mental relaxation for going into a Focusing session.

I have measured this with numerous students during my WBF workshops using my MyndPlay Brain Band technology. This is a simple two electrode EEG measuring machine, which aggregates the brain wave patterns throughout the whole brain, and the results are then displayed on my computer using a Bluetooth connection. My students are constantly amazed to see how changing their awareness and patterns of thought can change the readings showing their predominant brain wave patterns on the computer, and how they can shift from one-pointed focus in Beta, into expansive open focus in Alpha & Theta brain-wave activity.

The general principle is that there are two points of reference and the awareness has expanded to include the interconnecting space in between, which comes alive and expands when the energetic interconnection is there. This is exactly the principle that Dr Les Fehmi has proven after more than 40 years of research into how to induce alpha wave activity in the brain (Dr Les Fehmi, "The Open Focus Brain"). When Dr Fehmi was hooked up to his neurofeedback machine and was trying hard to induce alpha waves nothing was happening – except that he was getting very tense and stuck in Beta wave activity. Then *when he finally just gave up trying* and leant over to switch off his machine, he noticed that he had shifted into increased alpha wave activity. This gave him the clue that when he was in "narrow focus mode" and trying hard all he was doing was arousing his nervous system and getting ready for fight or flight. He discovered that when he *became aware of how he was paying attention* and started to soften the focus of his eyes, he could do two-pointing to allow a sense of space in his forehead between his eyes and then include more peripheral vision to either side of his head, as well as more sense of space in the body and in the environment surrounding him, observing it all as the neutral detached observer. Then the brain shifted into "open focus" mode and this resulted in more alpha-wave brain activity. There was a sense of ease and flow when in alpha wave activity, *like its doing you* rather than you are doing it, *an enjoyment of being* rather than all tension and doing. This all came from not trying and an awareness of the space in-between, and he proved how this principle works in many years of research and experiments.

What are these different brain wave rhythms and what states of consciousness do they correlate with? When neurons fire together they exchange charged elements that then produce electromagnetic fields and these fields are what are measured during an EEG brain scan. There are several types of brain-wave frequencies and the slower the brain wave state you are in the deeper you go into the world of the subconscious mind. In order of the slowest to the fastest the brain-wave states are: delta (deep restorative sleep), theta (a twilight state between sleep and wakefulness), alpha (creative imagination, relaxation), beta (conscious thought) and gamma (elevated states of consciousness, flashes of insight).

Brain Wave Frequencies

Heinrich Herz, German physicist who proved the existence of electromagnetic waves. 1 Herz = 1 cycle per second.

Delta 0-4 Hz: They are associated with deep restorative sleep and totally unconscious.

Theta 4-8 Hz: Predominant frequency during the transition stage between wakefulness & sleep. Theta waves are noted during deep meditation, a sense of peace, joy and merging with the oneness of all creation. You can access your subconscious mind most easily & influence it with positive affirmations and healing suggestions. In theta the analytical mind isn't operating.

Alpha 8-12 Hz: They are associated with a light state of meditation, imagination and creativity. This is a flow state where you can move calmly and smoothly to accomplish whatever task is at hand. In alpha the inner world starts to seem more real than the outer world. When alpha waves predominate you feel pleasantly calm and relaxed.

Beta 15-18 Hz: It is a very common brain-wave form associated with the alert waking state, when the thinking brain, is processing all the incoming data, creating meaning, solving problems, and making decisions. Beta waves predominate when you are in "get the job done" mode. This can range from interested attention during learning and studying to highly focused crisis mode when one particular task urgently needs completing. Beta is needed when dealing with the outer world, when making judgments, making decisions, processing information about the world and about us. But it can also occur as a sign of anxiety or apprehension.

Gamma 26-40 Hz: Associated with perception and consciousness, often around 40 Hz., but can be 26-70 Hz. Higher level cognitive activity and flashes of insight occurs when lower frequency gamma waves suddenly double into the 40 Hz range. Occurs during higher mental activity, higher reasoning and mental insights.

Most of the day we are moving back and forth between alpha and beta states. Alpha is your relaxation state, when you pay less attention to the outer world and pay more attention to your inner world. Beta is more focused on getting the job done in time. So there is this oscillation back and forth, however you can notice when you are getting too uptight and stressed and take time out to relax and induce more alpha wave activity, because the real aim is to be in a state of open focus, where you are "in the zone" a state which has been described by top athletes as being incredibly focused and yet totally relaxed and calm at the same time. So both are needed, and many different types of brain activity can be present at the same time.

I believe that exactly the same thing is happening during regular Focusing sessions, because there is a detached, observing consciousness (self) and the part that does not feel right. When the focuser can say "something in me is calling for attention", "it hurts, it feels like..." *and* yet there is also the observing self that is bigger than that, the observing self can contain the part that does not feel right in detached awareness and not get sucked in by it. It is the interplay between these two parts and the interconnected space in between, which actually allows the brain to go into alpha rhythms and allows the shift to take place. If the Focuser cannot do this for themselves, then they need help and one of the most vital interventions that the listener (or Focusing-oriented therapist) can make is to ask the Focuser to change their language to say "something *in me is feeling....*" and that then stops all of you from getting completely sucked into the emotional memory of the pain/trauma and helps to facilitate a shift. I have appreciated this type of intervention in the work of Ann Weiser Cornell and Joan Klagsbrun at the Focusing Institute Summer School and I have always noticed how effective it is in facilitating a shift.

The same thing happens in WBF, but in a slightly different way. A really crucial intervention that is often needed is when the listener/therapist asks the Wholebody Focuser to be aware of both (a) the sense of a part of the body that carries tension and does not feel right (and the exploration of meaning associated with that) and (b) also the sense of strength and support that you get from feeling the soles of the feet being in contact with the floor and being in grounded presence.

The request is to see if you can "hold both in equal positive regard" or "to hold both in a non-judgmental awareness". And of course I would also add to be aware of the space in-between and to let it come alive in its own time and in its own way.

In our research study during the WBF session Client X had become aware of a bodily felt sense of "not being connected

... I feel disconnected ... I feel empty ... I'm not connected with myself..."

After the listener had reflected back these words, Client X contacted even more of the felt sense: "I'm *not expressing ... not putting energy out into the world ... not connecting with the world ... not feeling supported."* So a really crucial intervention at this stage was when Client X was asked to sense where this part is in the body and to connect with the support of the ground through the soles of the feet at the same time: "to hold both with equal positive regard". Having done so in awareness for a period of time Client X began to experience something else happening.

That something else that Client X experienced during the course of the WBF session was revealed in the qEEG brain scans. What had happened is that during the course of the WBF session the brain went from normal Beta waves right into Alpha and even stronger Theta wave patterns. Also there was a shift into right brain domination, (as the right hemisphere of the brain is the more holistic, symbolic and artistic side of the brain), which is to be expected. As the clinical psychologist Dr Christine Kraus reported: "Overall, it appears that the therapy that was addressed within the various sessions increased visual and sensory awareness to one's self and increased the relaxed focused state. It appears that session 5 (the WBF session) also enhanced the super learning or creative spiritual thought process as Theta was increased as well" (Dr Kraus, Amen Clinic, Newport Beach). See Fig X below, with readings taken during a WBF session, deep into step 5.

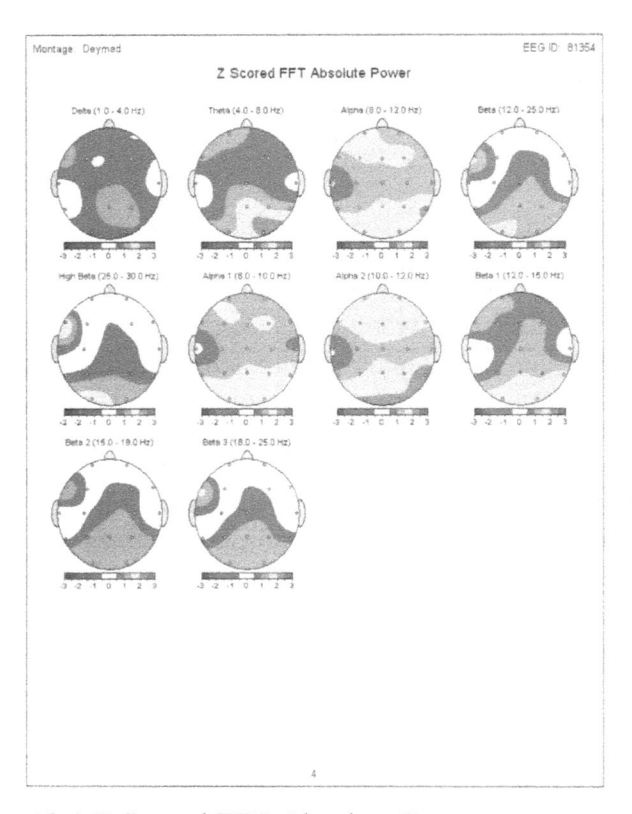

Fig. 13.1 Z Scored FFT Absolute Power

You would expect Alpha waves during a pleasantly relaxed, creative state, and during regular meditation periods, but Theta waves are normally only present during periods of very deep meditation by highly experienced meditators, or during deep hypnosis. During Theta (4 Hz – 7 Hz) there is deep calmness, a sense of peace and joy. Your awareness can access your subconscious mind most easily and influence it with positive affirmations and healing suggestions. There can also be a vibrant, living awareness of our ever- present spiritual connection with the whole of the Universe, or God, a feeling of oneness with all of life. At this stage of the WBF session,

Client X reported experiencing feelings of "joy, elation, ecstasy, feeling connected to something bigger that myself, a sense of unity with the whole of creation." So on the one side we have the trauma, the anxiety and depression – which is clearly indicated in the brain surface/brain interior SPEC scans and in the words, imagery, and body sensations of the WBF session (also in the initial reported attachment history of the client). On the other side we have a very clear indication of a sense of joy and a sense of connection. Something else has come into the client's field of consciousness and is offsetting the experience of trauma.

What is crucial in WBF is the intervention to ask the client to "hold both in equal positive regard," because there are now two points of reference that can be held in the field of neutral awareness and a whole new inter-connected energy comes out of that, something happens between them. This is in line with the expectations of Field Theory, which is actually "a region of mutual influence between two or more points in space, often via a force like gravity, electro- magnetism or a conscious human being." (Karen Whalen).

There is a blocked energy in the trauma that can now free up by connecting with this other place. There is a participation, an engagement of both, not a getting rid of something. The link between the joy and the trauma is what gets the client moving. And in this feeling of awakened new energy the self seems to want to experience itself more fully and explore its full potential. The suppressed energy within the trauma can now turn positive, when seen from a bigger perspective all the pain and suffering of the defended position and all the adaptations and desperate survival techniques are seen for what they are – just a way of defending a vulnerability that was not strong enough to stand unaided.

Another interesting result of the EEG scans was the left hemisphere/ right hemisphere story that emerges. This is what is to be expected. Focusing first starts to operate in the right hemisphere, as the right brain goes into Alpha wave patterns. It is the murky, unclear felt sense of the "whole thing" as "something that is not quite right" struggles to emerge into consciousness from the holistic and symbolic perceptions of the right hemisphere during the Focusing session. It is the right side of the brain that first goes into Alpha and Theta wave patterns and opens up to a sense of connection with a greater whole and a sense of knowing – even when this cannot be expressed cognitively yet. It is that sense of "I know something but I'm not sure what it is and I cannot express it fully yet." Then the Alpha and Theta brain wave pattern moves over into the left side of the brain to influence the cognitive functioning of the brain as the Focuser gropes to find the right word or phrase that will fit the image or the feeling. This is "finding a handle" in Focusing terms, but even at this stage there is still a slight right brain preponderance of Alpha and Theta wave patterns – which is exactly what the EEG results in this study have confirmed.

Not surprisingly, the 3D Active (interior) SPEC scan images, which look deep inside the brain to the more primitive, deep- seated emotional brain (in the basal ganglia and the focal thalamic system) show no change in the before/after scans and this reveals that the more fundamental, severe anxiety and depression issues were not dealt with in a single WBF session. This can be because the brain of this particular client is just hard-wired that way, or more likely, it is the result of deep childhood trauma that needs long-term work to sort it out. Its all a tangle, as the tentacles of this particular issue reach into many seemingly disconnected areas of life, but at root is a feeling of discouragement and disempowerment. The body, in all its wisdom, will need more time to resolve it and there needs to be action steps that will change conditions in his current life situation. Something tangible needs to change to bring a greater sense of security and empowerment in his outer living condition; otherwise no amount of therapy will help. Obviously these are big issues and no one would seriously expect a single WBF session to change all of this; but on the flip side of the coin there is a huge amount of positive, forward moving life energy that is waiting to be released.

SPEC Brain Scans on Client X after 2 years of WBF Therapy

After 2 years we went back to the Amen Clinic, in Costa Mesa California, for the follow-up brain SPEC scan to see if any permanent changes in brain function were apparent. The results of the WBF Brain Scan research pilot study, in both the 3D surface and active SPEC scans were very interesting. This particular client was diagnosed to be suffering from anxiety and depression two years ago. There were 3 main areas of particular concern.

Firstly, at the baseline scan on 3/13/12, there was decreased temporal lobe and parietal lobe brain activity, which made a partial improvement directly after one WBF session on 3/14/12 and a dramatic and long-term improvement is shown two years later on 3/17/14. (See brain scan images at the end of this chapter).

The Temporal Lobe regulates: emotional stability, understanding & use of language, retrieval of words, long-term memory, reading social cues, reading faces, picking up on verbal intonation, auditory & visual learning.

My client did recognize that he had memory problems, learning problems, language problems in finding the right words, social phobias when he could not correctly interpret facial expressions and verbal intonation, moods swings, headaches, periods of anxiety and periods of spaciness/confusion.

He now feels much more socially at ease, with greater mood stabilization, a greater ability to find the right words to express himself with and as a result increased self-confidence and emotional stability. He is also able to correctly interpret facial expressions and tone of voice without getting triggered (which would normally have then added to his suppressed anger and anxiety and so fuelled a vicious circle). His periods of anxiety and feeling spacey/confused have significantly decreased. He has said that he now feels in control of his life and much happier as a result.

The Parietal Lobe regulates how we process all of our sensory information, also spatial processing & sense of direction, ability to read maps, visual guidance of hands & limbs, distinguishing left from right, admitting when you have a problem.

My client recognized that he suffered from sensory overload at times, feeling ungrounded, trouble with directional sense and a right/left confusion, For large periods of his life he was also unaware that anything was wrong or that he had a problem - as it was always the other persons fault!

He now feels much more grounded for large parts of the day, able to process sensory information coming in with a sense of spaciousness and a greatly improved sense of direction and ability to navigate his car.

So improvements in these two areas - basically mood stabilization, improved ability to find the right words and sensory integration, are perfect for what you would expect from Focusing/Wholebody focusing therapy and integrating these insights into daily life. It still raises the question that if you had other problems in different areas of the brain and impaired brain function - would it help other areas as well? This is impossible to say from a pilot study and that's why we are going to need a large scale study to see if there would be generalized improvement in these specific areas alone or in other areas that were also malfunctioning.

We do have a partial answer here in this pilot study, in that **The Prefrontal Cortex,** the executive control function which regulates our ability to focus, plan, organize, think ahead, control impulses & make good decisions. This was showing areas of under-activity in the baseline scan on 3/13/12. Not much difference after 1 WBF session and it has even got slightly worse two years later.

My Client admits to still feeling slow to focus and confused at times, with bad time keeping and planning, also that he finds it difficult to make good long-term decisions.

So on a general level we could speculate that WBF, as it is taught at the moment, is not a technique that increases your concentration and cognitive alertness in the prefrontal cortex. The technique of WBF tends to bring you more into the right side of the brain, which is more holistic, symbolic, and more concerned with somatic and emotional awareness. It gives greater understanding and a new perspective. But unfortunately has never really included an action step. Some Focusing therapists are now including it and this will help to activate a sense of self agency – of making plans and being in control of your life. Energy and intention needs to be released into positive action steps, in order to confront and move towards change the outer situation, rather than backing off and just thinking about the problem. Some sort of clear direction, action that is supported from a grounded sense of self, is needed to change the situation. This would help to facilitate a deeper level of brain integration to the pre-frontal neo-cortex.

There are also active SPEC brain scans, which can see with great clarity deeper into the brain. My client showed greater than normal activity in the **Deep Limbic System/Thalamus region**. This is the survival response of the amygdala, which can trigger the fight/flight/freeze response. This area stores our most charged memories and is the seat of emotions in a person's life. It also modulates motivation, and sets the appetite/sleep cycles and regulates the libido.

My client acknowledges having low motivation/energy at times; sleep problems, low self-esteem and inward directed sadness, at times.

The same is true of the **Basal Ganglia System, which** sets the body's idle state when at rest, sets anxiety levels, mediates pleasure and modulates motivation.

My client admits to still feeling irritable, tense, very unmotivated and yet anxious and conflict avoidant at the same time.

This increased activity in the Deep Limbic System and the Basal Ganglia system has not improved over the 2 year period, which would either suggests that he still feels in crisis mode in his life situation and he may be caught in the freeze response, where there is both an arousal inside and a seeming relaxation on the surface at the same time, so the tension does not get released into outer activity.

There is also an increase in **Brainstem activity** in the active scan, which is good and to be expected as the WBF training increases sensory feedback, which is transmitted through the medulla to the Cerebrum and Cerebellum.

At first, I was a bit surprised at this second SPEC scan result because I really thought that Wholebody focusing would transform or at least modulate the trauma/survival response in the deeper emotional brain. This is clearly not the case here, but it is only one case so no conclusions can be drawn when n=1. There is some evidence that if the trauma was severe, and involved severed attachment, which took place early on in the childhood, it is much harder to treat than if it took place later in the adult life. I would speculate that there is some sort of trauma loop in operation here that still gets triggered. The preliminary evidence from these brain scans, is showing that Focusing alone does not heal this type of deep-rooted trauma, and that some methods of calming the arousal need to be taught to the client, as well as action steps to confront on-going problems rather than backing off from them.

The psychiatrist who analysed the results, Dr Garrett Halweg at the Amen Clinic was impressed. He noted the big improvements that had occurred over the last two years and said that deterioration in the temporal lobes and the parietal lobes normally just gets worse, not better - They very rarely see an improvement in these areas, so evidence of neuroplasticity here is very encouraging.

The Clinical Psychologist who performed the EEG evaluations, Dr Christine Kraus wrote: " Overall it appears that the therapy that was addressed within the various sessions increased visual and sensory awareness to one's self and increased the relaxed focused state. It appears that session 5 (the Wholebody focusing session) also enhanced the super learning or creative spiritual thought process as Theta was increased as well". (Dr Kraus, Amen Clinic, Newport Beach).

Brain Scan Images for Client X

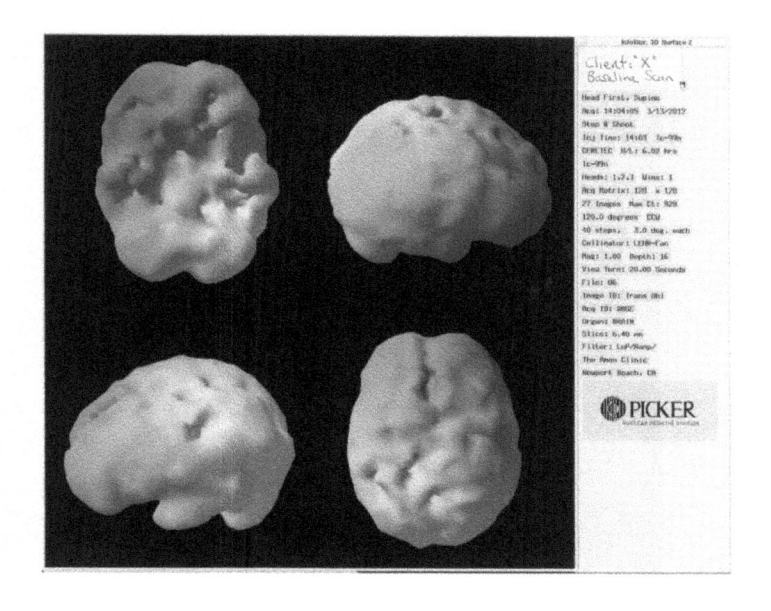

Fig. 1 X Surface Baseline Scan

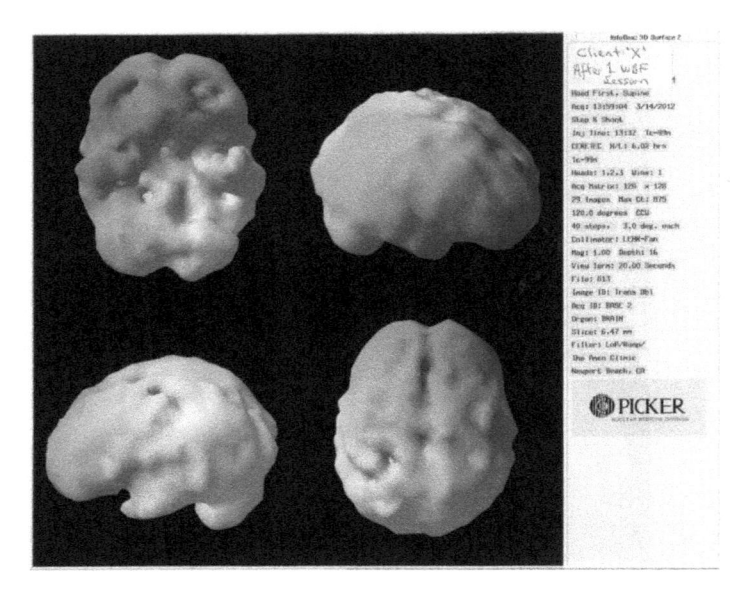

Fig. 2, X Surface after 1 WBF Session

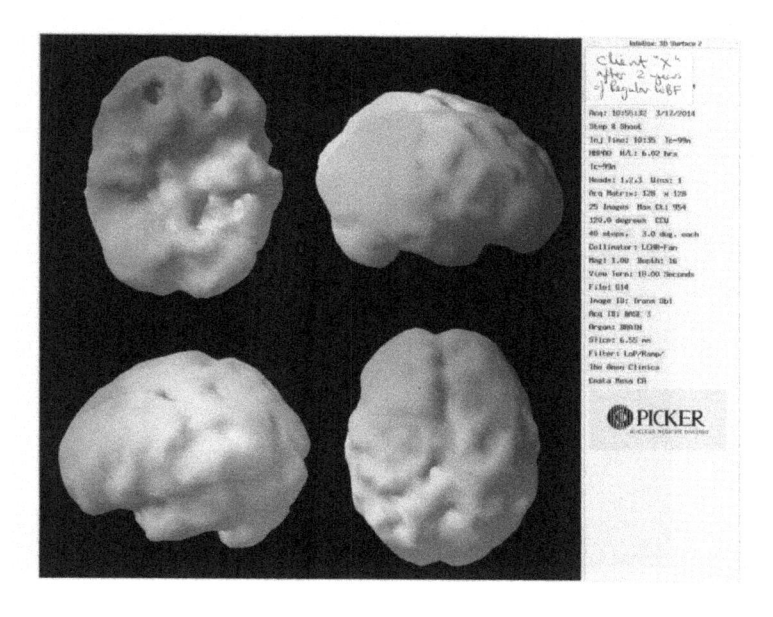

Fig. 3, After 2 years WBF Sessions

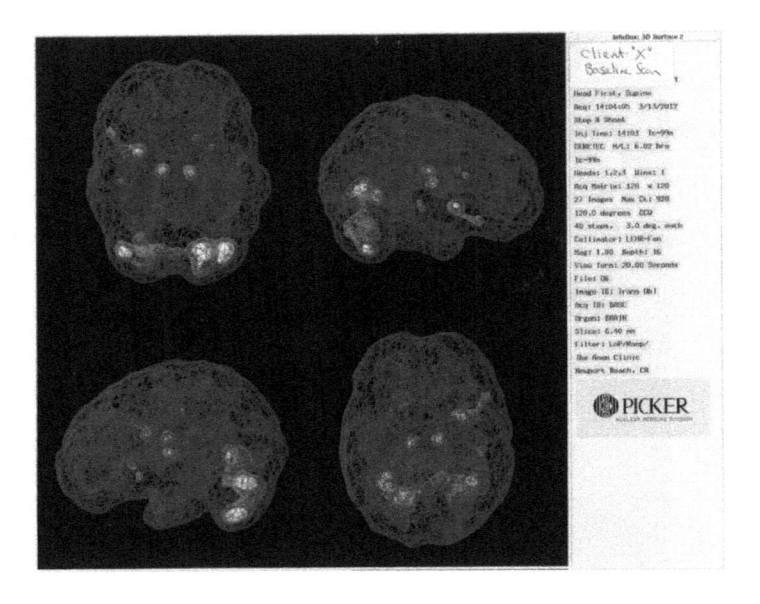

Fig. 4, X Active Baseline

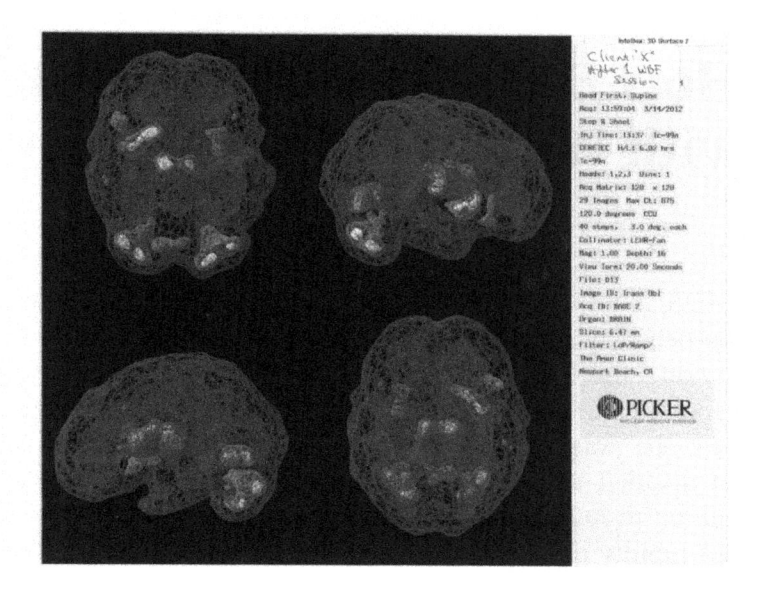

Fig. 5, X Active After 1 WBF Session

Chapter 14.
How EMDR can be integrated with WBF in the Treatment of Trauma

EMDR is an acronym for 'Eye Movement Desensitisation and Reprocessing'. EMDR is a powerful psychophysical treatment method that was developed by an American clinical psychologist, Dr Francine Shapiro, in the 1980s. As the story goes, she was suffering from some emotional trauma herself and decided to take a walk in the park one day. As she was walking in intense emotional pain she also started to move her eyes rapidly and as a result she noticed that she started to feel better. As a Senior Research Fellow at the Mental Research Institute, she decided to do some research into this phenomena and she published the first research data to support the benefits of the therapy in 1989.

In particular EMDR seems to be able to help with treating psychological trauma arising from experiences as diverse as war-related experiences, childhood sexual and/or physical abuse or neglect, natural disaster, assault, surgical trauma, road traffic accidents and workplace accidents. Since its original development there have been over 20 randomised controlled research studies consistently demonstrating the benefits of EMDR. E.g., the first study was by Dr Francine Shapiro in The journal of Traumatic Stress (1989). A subsequent study (Carlson et al., 1998) conducted at a Veterans Affairs facility used 12 treatment sessions and reported a 78 percent remission in P.T.S.D. Another study by Marcus et al., (1997, 2004) reported that after an average of six 50-minute sessions, 100 percent of the single-trauma victims and 77 percent of the multiple-trauma victims no longer had P.T.S.D. Bessel van der Kolk did a study reported in the Journal of Clinical Psychiatry (2007) to compare the effects of EMDR with standard doses of Prozac or a Placebo. After 8 EMDR sessions 1 in 4 were completely cured, (compared to 1 in 10 for the Prozac group) but the real improvement was long term, as eight months later 60 percent of those who received EMDR rated as being completely cured. This showed continuous improvement over time, whereas all those who had taken Prozac relapsed once they came off the drug. In other words the people who had EMDR felt better about themselves and were able to continue to make positive change in their lives.

The research is also showing how effective EMDR is in cases of trauma. Both Focusing and EMDR are mind/body therapies they work very well in combination because both refer back to the felt sense. I have worked with Client "X" using EMDR and he has responded well. The interesting thing with EMDR is the juxtaposition of memories, thoughts and images that takes place during the process. There is a memory of the initial trauma, the people involved, and the way that they all relate together. Then, as the client pays attention to that memory and is also moving their eyes to watch the moving finger of the therapist, something new happens in the visualization, instead of playing through the same old loop, the victim can suddenly break free and say or do something different. In the case of client "X", who had been emotionally abused by his mother, he was watching her speak and feeling the frozen terror that normally disempowered him. At the same time he suddenly felt a sense of his adult self being fully present and grounded in the present situation.

(C) "My feet feel contacting the ground. My pelvis is fully released into the support of the chair and my legs feel strong, my thighs feel alive. There is more energy in my shoulders and arms. I feel fully present in my adult self now and paying attention this memory from the past".

(T)"Just notice that".

(C) "I'm looking at my mother and I am curious and amazed. Who is this person? What motivates her?"

(T) "Just pay attention to that".

(C) "I'm feeling a mischievous impulse to say what I really think, and I'm not frightened of her. I'm just curious as to how she will react".

(Pause)

(C)"I'm not frightened anymore, I'm just curious and amused, how will she react and what will she say? Its more fun and I feel alive".

The actual practice of EMDR is an incredibly simple procedure. Let's say the client has reached a point of recalling some very painful, traumatic memory during the therapy session. They feel triggered by the memory; go into hyper-arousal and experience confusion and distress as some sort of emotional hijacking of the brain is clearly taking place. The practitioner sits in front of the client and moves a finger or a small baton in a regular rhythm from side to side, and asks the client to move their eyes, but not their head, as they follow the rhythm of the movements. (The rhythm is approximately moving from one side to the other and back again within 1 second). This does several things; firstly it stops the staring, rigid eyes that are so typical of people locked into shock or fear. Once the eyes can loosen up the body/mind unlocks and the memory becomes less intense and less able to suck you in. Secondly, as the body unfreezes there is more space and awareness of sensory input in the present moment. This enables the adult to be present in the room as well as the traumatised child. This is crucial as healing needs to take place in this twilight zone between accessing the memories from the past and still staying strongly grounded in the present moment with all your adult wisdom, strength and life experiences. Both of these two points link directly into how WBF works as a therapy.

Most importantly, there is a relaxation response because with REM (rapid eye movement) we imitate what happens at a certain stage of deep sleep. During REM the sleeping brain can reform memory by increasing the impact of emotionally relevant information whilst helping irrelevant information fade away. In dreams we forge new relationships between apparently unrelated memories. The essence of creativity is the ability to see new connections, by contrast PTSD sufferers are trapped in frozen associations – like women who shout at me are demanding and dominating, or anyone that dresses like an Arab is a potential terrorist and wants to kill me. It seems that REM, in sleep or in therapy situations, can integrate different memories and help the client to make new and sometimes bizarre associations, that help to give meaning and a sense of wholeness to life's experiences. In other words it helps to integrate the memory into the person's life experience by giving it a new meaning, a new perspective, so that the issue has then been resolved and there is a feeling of "its over now, its finished I can move on now." This link between EMDR and memory processing in dreams has been researched by Stickgold who concluded: " If the bilateral stimulation of EMDR can alter brain states in a manner similar to that seen during REM sleep there is now good evidence that EMDR should be able to take advantage of sleep-dependent processes, which may be blocked or ineffective in PTSD sufferers, to allow effective memory processing and trauma resolution." (R. Stickgold, "Journal of Clinical Psychology, 2002).

This all integrates beautifully with WBF, because in that new body-centered perspective there is a release of the frozen fear, the feeling of being trapped and unable to move forwards. The body becomes more alive as the body container comes into awareness and fills with energy. There is an awareness of the meaning of that incident in the whole of the life history and the also the awareness of choice, as in "I can do something different here, let's see how they react now". The client moves to a position of self-agency and empowerment, and the memory of that remains in similar situations in the future rather triggering off the trauma from the past.

Case History

I had been working with Michael for some time as a WBF client, but he was so aroused most of the time and then so easily triggered into hyper-arousal that I realized we needed to integrate some EMDR into the sessions to transform the root causes of the trauma. He was a very intelligent man but his survival technique had been to always think his way out of a threatening situation, which doesn't work when you are hyper-aroused because your amygdala has hijacked the neo-cortex so that you cannot think correctly anymore.

He came in one day with an issue about needing to change some old, dripping taps in his house, but not being a practical man he felt confused, out of his depth and fearful that he would do something wrong and his house would be flooded before he could get any help. His felt sense was of great physical tension all over his body and especially a tightness in his chest and breathing difficulty. The words that resonated for him were:

"confused", "paralysed with fear" and "I'm going to do something wrong".

T. " Do these words resonate for you? When else have you felt paralysed with fear, and that you were going to do something wrong?"

C. "I can remember going to school on public transport buses as a 5 year old child and getting on the wrong bus one day and ending up in a different part of the city. I was terrified..."

T. "You felt terrified..."

C. "Nobody would ask a 5 year old child to go alone on the buses now. I felt really confused and had to try and find another bus to take me home again."

(Pause)

C. "I can think of another example, I was at school and we all had to put our napkins in a special place after lunch. I put mine in the wrong place. I knew that I had done something wrong and was going to be found out. I felt trapped, terrified, but there was nothing I could do, because if I went up and took my napkin to put it in its proper place the teachers would see me and catch me and punish me. I couldn't move and I could hardly breathe".

T. "So you felt trapped and terrified. There was nothing you could do. You couldn't move and you could hardly breathe. Just stay with that whilst I do some EMDR with you, do you prefer me to move my finger from side to side in front of your eyes, or the bilateral stimulation of your own hand tapping *each leg alternately?"*

C. *"I prefer the tapping on my leg".*

T. *"OK so pay attention to that image of your 5 year boy at school in that situation whilst you tap each leg alternately. (About 1 beat per second)."*

(Period of Tapping)

C. *" I'm starting to feel anger. How could they put such pressure on a young child? My little boy feels trapped and all adults seem to be terrifying authority figures". (His face starts to crumple and he sobs silently).*

T. *"All adults seem terrifying and you feel sad. Pay attention to that."*

C. *" Yes, I sobbed twice."*
(Pause)
C. *"Now there is another adult there who seems very judgmental. He's like the internalized parent and he's saying that I shouldn't have made a mistake. It's all my little boy's fault".*

T. *"So another part of you, an internal parental figure seems judgmental. Pay attention to that and continue tapping."*

C. *"Yes, now my little boy is saying maybe you could help, maybe you could both help. He's speaking to those two parts."*

T. *" So your little boy is saying maybe you could help, maybe you could both help. Pay attention to that".*

C. *"My napkins in the wrong place, what are you going to do about it?"*

T. *"Are you asking them to do something about it?"*

C. *" No, I'm saying what's the worst thing that can happen, are you going to shoot me? I'm not afraid anymore."*

T. *"So your little boy is saying what's the worst thing that can happen in this situation? I'm not afraid of you anymore. There is a different energy in the situation now. Pay attention to that and continue tapping."*

C. *"Yes, I feel that there is a supportive connection now between my little boy and adult Michael here in the room. In a similar situation, when I feel overwhelmed I will appeal to the adult Michael for help and support".*

T. *"OK, you can stop tapping now. Just notice the different energy in your body and in the room now. You look different, how does it feel different inside you, what's different about your posture, your muscle tone, the spaces inside your body, your energy flow?"*

C. *"I feel calmer and more in control. It feels more relaxed in my chest, I've got more space across my chest and my breathing is longer and deeper. It's more measured, breathing in and out. I feel more supported."*

T. *" So just say thank you to your Inner Body Wisdom, and also notice that the story has a different ending now. This has a real influence on who you are and how you will react in similar situations."*

This little case history shows how important it is to integrate EMDR with WBF or some form of body-centered psychotherapy or experience of trauma therapy work. The client presented with an issue but underneath it was a deeper layer of quite severe childhood trauma. Working with EMDR brings alive the whole experience of that trauma and what was involved at the time. It is a fast track into the whole experience and a very powerful tool for change. On the one hand it does encourage the young child to be heard, but at the same time it helps the adult part of the client to be more present in the room, and allows new associations and unexpected possibilities to emerge from that session. However, it takes a lot of experience to keep those two parts in balance and also to read what has changed in the client's body and energy levels afterwards, so that the client can be consciously different in similar situations in the future. This is a very powerful tool, but it needs to be used with skill and caution by an experienced therapist who is also capable of being in grounded presence during the sessions. This is an essential skill to be able to model the ability to just let whatever comes up be there within the container of the body in a non-judgmental and self-compassionate way. Just by paying attention to it and using the bilateral stimulation to allow new associations and insights to emerge. Then when the shift comes it can be integrated into a new life – because it actually changes the way the story ends, which is now held in a new way in the long-term memory banks in the hippocampus. But it takes more follow-up sessions to be able to support the client in the way similar situations are dealt in future, before the client can truly say – "it's over, it's finished now" – and move forwards with their lives.

Chapter 15.
Short Meditation for Inducing Alpha Wave Rhythms in your Brain

OK, so lets take a moment to do a little meditation, and we are going to use specific techniques to induce alpha wave patterns in the brain.

…. So take your time and sway a little bit backwards and forwards as you are sitting on your chair..…

…Feel that you are well connected with your sitting bones and that you feel well balanced and aligned, as you sway backwards and forwards…

…You can get the feel of an upward thrust of energy, going up your spine from your sitting bones, right up to your head…

…Take a few deep breaths and every time you breathe out feel yourself getting heavier and sinking down….

…Waiting for the in-breath to come back in by itself…

…Now notice how you are sitting with your hands on top of your thighs, palms relaxed and be aware how the warmth of your hands is contacting the top of your thighs…allow your fingers to spread outwards…

…. Now travel down your legs in your awareness to the soles of your feet, which are flat on the ground….contacting the Earth…

Just notice that full contact of the soles of your feet with whatever is underneath them…

So I'm noticing a wooden floor underneath my feet and contacting the firmness and warmth of the wooden floor underneath me. You bring your awareness to notice whatever is underneath your feet right now…

Now just come back in your awareness to notice your hands on top of your thighs again…

…. Hold your awareness there and let your breath come and go just as it wants to. Maybe its slowed down by now and got very soft and deep. ….. Whatever it is, it is, just let it be that way…without trying to change it at all.

Now shift your awareness back to the soles of your feet on the floor…Stay there for a bit…

Now come back to noticing the warmth of your hands on top of your thighs…Stay there for a while….

And now try to be aware of both at the same time…Both the palms of your hands on top of your thighs and the soles of your feet contacting the floor. Be aware of both at the same time. Holding both in your awareness and allowing the space in-between to come alive in its own time and in its own way…So let's take a few minutes to do this….Holding both…holding both…in equal positive regard, being aware of the space in-between slowly coming alive...in its own time and in its own way...

You may notice a feeling of spaciousness beginning to spread throughout your whole body as your body becomes energetically alive and connected between these two points...

Feeling a sense of peace and spaciousness in the mind, as the mind starts to go into a deeper alpha wave pattern....

(Pause....)

Start to be aware of the space between your two eyeballs, across your forehead; there is space, a sense of lightness, a sense of spaciousness. As you allow these two points to connect... to become energetically connected through the space in-between.

(Pause...)

Then go back and be aware of the space between your hands and your feet....

Become aware that there is space in the chest, around your heart center, your chest seems to be expanding...expanding. There is space between the left and the right side of your chest, there is space between the front and the back of your chest...

There is space for the breath to flow easily and slowly and deeply....in and out of the lungs...in its own time....in its own way....you are just the observer....of your body breathing itself....It knows exactly how to do this if you don't try and interfere with it...

(Pause....)

Now be aware of the space surrounding you....be aware of the sounds in the distance...any sounds of birdsong, or the wind in the trees, or cars passing by...or any machines humming in the background...that's fine you can let them be just the way that they are...humming away in the distance...and you are centered here in your body, so you can just be aware of the sense of space between you and that sound....and that these two points are connected....and the way that the space between you and that sound can become energetically connected and alive.....in its own time....in its own way....

Notice the sounds of the birds, or the rain, or the wind in the trees....

Just let those sounds be there, the way that they are, and you are sitting here the way that you are right now.

(Pause...)

Notice how as your meditation deepens, the sense of connection to yourself deepens...

And now, you can take any one of your old issues, or belief patterns that are holding up your life...Just put it there in front of you. Hold it there. What is that belief pattern? Is there a word or a phrase that fits this? How does it feel in your body when this word or phrase is repeated back to you? ...

And now, just ground it through your feet, through your sense of connection with the Earth, allow all of that to be grounded, and hold both at the same time...be open to fresh possibilities, even though you do not know what they might be....

(Pause....)

Something can shift in your body...there is a feeling of shift, a different energy, a new way of being. See if you can find different words or if a different phrase comes up to fit this new way of being...

You may not know exactly how this is going to resolve itself but you are open to new possibilities...the infinite number of new possibilities that are out there waiting for you, when you let go of your old beliefs....your old habitual beliefs and attitudes.....those restricted patterns of thought that have kept you a prisoner.....So just let go and just open out to the infinite potential of the Universe that is waiting to manifest in your life right now, in a totally unexpected and yet perfect way.....

Be aware of that sense of expansion, hold onto that sense of new possibility, hold onto the clear intention that I don't need to do this anymore...and let go of these old beliefs and these old attitudes...These old restricted patterns of thought, belief and energy....and that something new is manifesting to take their place.

(Pause...)

Know that whatever happens you will be OK, that you are being supported, you are bigger than all of that, you are more spacious than all of that...you can contain all of that ......and transform it through awareness....

You have a sense of your expanded self, of openness, of possibility…You can welcome in new possibilities, as you recognize them and as they arise in your life…Be it in terms of health, well-being, or opportunities for greater abundance, opportunities to offer your gifts as a service to the world, opportunities to grow in wisdom, understanding and love… So find a way to link a clear intention for change with a trust in new possibility and get a sense of what that shift feels like in your body, mind and emotions, so that you can visualize it, and feel it, and know that it is happening right now in your body/mind.

Useful Addresses and Website Links

If you are interested in workshops, retreats or personal sessions/Skype sessions with me Alex Maunder, in Wholebody Focusing or the Alexander Technique, please look for details on my website. There are also free videos, useful links and meditation tapes on this website:
www.wholebodyfocusing.org

If you wish to have personal sessions in Focusing/Wholebody Focusing with somebody in your area please look on the Focusing Institute website. This is also a rich source of articles on different aspects of Focusing:
www.focusing.org

If you wish have personal lessons with an Alexander Technique Teacher in your area please visit the Society of Teachers of the Alexander Technique website at:
www.stat.org.uk

Meditation techniques, prayer requests and Kriya Yoga, as taught by Paramahansa Yogananda, can be learnt from Self-Realization Fellowship at:
www.yogananda-srf.org

BIBLIOGRAPHY

FM Alexander,
The Use of the Self
(Centerline Press, 1984)

John Amodeo & Kris Wentworth,
Being Intimate, a Guide to Successful Relationships
(Arkana Publications, 2012)

Ann Weiser Cornell
The Power of Focusing
(New Harbringer Publications, 2010)

Ann Weiser Cornell
Focusing in Clinical Practise The *Essence of Change*
(WW Norton & Company, 2013)

Richard J. Davidson,
The Emotional Life of Your Brain,
(Holder & Stoughton, 2012)

Dr Joe Dispenza,
You Are the Placebo
(Hay House Inc, 2014)

Karlfried Graf von Durkheim,
Hara
(Otto Wilhelm Barth Verlag, 1987)

Sebern F. Fisher
Neurofeedback in the Treatment of Developmental Trauma,
(W. W. Norton, 2014)

Viktor Frankl
Man's Search for Meaning
(Washington Square Press, 1959)

Eugene T. Gendlin
Focusing,
(Rider Books, 1978)

Daniel Goleman
Destructive Emotions,
(Random House, 2003)

James Kepner,
Body Process
(Jossy-Bass Publishers, 1995)

Bessel van der Kolk
(Allen Lane, 2014)
The Body Keeps the Score,

Alex Maunder
Let Your Life Flow – The Physical, Psychological & Spiritual Benefits of the Alexander Technique,
(C.W. Daniel, 2002)

Dr Shanida Nataraja
The Blissful Brain,
(Octopus Publishing Group, 2008)

Dr C Purton
The Focusing-Oriented Counselling Primer,
(PCCS Books, 2007)

Daniel J Siegel

The Mindful Brain,
(W.W. Norton & Co, 2007)

Daniel J Siegel
The Mindful Therapist,
(W.W. Norton & Co, 2010)

Daniel J Siegel
Pocket Guide Guide to Interpersonal Neurobiology,
(W.W. Norton & Co, 2012)

Paramahansa Yogananda,
Autobiography of a Yogi
(Self-Realization Fellowship, 1946)

www.ingramcontent.com/pod-product-compliance
Ingram Content Group UK Ltd.
Pitfield, Milton Keynes, MK11 3LW, UK
UKHW020619040625
6213UKWH00049B/465